Study Guide

to accompany

The Science of Psychology
An Appreciative View

Laura King

Prepared by

Chad Burton
University of Missouri, Columbia

Boston   Burr Ridge, IL   Dubuque, IA   Madison, WI   New York   San Francisco   St. Louis
Bangkok   Bogotá   Caracas   Kuala Lumpur   Lisbon   London   Madrid   Mexico City
Milan   Montreal   New Delhi   Santiago   Seoul   Singapore   Sydney   Taipei   Toronto

The McGraw·Hill Companies

McGraw-Hill Higher Education

Study Guide to accompany
THE SCIENCE OF PSYCHOLOGY: AN APPRECIATIVE VIEW
Laura King

Published by McGraw-Hill, an imprint of The McGraw-Hill Companies, Inc., 1221 Avenue of the Americas, New York, NY 10020. Copyright © 2008 by The McGraw-Hill Companies, Inc. All rights reserved.

1 2 3 4 5 6 7 8 9 0 QPD/QPD 0 9 8 7

ISBN: 978-0-07-330746-6
MHID: 0-07-330746-7

www.mhhe.com

Study Guide Introduction

This study guide has been designed in a unique manner that will help you succeed not only in your psychology class, but in all of your college classes. The first few chapters are fully outlined and will help you become familiar with how a textbook chapter should be outlined. As you progress through the text and the study guide, the outline structure is maintained but key information is removed. The removal of this information is gradual and allows you, the student, to actively participate in creating a chapter outline that will help you succeed. As you will learn in chapter 8 (Memory), the best way to study for exams is to *recall information on your own*, not simply recognize information that has been prepared for you. The active participation elicited by this study guide incorporates this technique as an example of how psychological research can be applied to your life in a way that will improve your study habits for life.

Each chapter in this study guide is broken up into the following sections:

Learning goals: Three broad goals for each chapter are listed first and provide you with the general concepts you should keep in mind while studying. Following the learning goals are a few statements regarding how the information in the chapter can provide you with an "appreciative view" of psychology.

Chapter outline: This section provides an outline of the most important information contained in each chapter.

Clarifying tricky points: Each chapter contains a few points that are difficult to fully understand based on the outline alone. This section breaks a few of those points down into a conversational, easy-to-understand manner that will help you to learn the most complicated or "tricky" points contained in each chapter.

An appreciative view of psychology and your life: A key element of your textbook and this study guide is helping you gain an appreciative view of psychology and how psychological concepts and research apply to your own life. This section features a brief activity that helps you see how each chapter contains information that is truly relevant to your own life.

Practice tests and answer key: Three practice tests with approximately 15 questions each are included for each chapter. The first test focuses on the first third of the chapter, the second test on the second third, and the third practice test focuses on the information contained in the last part of the chapter. An answer key for the practice tests is included at the end of each chapter. The questions in these practice tests are intended to cover the most basic information contained in each chapter. For more advanced questions that will help you better prepare for an exam, you should also consider completing the online quizzes found on your text's Online Learning Center (www.mhhe.com/king1).

Table of Contents

Chapter 1: What Is Psychology?

Learning Goals
1. Explain what psychology is and describe the positive psychology movement.
2. Discuss the roots and early scientific foundations of psychology.
3. Summarize the main themes of seven approaches to psychology.
4. Evaluate areas of specialization and careers in psychology.
5. Describe the connection between the mind and body.

After studying Chapter 1, you will be able to:
- Explain how psychology is more than common sense;
- Develop good study habits and critical thinking skills;
- Understand the connections between body and mind.

Chapter Outline
1. Defining Psychology
- Psychology is the scientific study of behavior and mental processes.
    - Psychology uses the systematic methods of science to observe behavior and draw conclusions.
    - Behavior is everything we do that can be directly observed.
    - Mental processes are the thoughts, feelings, and motives that each of us experience privately but cannot be observed directly.
- Psychology is more than common sense and indeed "what everybody already knows" is often wrong. Psychology can use the scientific method to systematically test questions of central interest to human beings.
- The positive psychology movement is a push during the last decade for a stronger emphasis on research involving the full range of human experience including positive outcomes such as hope, happiness, love, civility, tolerance, etc.

2. The Roots and Early Scientific Approaches of Psychology
- Psychology emerged from both philosophy and the natural sciences (biology and physiology) to become a discipline of its own. Wilhelm Wundt was the first to bring these two areas together to create the academic discipline of psychology.
- Wundt's approach to psychology was called structuralism because of its focus on identifying the structures of the mind.
    - Structuralism uses the method of introspection to study mental structures. For example, participants are asked to think (introspect) about what is going on mentally as various things happen and then describe what they felt. These studies focused primarily on sensation and perception of things such as the taste of different types of food.
- William James was the first American psychologist and had a different approach than Wundt's structuralism.
    - James' approach was called functionalism because it was concerned with the functions or purposes of the mind and behavior in adapting to the environment.
    - A functionalist approach does not believe in the existence of rigid structures of the mind (as Wundt and other structuralists do). Rather, James and the

functionalist perspective saw the mind as flexible and fluid, characterized by constant adaptation to the surrounding environment.
- Around the time of Wundt and James, Charles Darwin proposed the principle of natural selection, an evolutionary process that favors organisms' traits or characteristics that are best adapted to reproduce and survive.
  - o The functionalist perspective meshes well with Darwin's concept of natural selection.
- Today, most psychologists adopt more of a functionalist perspective than a structualist one.

3. Contemporary Approaches to Psychology
- Biological approach: focuses on the body, especially the brain and nervous system, and how physiological processes (such as sweating) are related to thoughts and feelings.
  - o Neuroscience: primary focus is on the nervous system.
- Behavioral approach: study of observable behavioral responses and their environmental determinants.
  - o J. B. Watson and B. F. Skinner were famous behaviorists.
- Psychodynamic approach: emphasizes unconscious thought, conflict between instinct and demands of society, and early family experiences.
  - o Sigmund Freud is the founding father of psychodynamics.
  - o Focus is almost exclusively on clinical applications rather than experimental research.
- Humanistic approach: emphasizes a person's positive qualities and the freedom for a person to choose his or her own destiny.
- Cognitive approach: focuses on the mental processes involved in awareness, perception, memory, and problem solving.
- Evolutionary approach: uses evolutionary ideas such as adaptation, reproduction, and "survival of the fittest" as the basis for understanding human behavior.
- Sociocultural approach: examines how social and cultural environments influence behavior. For example, in the United States it is culturally acceptable for women to behave in an assertive manner but in other cultures it would be inappropriate for a woman to be assertive.

4. Areas of Specialization in Psychology:
- Physiological psychology and behavioral neuroscience use animals (such as rats) to study processes that occur in but are difficult to study in humans, specifically the development of the nervous system.
- Developmental psychology concentrates on the biological and environmental factors that contribute to human development across the lifespan.
- Sensation and perception is an area of psychology that is primarily interested in the physical systems and psychological processes that allow us to interpret our environment through our senses.
- Cognitive psychology examines attention, consciousness, information processing and memory.
- Learning is the process by which behavior changes to adapt to changing circumstances and can be studied from both the behavioral and cognitive approaches.
- Motivation and emotion is an area interested in goal pursuit, how rewards affect motivation, brain processes underlying emotions, and emotional expression.

- Personality psychology focuses on enduring characteristics such as traits, goals, motives, genetics, and well-being.
- Social psychology deals with people's social interactions, relationships, social perceptions, and attitudes. How people work together in groups and ways to reduce racial prejudice are examples of topics a social psychologist would study.
- Industrial and organizational psychology (I/O psychology) is focused on the workplace. Human resource management and social and group influences of organizations are topics covered in this area of psychology.
- Clinical and counseling psychology is the most common area of specialization and primarily deals with diagnosing and treating people with psychological problems. Counseling psychology typically deals with less severe problems such as adjustment issues after major life transitions, whereas clinical psychology deals with depression, schizophrenia, and other psychological disorders.
- Health psychology studies psychological and lifestyle factors as they relate to health. Stress and coping are common areas of study in health psychology.
- Community psychology is concerned with providing accessible care for all people through community based mental health centers and outreach programs. Preventing problems through community involvement is also a focus.
- School and educational psychology deals with children's learning and adjustment in school. A school psychologist typically works for a school district and test children and makes placement recommendations.
- Environmental psychology studies the interactions of people with their environment. For example, the influence of building architecture and furniture arrangement on human behavior and thought is an area of study for an environmental psychologist.
- Psychology of women is an area that, not surprisingly, emphasizes research on women and integrating what we know about women with current psychological knowledge.
- Forensic psychology applies psychological knowledge to the legal system. Forensic psychologists often serve as expert witnesses in trials and advise lawyers on issues such as jury selection and defendant competency to stand trial.
- Sport psychology applies psychological principles to improving athletes' performance.
- Cross-cultural psychology studies the role of culture in understanding behavior, thought, and emotion. For example, people in individualistic cultures such as the United States hold different beliefs and attitudes than people in more collectivistic cultures such as Korea.
- Different psychologists spend their time differently. Some spend time seeing people with problems, some teach at universities and research, while others work for large companies designing more efficient criteria for hiring or evaluating employees.
- Majoring in psychology as an undergraduate can provide you with a variety of skills including research, measurement, problem solving, critical thinking, and writing.

5. Psychology and Health and Wellness
- The mind and body are intricately connected and one can influence the other. Your attitudes and thoughts about your health can affect the healthy (or not so healthy) behaviors you engage in. Similarly, the body can influence the mind. For example, it is hard to think clearly without a good night's rest.

Clarifying Tricky Points

<u>What everybody knows</u>

As a beginning student of psychology, it can be easy to dismiss psychological research as stuff everybody already knows. You are, after all, a person and psychology is the study of people. Psychology, however, is more specifically the *scientific* study of people. Everybody has their own theories about their childhood, their friend's problems, and people in general, but a psychologist uses the methods of science to test his or her ideas about people. Furthermore, and most importantly, "what everybody knows" is often just plain wrong. There was a time in American history when "everybody knew" that African Americans were intellectually inferior to whites and that women were morally inferior to men. These are examples of assumptions, and sometimes assumptions are right, but often they are not. Psychology is a scientific discipline that does not accept assumptions as true just because "everybody knows." Rather, psychology tests assumptions using advanced scientific methodology.

<u>More than just what is wrong with people</u>

Many average citizens only know psychology for its role in weekly therapy sessions to help people overcome depression, post traumatic stress disorder (PTSD), or many other mental health disorders. Though therapy is an important aspect, psychology is actually much more complex because it is defined as the scientific study of behavior and mental processes. That means all behavior and all thought falls in the realm of psychology, not just when things go wrong like in the case of depression or PTSD. Over the last decade or so, there has been a growing movement called positive psychology. Research has shown that most people are happy most of the time, so if psychology is truly about all human behavior and thought, then a large portion of the research must be about the good things in life. Because of the positive psychology movement, things like hope, optimism, love, and forgiveness are now commonly researched topics in psychology.

<u>Structuralism vs. Functionalism</u>

Wilhelm Wundt's approach to psychology was called structuralism. William James' approach was called functionalism. In the late 1800s, as psychology was essentially in its infancy, these two approaches dominated the field, but they were very different. Structuralism sought to look inside and identify the structures of the mind. For example, the sensation of taste was found to be structured according to four components: bitter, sweet, salty, and sour. James' took a very different approach and was interested in the functions or purposes of the mind. Rather than knowing how the sense of taste is structured in the mind, James and other functionalists were interested in knowing what is the function or purpose of even being able to taste in the first place. The functionalist perspective often inquires as to the adaptive nature of things. If we evolved to taste, then there must be a purpose for the sense of taste. Functionalists would seek out that purpose through scientific research.

<u>Specializations are not mutually exclusive</u>

As you learned in chapter one, psychology is divided into several different areas (social, developmental, cognitive, personality, etc.), but the boundaries between these areas are not fixed or rigid. Oftentimes some of the most interesting research spans two are more areas. For example, if you are interested in studying the way friendships and social interactions change from childhood to adolescence to adulthood, would you first talk to a social psychologist because they know a lot about social interactions, or would you contact a developmental psychologist because they know about how people change or develop over the life span? The answer is both. The areas of specialization in psychology are not mutually exclusive. Therefore, researchers often have to, and indeed are encouraged to, pull information from different areas and perspectives in order to fully articulate a complex phenomenon such as friendships across the lifespan.

An Appreciative View of Psychology and Your Life
In this first chapter, you learned some effective study habits that are based on psychological research. How will you employ these strategies in studying for your upcoming psychology exam?

Practice Test 1
1. Psychology is best defined as the
    a. study of perception and memory.
    b. investigation of the human psyche.
    c. scientific study of conscious and unconscious processes.
    d. scientific study of behavior and mental processes.

2. As you read the definition of psychology you begin to think about examples. Of the following, which one is the best example of behavior?
    a. planning your weekend activities
    b. adding two numbers in your head
    c. a two-year-old boy coloring a picture
    d. thinking about this question

3. The definition of psychology is made up of three main concepts. Which concept refers to thoughts, feelings, and motives?
    a. scientific study
    b. behavior
    c. contexts
    d. mental processes

4. What is the main difference between philosophers and psychologists?
    a. the types of questions they ask about human behavior
    b. the causes they presume for human behavior
    c. the debate of the question as to how people acquire knowledge
    d. the methods they use for obtaining evidence

5. The British naturalist Charles Darwin is best known for his suggestion that
    a. organisms that are best adapted to their environment survive and pass on their characteristics to their offspring.
    b. conscious experience is made up of structure.
    c. psychology should focus only on observable behavior, not the mind.
    d. people have freedom to choose their own destiny.

6. A structuralist would have been most interested in studying
    a. the unconscious.
    b. dreams.
    c. conscious thought.
    d. behavior.

7. According to Skinner, what is the ultimate test of who we are?
    a. our personality
    b. how we think
    c. what we do
    d. our level of happiness

8. Structuralism is to _____ as functionalism is to _____.
    a. Wundt; Titchener
    b. Skinner; Wundt
    c. James; Bandura
    d. Wundt; James

9. There are three key terms in the definition of psychology. Which of the three terms is the one defined as everything that we do that can be directly observed?
    a. thoughts
    b. science
    c. mental processes
    d. behaviors

10. Which of the following statements is consistent with the theories and arguments of Rene Descartes?
    a. Contemporary humans are part of an evolutionary process that has shaped their psychology.
    b. Sensations and perceptions combine to form our thoughts.
    c. The body and the mind are separate entities.
    d. How we think and behave is determined by our body type.

11. The conscious mental structures discovered by using the introspection method would be of most interest to a psychologist from the _____ perspective.
    a. structuralism
    b. functionalism
    c. behavioral
    d. psychodynamic

12.   Seligman and Csikszentmihalyi, in an article published in the year 2000, proposed that in the 21st century psychology ought to focus more on positive psychological experiences. Which of the following questions is more likely to be studied under this movement?
       a.   What personality characteristics contributed to Picasso's lifelong creativity?
       b.   What is the relationship between self-esteem and eating disorders?
       c.   What is the psychological profile of a terrorist?
       d.   Are women more likely to experience depression than men?

13.   Compared to other sciences, psychology is relatively young, because it is considered that modern psychology started approximately
       a.   50 years ago.
       b.   200 years ago.
       c.   100 years ago.
       d.   300 years ago.

14.   Which of the following contemporary approaches in psychology is reminiscent of the functionalist approach?
       a.   behavioral
       b.   cognitive
       c.   humanistic
       d.   evolutionary

15.   Structuralism is to _____ as functionalism is to _____.
       a.   purpose; parts
       b.   parts; purpose
       c.   unconscious; conscious
       d.   behaviors; mental processes

16.   Which of the following was the aspect of psychology most often studied during the first half of the 20th century?
       a.   thoughts
       b.   emotions
       c.   behaviors
       d.   motives

17.   Which of the following statements is NOT consistent with Darwin's concept of natural selection?
       a.   Natural selection determines our traits.
       b.   Natural selection tends to favor traits that are not adaptive for survival.
       c.   The process of natural selection can modify an entire species over time.
       d.   Giraffes have long necks because natural selection has selected the trait long necks, because that trait is necessary for survival in the giraffes' environment.

Practice Test 2

1.   You believe that the environment determines behavior. What approach would you be most likely to side with?
        a.   psychodynamic
        b.   humanistic
        c.   behavioral neuroscience
        d.   behavioral

2.   The _____ approach sees behavior as being influenced by the unconscious mind.
        a.   cognitive
        b.   humanistic
        c.   psychodynamic
        d.   evolutionary

3.   Of the following, which best summarizes the humanistic approach?
        a.   People are influenced by their unconscious mind and the conflict between their biological instincts and society's demands.
        b.   Consciousness is understood by examining its basic elements.
        c.   Ethnicity, gender, and culture are the primary determinants of behavior.
        d.   People have the freedom to choose their own destiny.

4.   Which of the following would make the best title for a presentation on humanistic psychology?
        a.   Be all that you can be.
        b.   The psychology of dancing tango
        c.   Explore your unconscious and you will find yourself.
        d.   People are pawns of their environment.

5.   Your professor says that memory, attention, problem-solving, and perception are key components of the _____ approach.
        a.   cognitive
        b.   sociocultural
        c.   evolutionary
        d.   functional

6.   Which of the following approaches emphasizes the brain and nervous system?
        a.   cognitive
        b.   behavioral neuroscience
        c.   information processing
        d.   behavioral

7.   According to the evolutionary psychology approach, why does the mind have the capacity to achieve specific goals?

    a.   The mind has evolved.

    b.   One's environment has shaped the mind.

    c.   The unconscious mind tends to create these goals.

    d.   The person has so decided to achieve specific goals.

8.   What is the main difference between a clinical psychologist and a psychiatrist?

    a.   their education

    b.   their theoretical approach

    c.   their research interests

    d.   their number of publications

9.   Which of the following statements is consistent with social cognitive theory?

    a.   Our early life experiences are the major determinants of our behaviors and mental processes.

    b.   Imitation is one of the main ways we learn about the world.

    c.   Psychology should only focus on behaviors.

    d.   Unconscious influences are the most important factor in understanding psychology.

10.   Which of the following factors is NOT addressed is the psychodynamic perspective?

    a.   instincts

    b.   culture

    c.   parenting

    d.   unconscious

11.   Which of the contemporary approaches in psychology is more likely to be associated with the statement: "Memory is written in a chemical code"?

    a.   behavioral neuroscience

    b.   sociocultural

    c.   behavioral

    d.   evolutionary

12.   Latinos in the United States are facing a variety of challenges that are resulting in higher numbers of high school dropouts than other ethnic groups. Which contemporary perspective in psychology would be appropriate to study this tendency?

    a.   behavioral

    b.   cognitive

    c.   evolutionary

    d.   sociocultural

13.   The humanistic perspective emerged in the middle of the 20th century and emphasized
    a.   the role of the psychotherapist in figuring out the psychological problems of others.
    b.   free will and the ability people have for self-understanding.
    c.   how external rewards determine what people do.
    d.   the role of unconscious determinants of our personality.

14.   Which of the following approaches should we use if we want to learn about the meaning of dreams and other psychological experiences that occur when we are not conscious and aware?
    a.   psychodynamic
    b.   behavioral
    c.   sociocultural
    d.   evolutionary

15.   Based on the sociocultural approach, we may wonder if
    a.   watching professional wrestling on TV could make children behave aggressively.
    b.   how we think about others influences how we think about ourselves.
    c.   the brain plays a role in learning.
    d.   a child from Canada behaves similarly to a child from Argentina.

16.   The psychodynamic approach is to _____ as the cognitive approach is to _____.
    a.   mental processes; unconscious experience
    b.   Freud; Skinner
    c.   unconscious experience; mental processes
    d.   Rogers; Freud

17.   The behavioral approach is to _____ as the psychodynamic approach is to _____.
    a.   external factors; internal factors
    b.   internal factors; external factors
    c.   20th century; 21st century
    d.   21st century; 20th century

18.   The behaviorist approach is to _____ as the humanistic approach is to _____.
    a.   external control; environment
    b.   environment; external control
    c.   external control; free will
    d.   free will; external control

19.   "Do our traits and goals affect our levels of stress?" Which two areas of specialization in psychology could be combined to best address this question?
    a.   personality and health
    b.   social and environmental
    c.   social and health
    d.   community and environmental

Practice Test 3

1. Chemical changes in the brain associated with anxiety would be of most interest to a(n)
    a. evolutionary psychologist.
    b. cognitive psychologist.
    c. sociocultural psychologist.
    d. behavioral neuroscientist.

2. The majority of psychologists have specialized in
    a. personality psychology.
    b. clinical and counseling psychology.
    c. health psychology.
    d. sports psychology.

3. Which of the following areas of specialization is more likely to use animals for research?
    a. social psychology
    b. industrial/organizational psychology
    c. developmental psychology
    d. behavioral neuroscience psychology

4. A psychologist that develops an after school program to prevent kids from spending time alone at home in the afternoons is probably a(n)
    a. industrial/organizational psychologist.
    b. community psychologist.
    c. environmental psychologist.
    d. clinical psychologist.

5. If you want to be a forensic psychologist, you will probably take some classes on
    a. law.
    b. medicine.
    c. language.
    d. engineering.

6. You are a psychologist and you study self-concept, aggression, and inner directedness. You most likely specialize in
    a. school and educational psychology.
    b. cross-cultural psychology.
    c. personality psychology.
    d. clinical psychology.

7. The specialist who works at a secondary school and consults with teachers about children's school achievement problems is most likely in which field of specialization?
    a. learning and memory
    b. motivation and emotion
    c. school psychology
    d. biological psychology

8.   According to research on happiness, how happy are people such as the Maasai in Africa and the Inuits in Greenland?

a.   They are not happy at all, because the environment is too harsh.

b.   They are about as happy as people in developed nations, such as the United States.

c.   They are somewhat happy but not as happy as people in Europe.

d.   Nobody knows because it's impossible to study groups that differ from traditional Western society.

9.   A forensic psychologist may be the best professional to consult if

a.   you are trying to figure out the psychology of a dead person.

b.   you are an M.D. specializing in forensic medicine.

c.   you are a defense attorney who needs to select a jury that will favor your client.

d.   you are a judge who needs psychological help.

10.   Which of the following is NOT true about effective studying strategies?

a.   Having music in the background while studying helps memory.

b.   Studying many times for shorter periods is better than studying one time for a longer period.

c.   Reading a summary of a chapter before reading the chapter enhances the reading and improves memory.

d.   Critical thinking contributes to memory.

11.   Which of the following is NOT consistent with critical thinking?

a.   figuring out what "the real problem is"

b.   sticking to one approach to psychology

c.   being open-minded

d.   being skeptical

12.   Critical thinking involves all the following except which one?

a.   thinking reflectively

b.   thinking productively

c.   thinking impulsively

d.   evaluating evidence

Answer Key

Practice Test 1 Answers

1.   a.   No; psychology is more than the study of just perception and memory.

b.   No, this is not the best definition.

c.   No; even though psychology does study conscious and unconscious processes, this is not the best answer

d.   THAT'S CORRECT; psychology is best defined as the scientific study of behavior and mental processes.

2.   a.   Planning is an example of a mental process, since it cannot be directly observed.

        b.   Adding is an example of a mental process, since it cannot be directly observed.

        c.   CORRECT; coloring a picture is behavior, since it can be directly observed.

        d.   Thinking is an example of a mental process, since it cannot be directly observed.

3.   a.   Scientific study refers to using systematic methods.

        b.   Behavior is anything you do that is directly observable.

        c.   "Contexts" is not a component of the definition.

        d.   YES; thoughts, feelings, and motives are examples of mental processes.

4.   a.   Philosophers and psychologists often ask the same questions.

        b.   No; both may acknowledge the same causes of behavior.

        c.   No; both debate

        d.   YES; philosophers think to obtain evidence; psychologists use the scientific method.

5.   a.   YES; this is the idea of natural selection.

        b.   This describes structuralism, not Darwinism.

        c.   Focusing on observable behavior was Skinner's suggestion.

        d.   Freedom to choose is a basic tenet of the humanistic approach.

6.   a.   No; structuralism focused on conscious thought.

        b.   No

        c.   YES; structuralism attempted to examine the structure of conscious thought.

        d.   No; the emphasis of structuralism was on conscious thought, not behavior.

7.   a.   No; Skinner was not interested in personality.

        b.   No; Skinner was not interested in cognitive psychology.

        c.   YES; Skinner was a behavioralist, so he believed that what we do is the ultimate test of who we are.

        d.   No; Skinner was unconcerned with how happy people feel.

8.   a.   Both Wundt and Titchener are associated with structuralism.

        b.   Skinner is associated with the behavioral approach; Wundt is associated with structuralism.

        c.   James is associated with functionalism; Bandura is associated with social cognitive theory.

        d.   THAT'S RIGHT; Wundt is associated with structuralism and James is associated with functionalism.

9. a. Thoughts are mental processes.
    b. Science is one of the key terms, but it refers to the systematic methods of research used in psychology.
    c. Mental processes cannot be directly observed.
    d. YES; behaviors can be directly observed and are an essential component in the definition of psychology.

10. a. This statement is consistent with the arguments of Charles Darwin.
    b. This statement is consistent with the beliefs of Buddha.
    c. YES; Descartes argued that the body and the mind are separate entities.
    d. This statement is more consistent with ancient thinkers who sought to find links between the body and the mind.

11. a. YES; this was the focus of the work of Wundt and Titchner.
    b. No; functionalists were more interested in why we have a consciousness and how it helps us adapt to the demands of the environment than they were in the parts of the consciousness.
    c. No; behaviorists would even oppose the study of consciousness, as it is not observable.
    d. No; the psychodynamic perspective focused in the unconscious.

12. a. YES; creativity should be one of the areas of study according to the positive psychology movement.
    b. This question focuses on the abnormal psychology of eating disorders, thus considered negative.
    c. This question focuses on terrorism, a phenomenon that involves negative behaviors such as aggression and violence.
    d. This question focuses on depression, a psychological disorder, thus considered negative.

13. a. No; by the 1950s there was already a great body of research in psychology.
    b. No; modern psychology started later, in 1879, with the establishment of the first psychology laboratory by Wilhelm Wundt.
    c. YES; about 120 years ago, the first set of scientific studies in psychology were performed at the Leipzig, Germany laboratory founded by Wundt.
    d. No; 300 years ago and even before then, the questions of psychology were being asked, but scientific methods were not being used in the process of answering the questions.

14. a. No
    b. No
    c. No
    d. YES; the evolutionary approach, like functionalism, explores the question of the role of adaptation in psychology.

15. a.   No
    b.   YES; structuralism focuses on the structure, dimensions, or "parts" of the mind, while functionalism asks what is the adaptive purpose of the mind and behaviors.
    c.   No
    d.   No

16. a.   No; the behavioral perspective dominated psychology during the first half of the 20th century, and this perspective ignored the role of thoughts in psychology, because they could not be directly observed.
    b.   No; for the same reason as item a.
    c.   YES; behaviors, which are everything that we do that is directly observable, were the main focus of behaviorists, who dominated psychology during the first half of the 20th century.
    d.   No; for the same reason as items a and b.

17. a.   No; this statement is consistent with Darwin's ideas.
    b.   CORRECT; this statement is not consistent with Darwin's concept of natural selection.
    c.   No; this statement is true.
    d.   No; this statement is true.

Practice Test 2 Answers

1. a.   The psychodynamic approach focuses on unconscious influences.
   b.   The humanistic approach says that people control their own lives, not the environment.
   c.   The behavioral neuroscience approach argues that the brain and nervous system determine behavior.
   d.   YES; environmental conditions determine behavior.

2. a.   The cognitive approach looks for the role of mental processes such as perception.
   b.   The humanistic approach asserts that people, not the unconscious mind, choose who they are.
   c.   RIGHT; the psychodynamicanalytic approach also focuses on biological instincts.
   d.   The evolutionary approach focuses on the survival of the fittest.

3. a.   This summary describes the psychodynamic approach.
   b.   This summary describes structuralism.
   c.   The sociocultural approach emphasizes ethnicity, gender, and culture.
   d.   YES; this view sees people as having the freedom and the capacity for self-understanding.

4. a.   GOOD; the humanistic perspective stresses growth and self-actualization.
   b.   This sounds more like the sociocultural approach.
   c.   The unconscious mind is the focus of the psychodynamic approach.
   d.   This title would be best for the behavioral approach.

5.   a.   THAT'S CORRECT; the cognitive approach focuses on mental processes.
        b.   The sociocultural view examines the role of ethnicity, culture, and gender.
        c.   This approach stresses natural selection.
        d.   The functional view examines how the mind adapts to the environment.

6.   a.   The cognitive approach emphasizes mental processes.
        b.   YES; those in this approach examine how the physical structures of the brain and nervous system influence behavior, thoughts, and emotion.
        c.   The information-processing approach focuses on attention, perception, and memory.
        d.   This approach examines the relationship between the environment and behavior.

7.   a.   THAT'S RIGHT; it is theorized that the mind has evolved in ways that would have benefited hunters and gatherers.
        b.   This option is best associated with the behavioral approach.
        c.   The psychodynamic approach would suggest this role of the unconscious mind.
        d.   This best describes the humanistic approach.

8.   a.   YES; a psychiatrist holds a degree in medicine; a clinical psychologist does not.
        b.   Both are interested in helping people.
        c.   Both professionals help improve the lives of people, and their research reflects this.
        d.   No; this is not important.

9.   a.   No; this statement is consistent with the psychodynamic perspective; social cognitive theory and in general the behavioral approach considers life-long learning experiences.
        b.   YES; Bandura argued that modeling and imitation are important ways of learning.
        c.   No; this statement is more consistent with the traditional behavioristic perspective.
        d.   No; this statement is consistent with the psychodynamic approach.

10.   a.   Instincts are important in the psychodynamic perspective.
        b.   YES; the psychodynamic perspective has been criticized for not properly addressing the role of culture in psychology.
        c.   Parenting, particularly in the first few years of life, was one of the factors addressed in Freud's original theories.
        d.   The unconscious is a concept central to the psychodynamic approach to psychology.

11. a. YES; behavioral neuroscience considers the biological basis of psychology; one of the areas of study is the nervous system and its chemical components.
     b. No; the sociocultural approach is more interested in broader social and cultural questions.
     c. No; memory is a mental process, and thus is not likely to be studied in the behavioral approach.
     d. No; the evolutionary perspective focuses on the adaptive role of behaviors.

12. a. No; the behavioral perspective is not associated with the study of ethnicity.
     b. No; the cognitive perspective is not associated with the study of ethnicity.
     c. No; the evolutionary perspective is not associated with the study of ethnicity; one of the main criticisms of this perspective is precisely that it does not account appropriately for cultural differences.
     d. YES; the sociocultural approach is dedicated to questions just like this, in which the relationship between culture, ethnicity, and a behavior (in this case, dropping out of high school) is studied.

13. a. No; this is more consistent with the psychodynamic perspective.
     b. YES; this is what distinguished the humanistic approach from other approaches such as the behavioral and the psychodynamic, which were dominating psychology during the first half of the 20th century.
     c. No; this issue is addressed by the behavioral perspective.
     d. No; this issue is addressed by the psychodynamic perspective.

14. a. YES; the psychodynamic approach focuses on the unconscious ("when we are not conscious and aware").
     b. No; the behavioral perspective focuses on what can be observed, and dreams and other unconscious experiences cannot be directly observed.
     c. No; this approach focuses on social and cultural factors of psychology.
     d. No; in general, evolutionary psychology focuses on behaviors and mental processes that are common to most, if not all humans, and the meaning of dreams is a very personal psychological experience.

15. a. No; social psychology would be interested in this.
     b. No; this pertains to the domain of the cognitive approach.
     c. No; this pertains to the domain of behavioral neuroscience.
     d. YES; the sociocultural approach is interested in cultural differences.

16.   a.   No; mental processes are the focus of cognitive psychology, while the unconscious is the focus of the psychodynamic approach.

      b.   No; Freud is associated with the psychodynamic perspective, but Skinner is associated with the behavioral perspective, not the cognitive approach.

      c.   YES; unconscious experiences are the focus of the psychodynamic perspective and mental process the focus of the cognitive approach.

      d.   No; Rogers is associated with the humanistic perspective and Freud with the psychodynamic.

17.   a.   YES; the behavioral approach focuses on the environmental or external factors that shape our behaviors, while the psychodynamic approach focuses on internal factors such as instincts and the unconscious.

      b.   It is the opposite, as explained in the previous item.

      c.   Actually, both the behavioral and the psychodynamic approach were developed and were widely popular during the first half of the 20th century.

      d.   Incorrect, as both approaches were developed in the 20th century.

18.   a.   No; while the behavioral approach is associated with the study of external factors that control behaviors and mental processes, the humanistic approach focuses more on internal factors, such as self-control, rather than on environmental or external explanations.

      b.   No; this item is similar to item a, but the order has been reversed; therefore, the explanation for item a also applies to item b.

      c.   YES; the behavioral approach is associated with external or environmental controls on our psychology, whereas the humanistic approach emphasizes our free will and ability to control our behaviors and mental processes.

      d.   No; this item presents the same concepts as in item c, but in a reversed order; therefore, the item is incorrect; behaviorists do not focus on free will, humanists do.

19.   a.   YES; personality psychology is the study of traits and goals while health psychology is the study of, among other things, stress and coping.

      b.   No

      c.   No

      d.   No

Practice Test 3 Answers

1.   a.   Probably not, because evolutionary psychologists are more interested in how behavior allows organisms to adapt to the environment.

      b.   A cognitive psychologist examines the role of mental processes.

      c.   This psychologist would study the roles that culture, ethnicity, and gender play.

      d.   SOUNDS GOOD; behavioral neuroscience studies how the brain and nervous system are important to behavior, thought, and emotion.

2. a. No
    b. YES
    c. No
    d. No; this is one of the most recent areas of specialization in psychology.

3. a. No; this area focuses on humans.
    b. No; this area focuses on humans in the workplace.
    c. No; this area focuses on the development, growth, and aging of humans.
    d. YES; this area focuses on the biological basis of psychology, and many times research involves the systematic study of the nervous systems of animals.

4. a. No; I/O psychologists do not work with school and or children; they focus on adults in the workplace.
    b. YES; this is a job for a community psychologist, someone who has been trained to explore community services and how they relate to the psychological well-being of all members of the community, including children.
    c. No; an environmental psychologist studies the relationship between psychology and the physical environment.
    d. No; a clinical psychologist works with individuals who have psychological problems.

5. a. CORRECT; forensic psychology applies psychological principles to the legal system.
    b. No
    c. No
    d. No

6. a. No; children's learning and adjustment in school take center stage in this specialization.
    b. No; cross-cultural psychology examines the role of culture.
    c. YES; these are examples of areas that a personality psychologist would study.
    d. No; a clinical psychologist studies and treats psychological problems.

7. a. Learning and memory are important in school, but this is not a field of specialization.
    b. While important in school, "motivation and emotion" is not the name of a specialization.
    c. CORRECT; school psychology is concerned about learning and adjustment in school.
    d. Biological psychology focuses on the relationships between brain and nervous and behavior, thought, and emotion.

8.　a.　No.

　　b.　YES; Diener and Biswas-Diener have found that, in all cultures, most people are happy most of the time.

　　c.　No.

　　d.　No; studying groups that are different from our own is not only possible but very important to psychology.

9.　a.　While a doctor who has specialized in forensic medicine does work with dead bodies, for example, performing autopsies, forensic psychology has nothing to do with people who have passed away.

　　b.　No; forensic psychology and forensic medicine are not related fields.

　　c.　YES; in this case a forensic psychologist, someone who has specialized in the psychological factors involved in the legal system, would be a great resource in the process of selecting a jury.

　　d.　No; a judge with psychological problems would have to seek the assistance of a clinical psychologist.

10.　a.　CORRECT; music may serve as a distraction, and distractions should be minimized when studying, thus this is not an effective strategy.

　　b.　Distributing studying sessions across time contributes to the consolidation of the knowledge and enhances memory.

　　c.　Having an idea of the order of the material and being aware of the goals of the chapter before reading it does make the reading and studying more effective.

　　d.　Reflecting, being thoughtful and open-minded does contribute to memory.

11.　a.　Finding "the real problem" requires thoughtfulness and attention; it requires critical thinking.

　　b.　CORRECT; sticking to one approach is similar to being close-minded and therefore inconsistent with critical thinking.

　　c.　This is part of the definition of critical thinking.

　　d.　Being skeptical sometimes requires questioning what other people don't question, and this is possible when the person is thinking critically.

12.　a.　This is a component of critical thinking.

　　b.　Critical thinking involves thinking productively.

　　c.　THAT'S RIGHT; critical thinking requires that we be reflective and not impulsive.

　　d.　Critical thinking requires that we evaluate evidence.

Chapter 2: Psychology's Scientific Methods

Learning Goals
1. Explain what makes psychology a science.
2. Discuss common research settings and the three types of research that are used in psychology.
3. Distinguish between descriptive and inferential statistics.
4. Discuss some research challenges that involve ethics, bias, and information.
5. Discuss scientific studies on human happiness and the nature of their findings.

After studying Chapter 2, you will be able to:
- Describe the key characteristics that make for a good scientist (curiosity, skepticism, objective, critical thinking) and how you can embrace those characteristics in your own study of psychology and other scholarly endeavors;
- Understand why you should be careful when interpreting psychological research reported in mass media outlets such as newspapers, magazines, TV, and the Internet;
- Describe how the content and pursuit of your personal goals affects your well-being.

Chapter Outline
1. Psychology's Scientific Methods
- Psychology is commonly represented in popular self-help books but it can be difficult to know if the advice provided by such best selling books is actually good and helpful. The scientific method provides psychologists with a way to test whether advice that *sounds* good really *is* good.
- Science is not defined by what it investigates but by how it investigates. The same scientific method used to study photosynthesis in biology is used to study psychology.
- A scientist is characterized by four attitudes: curiosity, skepticism, objectivity, and a willingness to think critically.
- Science is a collaborative effort. Different scientists may work from very different theories but all scientists are working towards the same goal of increasing our collective body of knowledge. The peer review process is critical to this collaborative effort because peer review means that before any piece of research is published in an academic journal it has first been thoroughly reviewed by knowledgeable scholars in the field who attest to the soundness of the research.
- The collaborative nature of research is also demonstrated by meta-analysis, which is a method by which researchers combine results across a variety of different studies to establish the strength of any given finding.
- Psychology used the scientific method to study phenomena. The scientific method is summarized by the following five steps:
    1. Observing some phenomenon
    2. Formulating hypotheses and predictions
    3. Testing through empirical research
    4. Drawing conclusions
    5. Evaluating conclusions

- Observing phenomena requires an operational definition of the variable under study. An operational definition is an objective description of how a research variable is going to be measured and observed.
- A hypothesis is a prediction arrived at logically from a theory and that can be tested.
- To test a hypothesis through empirical research, data must be collected. One of the most important decisions when a scientist is collecting data is who to choose as research participants.
- The entire group about which a researcher wants to draw conclusions is called the population. The subset that actually participates in the study is called the sample. In an effort to more closely mirror the population, an investigator would use a random sample, a sample that gives every member of the population an equal chance of being selected.
- To test a hypothesis, a scientist employs statistical analyses on the data collected from the sample. The conclusions drawn from a study are based on these statistical analyses
- The concept of a variable is central to all research. A variable is anything that varies between people such as height, happiness, IQ, and religious faith, just to name a few.

2. Research Settings and Types of Research

- Psychological research is conducted in different settings, specifically a laboratory or a natural setting. A laboratory is a controlled setting with many of the complex factors of the real world removed. Laboratory research allows a great deal of control but has some drawbacks such as:
    1. It is impossible to conduct research in the lab without the participants' knowing they are being studied.
    2. The lab is unnatural and therefore can cause the participants to behave unnaturally.
    3. People who are willing to go to a university laboratory may not fairly represent groups from diverse cultural backgrounds.
    4. Some aspects of the mind and behavior are impossible or unethical to examine in the lab.
- Naturalistic observation, or observing behavior in the real-world such as sporting events, daycare centers, malls, airports, etc., overcomes some drawbacks of laboratory research but naturalistic observation has less control than laboratory research.
- There are three general types of research: descriptive, correlational, and experimental.
- Descriptive research: Examples of descriptive research include observing behavior in a natural setting, observing videotaped lab sessions, surveys and interviews, standardized tests, and case studies. Descriptive research cannot prove what causes some phenomena but it can reveal important information about people's behavior and attitudes.
- Correlational research: Research that relies on systematic observation of variables and is concerned with identifying relationships between such variables in order to describe how variables change together is called correlational research. Not surprisingly, correlational research is based on the statistical technique of correlation.
    - A correlation coefficient (represented by the letter r) is a numerical value between -1 and 1 that represents the strength and direction of the relationship between two variables. The closer the number is to 1 or -1, the stronger the relationship is. A value of 0 represents no relationship at all. Whether the

correlation is positive or negative represents the direction of the effect. A positive value means that as one variable goes up, the other goes up as well. A negative value means that as one variable goes up, the other goes down.

- o Though a correlation describes how two variables are related it does not imply that one variable causes the other. Correlation does not imply causation.
- o Third variable problem: sometimes an extraneous variable that has not been measured accounts for the relationship between two other variables.
- o A multivariate approach, a method that involves more than just the two main variables of interest, can confront the problem of third variables.
- o Sophisticated correlational research can employ methods such as experience sampling method (ESM) and/or longitudinal design. ESM has people document, usually through a PDA (e.g., Palm Pilot), their daily experiences throughout the day or week and is a good way to study people in natural settings. Longitudinal designs approach the issue of causation by measuring the variables of interest in multiple waves over time (sometimes as long as several decades).

- Experimental research: Conducing experiments is a way to establish causality. An experiment is a carefully regulated procedure in which one or more variables are manipulated while all other variables are held constant.
  - o Experiments use random assignment to insure that the only difference between groups is the independent variable, or the variable that is being manipulated. A dependent variable is a factor that can change in an experiment in response to the changes in the independent variable.
  - o Experiments include two types of groups: experimental and control. The experimental group is a group whose experience is manipulated. A control group is treated in every way like the experimental group except for the manipulated factor. The control group provides a baseline against which the effects of the experimental condition can be compared.
  - o Validity refers to the soundness of the conclusions drawn from experiments. Ecological validity is the extent to which an experimental design is representative of the real world issues it is supposed to address. Internal validity is the extent to which changes in the dependent variable are due to the manipulation of the independent variable.
  - o Experimenter bias occurs when the experimenter (the person running the study) influences the outcome of the research through his or her expectations.
  - o Research participant bias occurs when the behavior being studied is influenced by how the participant thinks he or she is supposed to behave.
  - o A placebo is an innocuous, inert substance that has no specific physiological effect. Placebos are used in control conditions and a placebo effect occurs when control participants' expectations, rather than an experimental treatment, produce an experimental outcome.
  - o Double blind experiments are those experiments in which neither the experimenter nor the participant knows what condition participants are in. This method helps alleviate experimenter and research participant bias.

3. Analyzing and Interpreting Data

- Descriptive statistics are the mathematical procedures used to describe and summarize sets of data in a meaningful way.

- o Measures of central tendency: mean, median, and mode. Mean is the average and is calculated by adding all the scores in a set and then dividing by the number of scores in the set. Median is the score that falls exactly in the middle of the distribution of scores after they have been arranged from highest to lowest. Mode is the score that occurs most often in a set of data.
    - o Measures of dispersion give us a sense of the spread of scores, or how much the scores in a sample vary from one to another. Standard deviation measures how much the scores vary, on average, from the mean.
- Inferential statistics are the mathematical methods used to indicate whether or not data sufficiently support or confirm a hypothesis. Essentially, inferential statistics represent the probability that the differences revealed through data analysis are real and not simply due to chance.

4. The Challenges of Conducting and Evaluating Psychological Research

- Ethics is an important consideration for psychology. General principles have been established by the American Psychological Association (APA) and address four important issues:
    - o Informed consent: Participants must know what their participation will involve and what risks might develop.
    - o Confidentiality: All information gathered from psychological research must be kept confidential and, when possible, be anonymous.
    - o Debriefing: Upon completion of the study, participants should be informed of the study's purpose and methods that were used.
    - o Deception: Sometimes it is necessary for a researcher to deceive participants about the true nature of the experiment. Researchers however must insure that the deception will not harm the participants and that participants will be told the true nature of the study once the study is complete.
- Animal research has a different set of ethical guidelines that mandate researchers evaluate potential benefits against possible harm to the animals and avoid inflicting unnecessary pain.
- Gender and ethnicity bias in research is also an important consideration. Historically, the university student population, and therefore the pool of potential research participants, has been predominantly male. A similar phenomenon happens today regarding cultural and ethnic bias. Research samples are typically predominantly Anglo-American but researchers try to generalize to other ethnicities creating a source of bias.
- To be a wise consumer of psychological research you should:
    - o Distinguish between group results and individual results. Just because a study finds that divorced women tend to not cope as well as married women does not mean that any individual divorced woman cannot cope well, perhaps even better than a given married woman.
    - o Avoid generalizing from a small sample. A small sample may not accurately reflect the population and therefore conclusions must be generalized with caution.
    - o Look for answers beyond a single study. Generally speaking, no single study will provide conclusive answers to an important question, particularly answers that apply to all people.

      o Avoid attributing causes where none have been found. Correlational research describes relationships that often sound causal but actually correlations cannot speak to cause and effect.

      o Consider the source. Just like news reported in the *New York Times* is more trustworthy than news reported in the *National Enquirer*, research reported in peer reviewed academic journals is typically of a higher quality than research not reported in such prestigious outlets.

5. The Scientific Method, Health, and Wellness

- The scientific study of happiness typically focuses on a variable called subjective well-being.
- Hedonic treadmill: the concept that any aspect of life that enhances our positive feelings is likely to do so for only a short period of time.
- Everyday goals and the pursuit of them relates strongly to subjective well-being.

Clarifying Tricky Points

Psychology as Science

Science is not defined by what it investigates but by how it investigates it. Psychology, therefore, is a science because it employs the scientific method to study the thoughts and behaviors of people. Most psychologists involved in research spend their days observing phenomena, formulating hypotheses, testing those hypotheses by collecting data through correlational research or experiments, analyzing the data using advanced statistical procedures, and then drawing conclusions.

Scientific Theory

Most psychological research is driven by theory. A theory is a broad idea that attempts to explain certain behaviors. Theories are important to psychology because they help to make sense of the large number of research studies that are always being conducted. Furthermore, without a theory it would be difficult for a researcher to figure out where to go next. Uncovering or explaining an interesting phenomenon is great but once the data are analyzed and results reported, a researcher must decide what direction to take his or her research next. Theories can help inform what new directions are likely to be the most fruitful. Theories are not, however, infallible and are always subject to revision. Sometimes when reading about a theory, such as Self-determination Theory or Terror Management Theory (as mentioned in Chapter 2), it is easy to get wrapped into the ideas presented in the theory and take its tenets to be absolute. This, however, is not a good interpretation of any theory because scientists do not regard theories to be absolutely correct on all counts. Recall from Chapter 2 that one of the values a scientist should embrace is skepticism. A scientist should always question things others take to be absolute.

Sample vs. Population

Understanding the difference between a sample and the population can be tricky but it is important to know how both are defined. The population is the group of people in which a researcher is interested in knowing more about. Sometimes the population is defined as all people, sometimes just one gender, or sometimes it can be quite specific such as single women between the ages of 18 to 35 who immigrated to the United States from Mexico. Regardless of how the population is defined, a researcher almost never has access to the entire population. Therefore researchers select a sample from that population and the sample is the group of people that actually participate in the researcher's study. Statistical analyses are conducted on data collected from the sample and conclusions are cautiously generalized to the population. In an effort to make sure the sample is representative of the population of interest, samples are typically selected randomly. Random samples can be obtained through a variety of means such as approaching people in large public places like parks, movie theaters, airports, randomly calling people listed in the phonebook, etc.

Interpretation of Statistics
Interpreting statistics correctly can be very tricky and even very well educated people misinterpret statistics from time to time. Perhaps the most commonly misinterpreted statistic is the correlation coefficient. Recall from Chapter 2 that correlation coefficients describe the strength and direction of a relationship between two variables. Correlations do not however describe what causes the relationship. Just because marriage and happiness are positively correlated does not mean if you get married you will be happy. It is possible that married people are generally happier than non-married but, based solely on a correlation coefficient, it is equally likely that people who are already happy tend to get married more than unhappy people. The media often draws causal conclusions from correlational research, but it is your job as an informed and educated consumer of information to recognize correlational research when you see it and interpret such research accordingly.

An Appreciative View of Psychology and Your Life
- The pursuit of goals is strongly related to subjective well-being. Simply having important, valued goals is good, as is making progress towards them. Goal pursuit also provides meaningful connections to events in our lives given them a beginning, middle, and end.
- Goals should be moderately challenging and share an instrumental relationship with each other so that the pursuit of one goal facilitates the accomplishment of another.

What are the top 3 goals you are pursing right now?
1. _____
2. _____
3. _____

How does the pursuit of these goals affect your subjective well-being? _____

_____

_____

How challenging are these goals and is the level of challenge good? _____

_____

_____

Practice Test 1

1. What is the first step of the scientific method?
   a. draw conclusions
   b. analyze the data
   c. collect data
   d. observe

2. _____ are specific predictions that can be tested to determine their accuracy and are derived logically from theories.
   a. Correlations
   b. Experiments
   c. Observations
   d. Hypotheses

3. Ali and Michael are conducting a study in which they sit in the student center lobby and take notes on different students' hand gestures as they speak. What type of research method are they using?
   a. case study
   b. correlational study
   c. naturalistic observation
   d. experimental research

4. A research method typically used by clinical psychologists with unique individuals is called a(n)
   a. interview.
   b. random sample.
   c. experiment.
   d. case study.

5. Standardized tests
   a. give every member of the population an equal chance to be tested.
   b. are used only by clinical psychologists.
   c. provide information about individual differences among people.
   d. involve making careful observations of people in real-world settings.

6. What is the main advantage of using standardized tests?
   a. They have very good external validity.
   b. They can determine cause and effect.
   c. They provide information about individual differences.
   d. They contain no biases.

7. The research method that measures how much one characteristic is associated with another is known as
    a. classic experimentation.
    b. naturalistic observation.
    c. correlational strategy.
    d. standardized tests.

8. Which of the following statements is TRUE about science?
    a. Science is defined by what it investigates.
    b. Science is defined by how it investigates.
    c. Collaboration is not essential to the progress of science.
    d. Objectivity is not necessary in science.

9. Which of the following is NOT one of the ways in which scientists collaborate?
    a. doing presentations in conferences
    b. submitting their work for peer review and serving as peer reviewers themselves
    c. avoiding replicating studies identical or similar to those that others have already done
    d. publishing in professional journals

10. Which of the following is NOT one of the basic steps of the scientific method?
    a. publishing in a professional journal
    b. collecting data
    c. analyzing data
    d. drawing conclusions

11. A _____ is characterized by the unobtrusive observation of behaviors in real-world settings, such as parks, streets, and day care centers.
    a. naturalistic observation
    b. laboratory observation
    c. correlational study
    d. survey

12. What is the main difference between naturalistic observation and experiments?
    a. In naturalistic observation, the researcher manipulates the environment to see what happens and then describes it.
    b. In experimental methods, the researcher tries to be as unobtrusive as possible.
    c. In naturalistic observation, the independent variable cannot be manipulated.
    d. In experimental methods, the researcher actively manipulates the environment of the participant.

13. Which of the following is a valid criticism of standardized tests?
    a. They cannot be used to compare people.
    b. They may be biased and favor people from some cultures.
    c. They do not measure appropriately the performance of an individual.
    d. They are used to compare people, and this is not good.

Practice Test 2

1. A _____ is selected from the population.
    a. sample
    b. placebo
    c. dependent variable
    d. theory

2. Each of the following is a drawback of laboratory research, except
    a. participants know they are being studied.
    b. the laboratory setting might produce unnatural behavior.
    c. the participants are not likely to represent diverse cultural groups.
    d. laboratory settings do not permit control over complex real-world factors.

3. Participants' tendency to respond in a way that is intended to create a good impression, rather than to provide true information, is one of the problems with
    a. experiments.
    b. correlational studies.
    c. surveys.
    d. naturalistic observations.

4. The strength of the relationship between two or more events can be determined by
    a. experimental research.
    b. case study.
    c. physiological research.
    d. correlational research.

5. Which of the following research strategies allows for most control and precision?
    a. correlational
    b. naturalistic observation
    c. experimental
    d. interview

6. If you conduct research in which you manipulate a variable, while holding others constant and randomly assign participants to groups, what research method are you using?
    a. case study
    b. interview
    c. correlational research
    d. experimental research

7.   An experiment is being conducted to determine the effects of different teaching methods on student performance. The independent variable is _____, while the dependent variable is _____.
   a.   different teaching methods; number of students taking the test
   b.   student performance; grades on a test
   c.   different teaching methods; student performance
   d.   student performance; different teaching methods

8.   In an experiment, the _____ is the "cause" and the _____ is the "effect."
   a.   dependent; independent
   b.   independent; dependent
   c.   control; dependent
   d.   dependent; experimental

9.   In an experiment testing the effect of amphetamine on learning in rats, the amphetamine is the
   a.   dependent variable.
   b.   experimental variable.
   c.   independent variable.
   d.   extraneous variable.

10.   Manipulated factor is to _____ as measured factor is to _____.
   a.   experimental group; independent variable
   b.   control group; independent variable
   c.   dependent variable; experimental group
   d.   independent variable; dependent variable

11.   Experiments with people involve a comparison between at least two groups: a group that receives the special treatment and a group that receives a placebo or neutral treatment. This latter group is called the
   a.   control group.
   b.   representative sample.
   c.   experimental group.
   d.   random sample.

12.   Which of the following statements about psychological research methods is correct?
   a.   Only clinical psychologists are allowed to conduct experiments.
   b.   It would be inappropriate to combine observation and the correlational method.
   c.   Experiments usually involve standardized tests.
   d.   Correlational studies cannot be used to arrive at cause-and-effect conclusions.

13.   When Terror Management Theory researchers asked participants to complete the word fragment COFF_ _ to measure mortality salience, what was this an example of? (hint: COFF_ _ can be completed with either IN or EE)
      a.   a hypothesis
      b.   a statistical test
      c.   random sampling
      d.   operationalization of a variable

14.   Which of the following is NOT a good way to operationalize happiness?
      a.   the score on a self-report questionnaire
      b.   coding pictures for Duchenne smiling
      c.   a structured interview about sources of happiness in the participant's life
      d.   an individual's standard deviation on a standardized test

15.   Which of the following would be an appropriate sample if a researcher intends to generalize the results of the study to "all males"?
      a.   a sample of 100 members of the Sigma Epsilon fraternity
      b.   a sample of 100 male freshman psychology students
      c.   a sample of 100 males, 50 from a university in Russia and 50 from a university in the U.S.
      d.   a sample of 100 American males who have been randomly selected from the draft registry

Practice Test 3

1.   The use of statistical procedures allows researchers to
     a.   conceptualize the problem.
     b.   collect data.
     c.   analyze the data.
     d.   develop hypotheses.

2.   In a correlation coefficient, the _____ is the indicator of the direction of the relationship.
     a.   number
     b.   sign
     c.   level of statistical significance
     d.   statistic

3.   The _____ is the score that falls exactly in the middle of the distribution of scores after they have been arranged from highest to lowest.
     a.   mean
     b.   mode
     c.   median
     d.   range

4.   If you were a psychologist concerned about reducing gender bias in psychological inquiry, you would be least concerned about which of the following?
   a.   gender stereotypes
   b.   exaggeration of gender differences
   c.   gender of consumers of psychological research
   d.   selection of research topics

5.   In scientific studies, generalizations can be made only if the _____ is representative of the _____.
   a.   sample; random sample
   b.   random sample; sample
   c.   population; sample
   d.   sample; population

6.   _____ is the extent to which scientific research yields a consistent, reproducible result.
   a.   Generalizability
   b.   Reliability
   c.   Objectivity
   d.   Randomness

7.   Which of the following is NOT one of the basic types of research in psychology?
   a.   correlational
   b.   descriptive
   c.   experimental
   d.   philosophical

8.   The _____ is a measure of central tendency that is calculated by adding all the scores and dividing that total by the number of scores or participants.
   a.   mode
   b.   median
   c.   mean
   d.   range

9.   The mode is the
   a.   score right in the middle of the distribution of scores.
   b.   "average" score as we commonly know it.
   c.   most common score.
   d.   difference between the highest and the lowest score.

10.   What is a meta-analysis?
   a.   a statistical procedure used to study meta-phenomena
   b.   a method of combining results across different studies
   c.   a special way to cheat at statistics
   d.   a specific form of critical thinking

11. If the correlation coefficient of the relationship between class attendance and final grade in a class is +.75, that means that
    a. there is no relationship between going to class and the final grade.
    b. going to class makes people get better grades.
    c. the lower the class attendance, the lower the final grade in the class.
    d. the less people attend class, the higher the final grade in the class.

12. Which of the following is an accurate list of the ethical guidelines for research using human participants as proposed by the American Psychological Association (APA)?
    a. informed consent, confidentiality, debriefing, deception
    b. informed consent, confidentiality, deception, anonymity
    c. informed consent, anonymity, debriefing
    d. Informed consent is the only guideline the APA proposes.

13. Why do surveys in magazines not have good generalizability?
    a. Magazines can use random sampling.
    b. People who choose to buy the magazine and choose to send in their answers may have characteristics that are particular to, and different from, the characteristics of those who do not complete the survey.
    c. Surveys in magazines are poorly constructed and are about topics that cannot be generalized.
    d. Magazine articles are silly and meaningless.

14. Which of the following is a true statement regarding Dr. Pennebaker's research where he randomly assigned one group to write about their most traumatic life event and another groups to write about their plans for the day?
    a. This research was unethical and shut down by the APA.
    b. This research is correlational but Dr. Pennebaker concluded that writing caused people to feel better.
    c. This is an example of an experiment.
    d. Writing about traumatic life events is bad for one's physical health.

15. Which of the following would be consistent with a –.68 correlation coefficient?
    a. The colder it is outside, the less people go outside.
    b. The more hours I study, the better my grade is on the test.
    c. The lower the ice cream sales, the lower the number of assaults reported at the police station.
    d. The number of books a person owns has no relationship with how knowledgeable he or she is.

16. In a correlation coefficient the _____ is an indicator of the strength of the relationship between the two factors being studied.
    a. number
    b. sign
    c. level of statistical significance
    d. statistic

17 .In political elections, which measure of central tendency would be more consistent with the method of determining who is elected?
   a.   mean
   b.   median
   c.   mode
   d.   standard deviation

18. The statistic that measures how closely the scores are clustered around the mean is the
   a.   mean.
   b.   range.
   c.   standard deviation.
   d.   mode.

19. _____ statistics are the mathematical methods used to draw conclusions and test hypotheses.
   a.   Descriptive
   b.   Inferential
   c.   Psychological
   d.   Mathematical

Answer Key

Practice Test 1 Answers
1.   a.   Drawing conclusions is the last step.
     b.   No; this is third step.
     c.   No; collecting data is the second step.
     d.   RIGHT; the first step in the scientific method is to conceptualize a problem.

2.   a.   Correlations are statistical assessments, not predictions.
     b.   Experiments are research methods, not predictions.
     c.   Observations are part of the process of collecting data and are not predictions.
     d.   TRUE; a hypothesis is a specific assumption or prediction that can be tested.

3.   a.   No; a case study involves an in-depth examination of one person.
     b.   No; a correlational study examines the relationships of two or more events or characteristics.
     c.   YES; this is the method by which behavior is observed in real-world settings.
     d.   No; experimental research consists of the manipulation of variables and groups of subjects.

4.   a.   No; an interview is a face-to-face method whereby the participant is asked questions.

b.   No; a random sample is a sample that is selected from the population at random.

c.   No; an experiment involves the manipulation of variables and subject groups.

d.   YES; a case study is an in-depth look at a single individual.

5.   a.   This option describes a random sample.

b.   Standardized tests are used by several different types of psychologists.

c.   CORRECT; these tests provide information about individual differences.

d.   Standardized tests are not given in real-world settings.

6.   a.   This may be true, but it is not the main advantage.

b.   Only experimentation can determine cause and effect.

c.   THAT'S RIGHT; standardized tests give information about individual differences.

d.   Standardized tests can be biased against certain groups of people.

7.   a.   The experiment determines cause-and-effect relationships.

b.   No, since naturalistic observation does not attempt to control variables.

c.   YES, THAT'S RIGHT; correlational research attempts to determine the relationship between variables.

d.   This is incorrect.

8.   a.   No; philosophers may address the same issues, but they are not subject to the scientific methods that define a science.

b.   YES; the way the information is collected, in other words, the methods used, are what define and distinguish a science from other approaches.

c.   Incorrect; collaboration is very important in the development of a science.

d.   Incorrect; objectivity is one of the four ideals that are central to the scientific approach.

9.   a.   This is one of the best ways to collaborate, by sharing information and taking advantage of the feedback that they may receive during the conference.

b.   This is also one of the main ways in which scientists collaborate.

c.   RIGHT ANSWER; avoiding replicating the studies of others is not in the spirit of collaboration; when scientists replicate the studies of others they add very important information that can serve to support or disprove the hypotheses and theories proposed by others.

d.   This is also a common form of collaboration; however, publishing in a prestigious journal requires a lot of work on the part of the scientist.

10.   a.   CORRECT; while this is an important activity that contributes to scientific collaboration, it is not an essential step of the scientific method.

b.   This is the second step of the scientific method.

c.   This is the third step of the scientific method.

d.   This is the fourth step of the scientific method.

11.   a.   CORRECT; notice that unobtrusive means that investigators try not to exert any influence or affect on those that are being observed; instead, they try to blend into the situation.
      b.   No; in laboratories the observations are obtrusive, since the participants do know that they are being observed and studied.
      c.   No; data collected through naturalistic observation may be analyzed with the correlational statistical procedure, but the correlational method is not limited to the use of data collected in real-world settings or in unobtrusive manners.
      d.   No; surveys may be collected in real-world settings, such as the mall, but they are obtrusive, since the participants do know that they are being studied.

12.   a.   No; naturalistic observation does not manipulate the environment.
      b.   No; experimental methods are obtrusive.
      c.   No; there is no independent variable to be manipulated in naturalistic observation.
      d.   YES; experimental methods are characterized by this manipulation of the environment in which the observations take place.

13.   a.   No; standardized tests are designed for the purpose of comparing people.
      b.   YES; unfortunately, if a test is standardized based on scores of individuals from one culture, the standardization may not apply to people from another culture.
      c.   No; standardized tests do measure appropriately the performance of an individual.
      d.   No; comparing people in psychological factors is a valid research endeavor.

Practice Test 2 Answers
1.   a.   YES; a sample is a subset of the population.
      b.   A placebo is an inert treatment that has no real effect.
      c.   The dependent variable is the variable that is being measured.
      d.   A theory is a set of interrelated ideas.

2.   a.   This is a drawback; participants will know they are being studied.
      b.   This is a drawback; being in a laboratory can cause participants to behave unnaturally.
      c.   This is a drawback.
      d.   CORRECT; the laboratory does in fact permit control over factors.

3.   a.   No, this is usually not a problem in an experiment.
      b.   No, this tendency is unrelated to correlational studies.
      c.   YES, this is one of the problems of surveys.
      d.   Incorrect

4.   a.   Experimental research consists of manipulation of variables and subject groups.
      b.   Case studies provide an in-depth look at an individual.
      c.   Physiological research studies the biological basis of behavior.
      d.   TRUE; correlational research examines relationships.

5. a. Correlational research only determines relationships among variables, and it is usually used when the researcher cannot control the factors of interest.
    b. This method by definition does not have any control over the factors influencing the observations.
    c. RIGHT; experimental research can determine cause and effect between events, because it controls factors and manipulates precisely the variables of interest.
    d. No; in an interview, the researcher chooses which questions to ask but does not seek to control every aspect of the procedure.

6. a. A case study consists of an in-depth analysis of a single individual.
    b. An interview is a face-to-face questioning of another person.
    c. In correlational research, we examine the relationship between two or more events.
    d. CORRECT; the experiment can help psychologists determine the causes of behavior.

7. a. Partially correct; the different teaching methods are the independent variable, but the dependent variable is not the number of students taking the test, which is irrelevant.
    b. Partially correct; student performance is not the independent variable, but student performance could be measured by grades on a test.
    c. TOTALLY CORRECT; the different teaching methods are being manipulated (cause), and student performance is the dependent variable (effect); it is being measured.
    d. No; they are backward.

8. a. No; the dependent variable is being measured to detect change that the manipulation of the independent variable might have caused.
    b. CORRECT; the cause is the independent variable and the effect is the dependent variable.
    c. No; the control group acts as a comparison; the dependent variable is the effect that is being measured because of changes to it due to manipulation.
    d. No; the dependent variable is being measured to detect change that the manipulation of the independent variable might have caused; the experimental group is the group that receives the manipulation.

9. a. No; the dependent variable is learning.
    b. No
    c. YES; the amphetamine is the "cause" that is being manipulated.
    d. No

10.   a.   The experimental group receives the manipulation; the measured factor is the dependent variable.

       b.   The control group acts as a comparison group; the measured factor is the dependent variable.

       c.   The manipulated factor is the independent variable; the experimental group receives the manipulation.

       d.   THAT'S RIGHT; the experimenter manipulates the independent variable and determines what, if any, changes occurred in the dependent variable.

11.   a.   RIGHT; this is the control group.

       b.   The sample that is selected from the population should be a representative sample.

       c.   The experimental group receives the special treatment.

       d.   Both groups make up the random sample.

12.   a.   Psychologists from all specializations conduct experiments.

       b.   Combining methods is something that is often done and is appropriate when required.

       c.   Experiments involve the independent variable and the dependent variable.

       d.   Correct, correlations do not indicate causation.

13.   a.   Incorrect, hypotheses are the predicted findings.

       b.   Incorrect, this is not a statistical test.

       c.   Incorrect, random sampling describes the way participants are selected.

       d.   CORRECT; this is how TMT researchers operationalized the variable of mortality salience.

14.   a.   No, this is actually a very good way to operationalize happiness and is the method Ed Diener uses in his research on happiness.

       b.   No; this is also a good way to operationalize happiness and has been used in past research.

       c.   No; while interviews do have the issue of self-serving bias they can be used to operationalize variables.

       d.   CORRECT; while if there is a standardized test for happiness, a person's score could be used to operationalize happiness, the standard deviation cannot.

15.   a.   No; this sample of males is not representative of all males.

       b.   No; while this would be the most common way to recruit participants for a study, this would not be a representative sample of all males.

       c.   No; while this option is better than option b, because it integrates males from different cultures, it is still limited to males from universities in powerful countries.

       d.   YES; while this sample has only American males, the fact that it is randomly selected from a list that includes males older than 18 would allow the researchers to get participants of various ages and from all of the United States.

Practice Test 3 Answers

1.   a.   Statistical procedures are not involved in conceptualizing research problems.
       b.   Collecting data is accomplished through research methods.
       c.   THAT'S RIGHT; statistical methods help psychologists understand the meaning of data.
       d.   Hypotheses are developed in the process of conceptualizing the problem, and thus before the data is analyzed with statistics.

2.   a.   No; the numbers of the correlation coefficient range from -1 to $+1$, and the farther away the number from 0, the stronger is the relationship between the two factors.
       b.   YES; the sign is the indicator of the direction of the relationship; if the sign is positive, the factors vary in the same direction, and if the sign is negative the factors vary in opposite directions.
       c.   No; the level of significance is a measure relevant to inferential statistics and is not used in correlations.
       d.   No; the correlation coefficient is a statistic, but placing the concept "statistic" at that point in the sentence does not make sense.

3.   a.   No
       b.   No
       c.   YES
       d.   No

4.   a.   No; this is a very important issue.
       b.   Gender differences are often exaggerated.
       c.   YEAH; this is the least important.
       d.   Research topics often reflect a male bias.

5.   a.   No
       b.   No
       c.   Incorrect; the population is larger than the sample; therefore, the statement does not make sense.
       d.   CORRECT; in almost all scientific studies, the scientist cannot study the complete population of interest and therefore must select a sample; in order to generalize the findings to the population, however, the sample must be representative.

6.   a.   No; generalizability is the extent to which the results of one study with a sample can be generalized to the population.
       b.   CORRECT
       c.   No; objectivity is one of the four ideal approaches to science.
       d.   No; randomness refers to the extent to which an event is due to chance.

7.   a.   No
   b.   No
   c.   No
   d.   CORRECT; while philosophers may address many of the same issues as psychologists, they do not use the scientific method in the same manner.

8.   a.   No; this is the most common score.
   b.   No; this is the score right in the middle of the distribution of scores.
   c.   YES; this is what we commonly associate with an average score.
   d.   No; this is a measure of variability, not of central tendency.

9.   a.   No; this is the median.
   b.   No; this is the mean.
   c.   YES; the mode is the most common or typical score.
   d.   No; this is the range.

10.   a.   No; there is no such thing as "meta-phenomena.
    b.   YES; meta-analysis combines the results of many studies to find the strength of an effect.
    c.   No, meta-analysis is not cheating.
    d.   No, this is not a form of thinking.

11.   a.   Incorrect; a correlation coefficient of 0 means that there is no relationship.
    b.   Incorrect; this statement suggests causation, which cannot be concluded from a correlation coefficient.
    c.   YES; the positive and strong correlation coefficient says that these two factors vary in the same direction; we could also say that the higher the attendance, the higher the final grade in the class.
    d.   Incorrect; this statement is consistent with a negative correlation coefficient.

12.   a.   CORRECT; these are the correct guidelines for ethical research.
    b.   No; this list is missing debriefing and anonymity is not a separate guideline.
    c.   No, this list is missing confidentiality and deception and anonymity is not a separate guideline.
    d.   No; confidentiality, debriefing, and deception are also guidelines for ethical research.

13.   a.   No; magazines are chosen by the reader and cannot use random sampling.
    b.   YES; generalizability to the people that did not complete the survey is compromised by the specific characteristics of those who did complete the survey.
    c.   No; surveys in magazines can be very good, and they can be about important topics, they are just not likely to get a representative sample, unless their population of interest is only the people that choose to answer the survey.
    d.   No; surveys in magazines can be very well constructed.

14 a. No; this research is perfectly ethical.

b. No; this research is not correlational.

c. CORRECT; because participants were randomly assigned to groups, it is an experiment.

d. No, Dr. Pennebaker's research actually found the opposite.

15. a. CORRECT; -.68 is a strong negative correlation between cold, which goes up, and people going outside, which goes down. Notice that the item does not make reference to measuring of temperature. Change the item to mean the same, but instead of using "cold" use the corresponding description of temperature, "lower temperature," and see how the correlation coefficient changes.

b. No; this is a positive correlation.

c. No; this is a positive correlation.

d. No; this presents no correlation.

16. a. YES; the numbers of the correlation coefficient range from –1 to +1, and the farther away the number from 0, the stronger the relationship between the two factors.

b. No; the sign is the indicator of the direction of the relationship.

c. No; the level of significance is a measure relevant to inferential statistics and is not used in correlations.

d. No; the correlation coefficient is a statistic, but placing the concept "statistic" at that point in the sentence does not make sense.

17. a. No; in elections we don't average votes.

b. No; this measure would be irrelevant.

c. YES; the mode is the score that occurs most often in a set of data; each time a person votes for candidate A this can be considered a score for A and the same for candidate B, etc.; the score that occurs more often (A, B, or C) determines who wins.

d. No; this is irrelevant.

18. a. No; this is a measure of central tendency, and the statement is asking about a measure of variability.

b. No; while this is a measure of variability, it does not assess the extent to which the scores vary from the mean.

c. YES; the standard deviation does measure how much, on the average, scores vary around the mean.

d. No; this is a measure of central tendency.

19.   a.   No; descriptive statistics are not used to test hypotheses, just to summarize the data.

          b.   YES; these types of statistics are used to draw inferences and test if the proposed hypotheses are supported by the data collected.

          c.   No; while there are some statistical procedures that are almost exclusively used by psychologists, "psychological statistics" is not the same as inferential statistics.

          d.   No; "mathematical statistics" is a redundant and incorrect concept because statistics *are* mathematics.

Chapter 3: Biological Foundations of Behavior

Learning Goals
1. Discuss the nature and basic function of the nervous system.
2. Explain what neurons are and how they process information.
3. Identify the brain's levels and structures, and summarize the functions of its structures.
4. State what the endocrine system is and how it affects behavior.
5. Describe the brain's capacity for recovery and repair.
6. Explain how genetics increases our understanding of behavior.
7. Describe the role of the biological foundations of human psychology in the body's stress response.

After studying Chapter 3, you will be able to:
- Explain the brain's incredible capacity for plasticity and repair;
- Understand that by changing how you think about things, you can actually change your brain;
- Describe the relationship between stress and the nervous system and how things like mindfulness mediation and self-talk can help to manage stress.

Chapter Outline
1. The Nervous System
- The brain can be changed by experience. When you "change the way you think," you are actually changing physical aspects of your brain.
- The nervous system contains billions of cells that make up the body's electrochemical communication network.
- These characteristics of the brain and nervous system allow it to direct our behavior:
  - Complexity: Billions of cells work together to simultaneously regulate breathing, interpret your visual surroundings, think about what you are reading, etc.
  - Integration: The brain takes information from all your senses (and even your genes) and integrates this information to determine how you function and behave in any given situation.
  - Adaptability: Nerve cells are not fixed and unchangeable. Rather nerve cells, and the brain more generally, can adapt to changes in the body and environment. This capacity for change is called plasticity.
  - Electrochemical transmission: Electrical impulses and chemical messengers carry messages throughout the nervous system. This electrochemical system however can be disrupted by disorders such as epilepsy which causes abnormal electrical discharges in the brain.
- Pathways in the nervous system are made up of afferent nerves, efferent nerves, and neural networks.
  - Afferent nerves carry information to the brain.
  - Efferent nerves carry information from the brain.
  - Neural networks make up most of the brain and integrate sensory input and motor output.
- The central nervous system is made up of the brain and spinal cord.

- The peripheral nervous system connects to the brain and spinal cord to the other parts of the body and is responsible for bringing information to and from the brain. The peripheral nervous system is composed of two major divisions:
  - Somatic nervous system consists of sensory nerves and conveys information about pain and temperature.
  - Autonomic nervous system takes messages to and from the body's internal organs and monitors breathing, heart rate, and digestion. The autonomic nervous system is divided into two parts:
    - Sympathetic nervous system arouses the body and prepares it for action.
    - Parasympathetic nervous system calms the body down.
- Neurons are the nerve cells responsible for processing information.
- Glial cells provide support and nourishment to neurons.

2. Neurons
- Structure of a neuron (see the tour included in this chapter for a visualization of how neurons are structured and how they relay information):
  - Cell body contains the nucleus which directs growth and maintenance of the cell.
  - Dendrites are treelike branches that receive and orient information toward the cell body.
  - Axon is the part that carries information away from the cell body towards other cells.
  - Myelin sheath is a layer of fat cells that insulates the axons in order to speed transmission of information. Multiple sclerosis is a neurological disease that causes the myelin sheaths to harden thereby disrupting communication between neurons.
- Neurons send information down the axon using neural impulses which are created by positively and negatively charged ions in the neuron.
- Resting potential is the stable, negative charge of an inactive ion.
- Action potential is the brief wave of positive charge that sweeps down the axon. When a neuron sends an action potential, it is said to be "firing."
- Synapses are tiny junctions between neurons and the gap between neurons is the synaptic gap. Neurotransmitters are responsible for communicating information through the synaptic gaps.
- There are different types of neurotransmitters and each performs a specific role. There are 50 known neurotransmitters, but more are likely to be discovered. Here are a few of the most common:
  - Acetylcholine: stimulates the firing of neurons and is involved in the action of muscles, learning, and memory.
  - GABA: inhibits the firing of neurons and therefore helps control the preciseness of the signal being carried between neurons. Low levels of GABA are linked to the experience of anxiety.
  - Norepinephrine: inhibits the firing of neurons in the central nervous system but excites the heart, intestines, and urogential tract. Too little norepinephrine is associated with depression but too much is associated with manic states.
  - _____: inhibits the firing of neurons and controls voluntary movement. It also affects sleep, mood, attention, and learning.

- o Serotonin: inhibits the firing of neurons and is similar to dopamine in that it too is involved with regulating sleep, mood, attention, and learning.
  - o Endorphins: stimulate neurons and shields the body from pain as well as elevates feelings of pleasure.
  - o _____: is both a hormone and neurotransmitter that plays a role in emotional bonds such as love. Mothers experience a surge of this after giving birth.
- Most drugs that influence behavior do so by either mimicking or blocking the effects of neurotransmitters.
  - o An agonist is a drug that mimics the effects of a neurotransmitter.
  - o An antagonist is a drug that blocks the effects of a neurotransmitter.
- Information, such as a person's name, is embedded in many neurons that are connected, or a neural network. The strength of these connections determines how well you remember the information.

3. Structures of the Brain and Their Functions

- Brain lesioning is an abnormal disruption in the tissue of the brain resulting from injury or disease, the study of which has provided researchers with clues about how different parts of the brain function.
- Electroencephalograph (EEG) records electrical activity in the brain through electrodes placed on the scalp. EEGs can be used to assess brain damage and certain neurological disorders.
- Positron-emission tomography (PET) measures the amount of glucose in various areas of the brain and can be used to determine which parts of the brain are active when engaging in different activities.
- _____ uses a magnet to measure the amount of hydrogen in specific areas of the brain and can create very detailed images of the brain.
- Functional magnetic resonance imaging (fMRI) is a powerful technique used by researchers to measure activity in the brain. fMRI works by detecting the amount of oxygenated blood in different areas of the brain.
- Organization of the brain (see the tour included in this chapter for a complete visualization of the brain:
  - o Hindbrain: rear of the skull
    - ▪ Medulla: begins where the spinal cord enters brain; regulates breathing and reflexes that allow us to stand upright.
    - ▪ Cerebellum: rear of hindbrain, above medulla; responsible for motor coordination.
    - ▪ Pons: a bridge in the hindbrain; responsible for sleep and arousal.
  - o Midbrain: between hindbrain and forebrain; relays information between the brain and eyes and ears.
    - ▪ Reticular formation: diffuse collection of neurons involved in behavior patterns such as walking, sleeping, and turning in response to noise.
    - ▪ Brain stem: includes part of the hindbrain and midbrain; determines alertness and relates basic survival functions such as breathing, heartbeat, and blood pressure.
  - o Forebrain: highest level of the brain and its development differentiates us from other animals.

- Limbic system: loosely connected network of structures responsible for memory and emotion.
  - Amygdala: involved in the discrimination of objects that are necessary for survival such as appropriate food, mates, and rivals. The amygdala is also involved in emotional awareness and expression.
  - Hippocampus: responsible for the storage of memories
- Thalamus: a relay station that sorts information and sends it to the appropriate region of the brain.
- Basal ganglia: works with cerebellum and cerebral cortex to control voluntary movements such as riding a bicycle.
- _____: monitors the pleasurable activities of eating, drinking, and sex. It is also involved in emotional states and the regulation of stress.
- Cerebral cortex: evolutionarily speaking, this is the most recently developed part of the brain. It is responsible for thinking and planning. The cerebral cortex is divided in to two hemispheres (left and right). Each hemisphere is further divided into several regions or lobes:
  - Occipital lobe: responds to visual stimuli
  - Temporal lobe: hearing, language processing, and memory
  - Frontal lobe: voluntary muscles, intelligence, and personality; a special area of the fontal lobe is the prefrontal cortex which is responsible for planning and reasoning. The prefrontal cortex is therefore sometimes referred to as the executive control system.
  - Parietal lobe: spatial location, attention, motor control
  - Somatosensory cortex: processes information about body sensations.
  - Motor cortex: processes information about voluntary movement.
  - _____: part of the frontal lobe and makes up 75% of the cerebral cortex. It is responsible for integrating information and is therefore responsible for intellectual functions such as thinking and problem solving.
  - Broca's area: located in the left hemisphere and responsible for the production of speech.
  - Wernicke's area: also in the left hemisphere but is responsible for comprehending language.
  - Corpus callosum: a large bundle of axons that connects the brain's two hemispheres.
- Hemisphere specialization: somewhat paradoxically, the left hemisphere receives information from the right side of the body whereas the right hemisphere receives information from the left side of the body. Each hemisphere has developed areas of specialization.
  - Verbal processing (such as speech and grammar) is localized in the left hemisphere.

- Nonverbal processing (such as spatial perception, visual recognition, and emotion) is localized in the right hemisphere.

4. The Endocrine System

- The endocrine system is a set of glands that regulate the activities of certain organs by releasing hormones into the bloodstream. These hormones serve as chemical messengers.
  - Pituitary gland: controlled by the hypothalamus and located at the base of the skull. This gland controls growth and regulates the other glands so it is sometimes called the master gland.
  - Adrenal glands: instrumental in regulating moods, energy level, and the ability to cope with stress. These glands release epinephrine and norepinephrine (also called adrenaline and noradrenaline respectively).

5. Brain Damage, Plasticity, and Repair

- The human brain has a remarkable capacity to repair itself, but it shows the most plasticity in young children.
- The brain repairs itself using three different methods:
  - Collateral sprouting: axons of healthy neurons next to damaged cells grow new branches.
  - Substitution of function: the functions of the damaged area are taken over by another area of the brain.
  - _____: is the creation of new neurons. This was once thought impossible but recent research has found that human adults can generate new neurons.
- When the brain cannot repair itself, brain grafts, which are implants of healthy tissue into damaged areas, can be used. However, donors of healthy brain tissue are understandably difficult to find. Aborted fetuses pose one potential source, but such a procedure is controversial and raises ethical issues.
- Stem cells are unique cells because they have the capacity to develop into most types of human cells. The use of stem cells in the treatment of brain and spinal cord injuries has great potential but is also very controversial because stem cells are typically taken from extra embryos left over from in vitro fertilization procedures.

6. Genetics and Behavior

- Chromosomes are threadlike structures that are located in the nucleus of every cell in the human body and contain our DNA. Genes, which contain our hereditary information, are short segments of chromosomes composed of DNA.
- Dominant-recessive genes principle explains how a pair of genes (one from each parent) interacts to form an observable trait such as eye color. If one dominant gene and one recessive gene are present, the dominant gene will dictate the trait. If two recessive genes are present then the recessive trait will be exhibited.
- Polygenic inheritance: unlike eye color, complex human characteristics such as personality and intelligence are influenced by many different genes.
- Molecular genetics: involves the manipulation of genes using technology to determine their effect on behavior.
- Genome: the complete set of instructions for making an organism (see Psychology and Life section in Chapter 3 for more information on the Human Genome Project which mapped much of the human genome).

- Selective breeding: a method in which organisms are chosen for reproduction based on how much of a particular trait is displayed. Selective breeding in rats has shown the important influence of genes on behavior but has simultaneously shown how the environment can also influence behavior.
- _____ is the study of the degree of heredity's influence on behavior.
  - Researchers have studied identical twins raised in the same household versus twins who were separated at birth to investigate the role of genes and environment in determining behavior. Identical twins have the exact same genetic code so if twins that are raised apart behave the same way, genes probably played an important role. However, if twins raised apart behave differently, the environment probably played an important role.
- Genotype is a person's actual genetic material or blueprint.
- Phenotype is a person's observable characteristics and is influenced by both the genotype and the environment.

7. Psychology's Biological Foundations, Health, and Wellness

- Stress is the response of individuals to stressors, which are circumstances that are threatening.
- When experiencing stress, out body readies itself to handle the stress through actual physiological changes.
  - Heart pounding, sweaty hands are evidence that the sympathetic nervous system is engaged to prepare the body to handle a stressor.
  - Such preparation for acute stress, or stress that goes away quickly is a good thing. But chronic stress is bad because it goes on continuously and therefore causes the autonomic nervous system to be continuously active which is associated with a breakdown of the immune system.

Clarifying Tricky Points
Definitions
The most challenging aspect of this chapter is all the definitions. You need to know the divisions of the nervous system, components of a neuron, the parts of the brain, neurotransmitters, and a few hormones. Learning all these definitions can seem daunting but, fortunately, there are several figures and even a tour of the nervous system in Chapter 3 that can help. Use these figures (particularly 3.1, 3.2, and 3.5, and the tour) to create visual representations in your mind of the nervous system, neurons, and the brain. While thinking about what a neuron looks like, also try to describe to yourself what each part does (do the same for the brain). Then challenge yourself by sketching your own figures of a neuron and brain, then try to label all the parts. Many students find that they learn best with visual representations of complex material. The tour included in this chapter is particularly useful in this sense. Try referring to it while you are reading to help you visualize how neurons and synapses work to relay information, how the brain is organized, and how the central and peripheral nervous systems operate.

Specialization in the Brain
Though much of your job in studying Chapter 3 involves memorizing what goes on in each part of the brain, it is important to keep in mind two of the key characteristics of the brain and nervous system: complexity and integration. This means, for example, that while visual stimuli

are processed in the occipital lobe, the occipital lobe is connected to many other parts of the brain and therefore the occipital lobe is not exclusively involved in our sense of sight. Neural networks are complex, often spanning across sections of the brain, therefore multiple areas of the brain are involved in forming any of our thoughts or processing any information. Recall from Chapter 3 the myth that the left hemisphere of the brain is logical and right hemisphere of the brain is creative. Most of human activity is complex enough that both hemispheres are required. For example, while the left hemisphere understands language syntax and grammar rules, the right hemisphere understands the intonation and emotion of language. Therefore, to fully understand a story you are reading or hearing from a friend, both hemispheres are necessary.

Dominant vs. Recessive Genes

Your characteristics that are said to be genetic (ex., eye color) are actually dictated by multiple genes. Some genes are dominant while others are recessive. Naturally, if a dominant gene is present then that gene determines the characteristic. But you also have in your genetic code many recessive genes that, while not exhibited by your physical features, are still present inside you and able to be passed on to your offspring. For example, even if you have brown eyes, you may carry the gene for blue eyes. It's just that the gene for blue eyes is recessive so, in the presence of the dominant brown eye gene, your eyes are brown. But, if you inherit two recessive genes, then the recessive trait (blue eyes in this example) will be displayed. While scientists have been able to accurately decode the genes that determine simple traits like eye color, more complex traits like personality are far more complicated to understand through the study of genes, because such complex traits are determined not only by multiple genes but also by the way proteins and hormones interact in your body to "activate" genes.

Genotype and Phenotype

Your genotype is the genetic blueprint for you. If genes could dictate everything, you would look and behave exactly how your genotype says you should. But, from Chapter 3, you know that the environment plays an important role in genetic expression. Your phenotype is how your genes are expressed given your environment. Phenotype is how you actually are, not just how your genes say you should be. A simple example is if your genotype indicates you should have brown hair but you dye it blonde, then your phenotype is blond hair but your genotype remains brown.

An Appreciative View of Psychology and Your Life

Think back to a time when you felt particularly stressed. Maybe this was when you had a big test, when you started college, or maybe just when you had too much going on and felt that you just couldn't possibly do any more.

Based on what you learned in chapter 3, describe how your body reacted to this stress including your heart, nervous system, hormones, and immune system.

_____

_____

_____

Now describe some of the techniques mentioned in chapter 3 that can help you deal more effectively with this stressor in the future.

_____

_____

_____

_____

_____

Practice Test 1

1.   The nervous system is made up of _____ (of) interconnected cells.
        a.   approximately ten thousand
        b.   billions
        c.   approximately one million
        d.   less than one million

2.   Which of the following types of nerves carry input to the brain?
        a.   sensory nerves
        b.   motor nerves
        c.   interneurons
        d.   foreneurons

3.   The majority of the brain consists of which type of nerves?
        a.   sensory nerves
        b.   motor nerves
        c.   neural networks
        d.   axons

4.   The brain and the spinal cord constitute the
        a.   central nervous system.
        b.   peripheral nervous system.
        c.   autonomic nervous system.
        d.   sympathetic nervous system.

5.   When you accidentally touch a hot burner on a stove, which part of your nervous system carries the pain message from your skin to your brain?
        a.   the autonomic nervous system
        b.   the sympathetic nervous system
        c.   the parasympathetic nervous system
        d.   the somatic nervous system

6. The physiological arousal that you feel as you enter a classroom to take an exam is produced by the _____ nervous system.
    a. parasympathetic
    b. sympathetic
    c. somatic
    d. central

7. Messages from other neurons are collected by the _____ of the receiving neuron.
    a. axon
    b. synapse
    c. neurotransmitter
    d. dendrite

8. The part of the neuron that carries messages away from the cell body is called the
    a. nucleus.
    b. axon.
    c. dendrite.
    d. neurotransmitter.

9. The _____ is the brief wave of electrical change that races down the axon.
    a. action potential
    b. achievement potential
    c. all-or-none principle
    d. ion

10. If a person has a low level of dopamine, this would most likely cause which problem?
    a. The person would have difficulty with walking.
    b. The person would suffer from anxiety.
    c. The person would suffer from depression.
    d. The person would have sleep problems.

11. The part of the nervous system that includes the brain and the spinal cord is the
    a. central nervous system.
    b. peripheral nervous system.
    c. autonomous nervous system.
    d. somatic nervous system.

12. Glial cells
    a. are fewer in number than neurons.
    b. have dendrites just like neurons.
    c. provide supportive and nutritive functions in the brain.
    d. are specialized to send and receive information.

13. Which division of the nervous system is the one involved in relaxation and the calming of the body?
   a. somatic
   b. central
   c. sympathetic
   d. parasympathetic

14. The layer of fat cells that insulate most axons is the
   a. myelin sheath.
   b. cell body.
   c. plasticity.
   d. ion.

15. Which neurotransmitter is the one that is involved in the action of muscles, learning, and memory?
   a. dopamine
   b. acetylcholine
   c. GABA
   d. norepinephrine

16. Multiple sclerosis (MS) is the deterioration of what part of the nervous system?
   a. parasympathetic nervous system
   b. spinal cord
   c. dendrites
   d. myelin sheath

17. The _____ is the stable, negative charge of a neuron and the _____ is the wave of positive charge in a neuron.
   a. neurochemical; synapse
   b. action potential; resting potential
   c. resting potential; action potential
   d. synapse; neurochemical

18. The input is to the _____ as the output is to the _____.
   a. axon; dendrite
   b. cell body; dendrite
   c. dendrite; cell body
   d. dendrite; axon

19. Which of the following neurotransmitters is not involved in the regulation of sleeping patterns?
   a. endorphins
   b. serotonin
   c. norepinephrine
   d. acetylcholine

Practice Test 2

1. The hindbrain structure that helps to control our breathing is called the
   a. pons.
   b. reticular formation.
   c. medulla.
   d. cerebellum.

2. The _____ is the forebrain structure that monitors eating, drinking, and sexual behavior.
   a. thalamus
   b. hypothalamus
   c. neocortex
   d. cerebellum

3. A forebrain structure that plays an important role in the storage of memories is the
   a. hippocampus.
   b. amygdala.
   c. thalamus.
   d. limbic system.

4. Research about various brain areas indicates that higher mental processes such as thinking and problem solving are located within the
   a. association area.
   b. parietal sulcus.
   c. limbic system.
   d. thalamic nuclei.

5. The two hemispheres are connected by which structure?
   a. corpus callosum
   b. thalamus
   c. hypothalamus
   d. reticular formation

6. Which of the parts of the hindbrain is the one that is involved in motor coordination?
   a. medulla
   b. cerebellum
   c. pons
   d. reticular formation

7. This system in the midbrain is involved in the control of walking, sleeping, and turning to attend sudden noise.
   a. pons
   b. brain stem
   c. reticular formation
   d. hypothalamus

8.   The "pleasure center" of the brain is found in the
        a.   thalamus.
        b.   midbrain.
        c.   hippocampus.
        d.   hypothalamus.

9.   The lobe that is associated with the control of voluntary muscles, intelligence, and personality is the _____ lobe.
        a.   frontal
        b.   occipital
        c.   temporal
        d.   parietal

10.   Which of the following functions has NOT been associated with the left hemisphere of the cerebral cortex?
        a.   speech
        b.   grammar
        c.   humor
        d.   mathematics

11.   The _____ controls growth and regulates other glands, and part of it is controlled by the hypothalamus.
        a.   adrenal gland
        b.   spinal cord
        c.   pituitary gland
        d.   thalamus

12.   The hypothalamus can be described best as a(n)
        a.   screen.
        b.   subordinate.
        c.   regulator.
        d.   advisor.

13.   The most common myth about hemispheric specialization is that
        a.   speech and grammar are localized in the left hemisphere.
        b.   the right hemisphere is more dominant in processing nonverbal information.
        c.   humor is localized in the right hemisphere.
        d.   the left hemisphere is logical and the right hemisphere is creative.

14.   What type of scan allows researchers to see pictures of the brain and literally see what is happening in the brain while it is working?
        a.   MRI
        b.   CT
        c.   fMRI
        d.   X ray

15. What area of the brain is responsible for emotions?
    a. amygdala
    b. GABA
    c. basal ganglia
    d. temporal lobe

16. The _____ lobe is linked to personality.
    a. frontal
    b. parietal
    c. hind
    d. cortex

17. What is NOT a responsibility of the endocrine system?
    a. controlling adrenaline
    b. managing hormones
    c. motor control
    d. regulate activities of certain organs

Practice Test 3

1. _____ is the brain's capacity to modify and change.
    a. Plasticity
    b. Integration
    c. Electrochemical transmission
    d. Evolution

2. Genes are short segments of _____ that are composed of _____.
    a. neurons; glial cells
    b. chromosomes; dopamine
    c. chromosomes; DNA
    d. DNA; chromosomes

3. The dominant-recessive genes principle applies to all the following except which one?
    a. A recessive gene exerts its influence only if both genes of a pair are recessive.
    b. Dominant genes override the effect of a recessive gene.
    c. If one gene of a pair is dominant and one is recessive, the dominant gene exerts its effect.
    d. If both genes of a pair are dominant, the effect converts into a recessive trait.

4. Which of the following statements is NOT true about chromosomes?
    a. The nucleus of each human cell contains 46 chromosomes, or 23 pairs.
    b. Each pair of chromosomes comes from one of the parents.
    c. Chromosomes contain DNA.
    d. Genes are short segments of chromosomes.

5. _____ is the genetic research method in which organisms are chosen for reproduction based on how much of a particular trait they display.
   a.   Molecular genetics
   b.   Behavioral genetics
   c.   Selective breeding
   d.   Evolution

6. Neurogenesis is the _____ and is (has) _____.
   a.   grafting of new parts of the brain onto old parts; been recently found to be possible
   b.   creation of new neurons; been recently found to be possible
   c.   creation of new neurons; impossible
   d.   grafting of new parts of the brain onto old parts; impossible

7. Stem cell research uses special cells taken from _____.
   a.   infants
   b.   sperm
   c.   embryos
   d.   adults

8. Why are stem cells unique?
   a.   Stem cells have the capacity to develop into almost any type of cell in the human body.
   b.   Stem cells are actually not unique and are the most common type of cell in the adult human body.
   c.   Stem cells are very rare and only found in certain people.
   d.   Stem cells can re-grow a spinal cord but nothing else.

9. One reason chronic stress is bad for the body is because the _____ nervous system is continuously activated and releases _____ which ages the brain.
   a.   parasympathetic; epinephrine
   b.   parasympathetic; serotonin
   c.   endocrine; GABA
   d.   autonomic; testosterone

Answer Key

- When faced with a stressor, the body responds by activating the sympathetic nervous system, increasing your hear rate, and releasing testosterone. When the stressor is chronic, rather than acute, your immune system begins to break down leaving your body vulnerable to infection.
- Self-talk is an effective way to manage chronic stress because it involves cognitive restructuring, which is the act of modifying thoughts that sustain your problems. By using statements like "This isn't so bad. I can handle this challenge," rather than statements like

"I just can't do this. I'm so stupid," you can actually reduce the negative impact of stress on your body.

Practice Test 1 Answers

1. a.   No; a single cubic centimeter of the human brain has well over 50 million nerve cells.
    b.   YES; the total number varies from person to person, but it is in the billions.
    c.   No; this would not account for even one cubic centimeter of the human brain.
    d.   No; this would not account for even one cubic centimeter of the human brain.

2. a.   YES; sensory nerves carry sensory information to the brain.
    b.   No; sensory nerves carry motor messages from the brain.
    c.   No; interneurons mediate sensory input and motor output.
    d.   No

3. a.   No; sensory nerves carry information to the brain.
    b.   No; motor nerves carry the brain's output.
    c.   YES; most of the brain comprises neural networks.
    d.   No; an axon is a part of a neuron, not a nerve.

4. a.   THAT'S RIGHT; the central nervous system is made up of the brain and the spinal cord.
    b.   No; the peripheral nervous system is made up of the somatic nervous system and the autonomic nervous system.
    c.   No; this is part of the peripheral nervous system.
    d.   No; the sympathetic nervous system is part of the autonomic nervous system.

5. a.   No; the autonomic nervous system regulates internal organs.
    b.   No; while the sympathetic nervous system will likely be involved in your reaction to the pain, it is not involved in the sending of the sensory pain information to the brain.
    c.   No; the parasympathetic nervous system calms the body.
    d.   YES; the somatic nervous system contains sensory neurons.

6. a.   No; the parasympathetic nervous system calms the body.
    b.   THAT'S RIGHT; during stressful situations, the sympathetic nervous system increases the body's arousal.
    c.   No; the somatic nervous system provides sensory information to the central nervous system.
    d.   No; the central nervous system is made up of the brain and spinal cord.

7. a.   No; the axon carries information away from the cell body to other cells.
    b.   No; the synapse is the space between neurons.
    c.   No; neurotransmitters are involved in the transmission but are not the recipients of the message.
    d.   YES; the dendrites collect information.

8. a.   No; the nucleus is part of the cell body.
    b.   CORRECT
    c.   No; the dendrite receives information.
    d.   No; neurotransmitters are not a part of the neuron.

9. a.   YES; the action potential is caused by the exchange of ions across the neuron's membrane.
    b.   No
    c.   No; the all-or-none principle describes the action potential.
    d.   No

10. a.   YES; dopamine is involved in voluntary movement.
    b.   No; the neurotransmitter GABA is involved with anxiety.
    c.   No; depression and serotonin and norepinephrine are related.
    d.   No; sleep problems are associated with serotonin.

11. a.   YES; the central nervous system includes the brain and spinal cord.
    b.   No; the peripheral nervous system connects the brain and the spinal cord with the rest of the body and external stimuli.
    c.   No; this is a division of the peripheral nervous system.
    d.   No; this is a division of the peripheral nervous system.

12. a.   No; there are more glial cells than neurons.
    b.   No; glial cells do not have dendrites or axons.
    c.   YES; these are the functions of glial cells.
    d.   No; glial cells do not send and receive information.

13. a.   No
    b.   No
    c.   No; this division of the autonomous nervous system is involved in arousal.
    d.   YES; this is the division of the autonomous nervous system that calms the body.

14. a.   YES; the myelin sheath speeds up transmissions.
    b.   No; the cell body is a part of the neuron.
    c.   No; plasticity is the capacity of the brain to modify and change.
    d.   No; an ion is an electrically charged particle.

15. a.   No; while dopamine is associated with learning, it also affects sleep, mood, and attention.
    b.   YES; these are some of the psychological factors associated with acetylcholine.
    c.   No; GABA has been linked to anxiety.
    d.   No; while this neurotransmitter works with acetylcholine, it is associated with depression and mania.

16.   a.   No; this is not affected by MS.
      b.   No
      c.   No
      d.   YES; MS causes the myelin sheaths of neurons to deteriorate.

17.   a.   No
      b.   No; it's actually vice versa.
      c.   YES; this statement is correct.
      d.   No

18.   a.   No; the opposite is true.
      b.   No; while the cell body may initiate messages, the dendrites would not be the source of output.
      c.   No; while dendrites do receive the message and can be considered "input," the cell body is an intermediary and not the sender of the message.
      d.   YES; this analogy is the correct one.

19.   a.   YES; endorphins are associated with increasing pleasure and reducing pain.
      b.   No; serotonin works with norepinephrine and acetylcholine to regulate the states of sleeping and wakefulness.
      c.   No; norepinephrine works with serotonin and acetylcholine to regulate the states of sleeping and wakefulness.
      d.   No; acetylcholine works with norepinephrine and serotonin to regulate the states of sleeping and wakefulness.

Practice Test 2 Answers
1.   a.   No; the pons is a structure in the hindbrain that is involved in sleep and arousal.
      b.   No; the reticular formation is involved in stereotyped behaviors.
      c.   YES; the medulla controls breathing and other reflexes.
      d.   No; the cerebellum plays a role in motor behavior.

2.   a.   No; the thalamus is not involved in these behaviors.
      b.   CORRECT; the hypothalamus monitors eating, drinking, and sexual behavior.
      c.   No; the cerebral cortex is another portion of the forebrain.
      d.   No; the cerebellum is involved in motor behavior and is in the hindbrain.

3.   a.   RIGHT; this structure plays a role in the storage of memories.
      b.   No; the amygdala plays a role in emotions.
      c.   No; the thalamus serves as a rely-station-like function for sensory information.
      d.   No; the limbic system is a network of structures.

4.   a.   YES; association areas are involved in the highest intellectual functions.
      b.   No
      c.   No
      d.   No

5.   a.   CORRECT; the corpus callosum, a large bundle of fibers, connect the hemispheres.
      b.   No; the thalamus serves to relay sensory information.
      c.   No; the hypothalamus is involved in eating, drinking, and sex.
      d.   No; the reticular formation plays a role in stereotyped behaviors.

6.   a.   No; the medulla is involved in breathing and reflexes.
      b.   YES; leg and arm movement is coordinated at the cerebellum.
      c.   No; the pons is involved in sleep and arousal.
      d.   No; this is a part of the midbrain.

7.   a.   No; this is a part of the hindbrain.
      b.   No; while this is a part of the midbrain, it is involved in alertness, breathing, heartbeat, and blood pressure.
      c.   YES; it is a diffuse collection of neurons associated with those functions.
      d.   No; the hypothalamus is part of the forebrain.

8.   a.   No; the thalamus relays sensory information to the appropriate areas of the brain.
      b.   No; this "pleasure center" is in a part of the forebrain.
      c.   No; the hippocampus is linked to memory.
      d.   YES; the hypothalamus is involved in pleasurable feelings.

9.   a.   YES; damage to the frontal lobe can affect personality, as in the case of Phineas T. Gage.
      b.   No; this lobe is associated with the processing of visual information.
      c.   No; this lobe is associated with the processing of auditory information.
      d.   No; this lobe is associated with the processing of special location, attention, and motor control.

10.   a.   No; speech is localized in the left hemisphere.
      b.   No; grammar is localized in the left hemisphere.
      c.   YES; our sense of humor resides in the right hemisphere.
      d.   No; the left hemisphere participates more in the kind of logic used to prove geometric theorems.

11.   a.   No; the adrenal gland regulates moods, energy level, and the ability to cope with stress.
      b.   No; this is a part of the central nervous system, not a gland.
      c.   YES; the anterior part of the pituitary gland is also referred to as the master gland.
      d.   No; the thalamus is not a gland.

12. a. No
     b. No
     c. YES; the hypothalamus regulates several behaviors by its interaction with the pituitary gland.
     d. No

13. a. No; this is true.
     b. No; this is true.
     c. No; this is true.
     d. YES; this is a myth—logic and creativity are really broad capabilities, and we can be logical and creative about many things; therefore, logic and creativity are involved in the activity of both hemispheres.

14. a. No; MRI is close but pure MRI does not allow researchers to see   the brain while it is working.
     b. No
     c. YES
     d. No

15. a. YES
     b. No; GABA is a neurotransmitter, not and area of the brain.
     c. No; the basal ganglia coordinates voluntary movement.
     d. No; the temporal lobe is associated with hearing and language processing.

16. a. YES; the frontal lobe is associated with personality.
     b. No; the parietal lobe is associated with spatial orientation.
     c. No; there is no hind lobe.
     d. No; there is no cortex lobe.

17. a. No; the endocrine system is involved in this.
     b. No; the endocrine system is involved in this.
     c. CORRECT; the endocrine system is not involved in motor control.
     d. No; the endocrine system is involved in this.

Practice Test 3 Answers

1. a. YES; this is the correct term used to refer to the capacity of the brain to change.
    b. No; this is the brain's capacity to organize complex information into integrated experiences.
    c. No; this is the method of communication in the nervous system.
    d. No; evolution may have caused changes in the brain across millions of years, but it is not the process of change and modification of the brain within a person's lifespan.

2. a. No
    b. No; dopamine is a neurotransmitter.
    c. CORRECT
    d. No; it is the other way around.

3. a. No; this statement is correct.
    b. No; this statement is correct.
    c. No; this statement is correct.
    d. YES; this statement is incorrect.

4. a. No; this is true.
    b. CORRECT ANSWER; in each pair of chromosomes, one member of each pair comes from each parent: one chromosome comes from the biological mother and the other chromosome comes from the biological father.
    c. No; this is true.
    d. No; this is true.

5. a. No; this method involves the manipulation of genes using technology to determine their effect on behavior.
    b. No; this method is the study of the degree to which nature influences behavior.
    c. YES; selective breeding is what Mendel used in his study of pea plants.
    d. No; this is not a research method.

6. a. No
    b. CORRECT
    c. No; recent research has found that the creation of neurons is possible.
    d. No

7. a. No
    b. No
    c. YES; stem cells are found in embryos.
    d. No

8. a. CORRECT
    b. No
    c. No; all embryos contain stem cells.
    d. No; stem cells can turn into cells contained in the spinal cord but can also become other types of cells.

9. a. No
    b. No
    c. No
    d. CORRECT

Chapter 4: Human Development

Learning Goals
1. Explain how psychologists think about development.
2. Describe children's development from prenatal stages to adolescence.
3. Identify the most important changes that occur in adolescence.
4. Discuss adult development and the positive dimensions of aging.
5. Discuss important factors in successful adult psychological development.

After studying Chapter 4, you will be able to:
- Identify the unique challenges associated with period of development known as emerging adulthood;
- Describe how intellectual activities can ward off Alzheimer's disease;
- Outline the principles at work in successful marriages.

Chapter Outline
1. Exploring Human Development
- Development refers to the pattern of continuity and change in human capabilities that occurs throughout the course of life.
- Development involves:
  - Physical processes: changes in biological nature
  - Cognitive processes: changes in thought, intelligence, and language
  - socioemotional processes : changes in relationships, emotions, and personality
- Nature refers to an organism's biological inheritance.
- nurture refers to an organism's environmental experiences.
- Development is neither nature nor nurture. Rather, it is a complex interaction of the two.
- The *early-experience* doctrine contends that, after a period of early development, we become relatively fixed and permanent in our makeup. According to this perspective, infants who do not receive warm, nurturant caregiving in the first year of life cannot develop to their full potential.
- Advocates of later-experience doctrine argue that children are malleable and that sensitive caregiving is just as important later as earlier.

2. Child Development
- Prenatal development
  - Conception occurs when a single sperm penetrates the ovum (egg). This process is called fertilization and the product of fertilization is a zygote.
  - Germinal period: weeks 1 and 2; zygote begins as a single cell but ends this period with 100-150 cells and attaches to the uterine wall.
  - embryonic period : weeks 3-8; beginnings of organs appear, arm and leg buds emerge, towards the end of this period the heart begins to beat.
  - fetal period : months 2-9; organs mature to the point life could be sustained outside the womb, irregular breathing begins.
- Teratogen is any agent that causes a birth defect. Certain prescription drugs, alcohol, and nicotine are examples.

- Preterm infant is a baby born prior to 38 weeks after conception and experiences greater risk of having developmental problems later in life.
- Physical development in childhood:
    o Infancy is the developmental period between birth and 18 months and is second only to prenatal development in terms of the extensive physical changes that occur.
    o Newborns are born with instincts necessary for survival such as swallowing, holding breath under water, etc.
    o Motor skills develop as an interaction of nature and nurture. Some aspects of motor development are genetically programmed but the infant is motivated and supported by the environment to actually do something with his or her new found motor skills.
    o Imitation is a way babies learn a vast amount of information. Clapping, waving goodbye are examples of behaviors that are learned through imitation.
    o Preferential looking is a technique used by researchers to study infant perception. It involves giving the infant a choice of what to look at. If the infant shows a preference for a particular object and the object is moved but the infant still shows a preference for the particular object over other objects, then the infant has the perceptual skills to tell objects apart.
    o _Habituation_ is the name given to decreased responsiveness to a stimulus after repeated presentations. If an infant habituates to a stimulus, or finds it less interesting upon subsequent presentations, then the infant can clearly tell that object apart from other objects.
    o Myelination, or the process of creating the myelin sheath around axons, begins prenatally but continues over the course of childhood.
    o There is a dramatic increase in synaptic connections in the brain during childhood.
    o Brain imaging studies have found that the amount of brain material in some areas can nearly double within as little as a year during childhood. This is followed by a drastic loss of tissue as unneeded cells are purged and the brain continues to reorganize itself.
- Jean Piaget's theory of cognitive development in childhood
    o Cognitive development refers to how thought, intelligence, and language processes change as people mature.
    o A _____ is a concept or framework that already exists at a given moment in a person's mind and that organizes information and provides a structure for interpreting it.
    o Two processes are responsible for how people use and adapt their schemas.
        ▪ Assimilation: occurs when individuals incorporate new information into existing knowledge.
        ▪ _____ occurs when individuals adjust their schemas to new information.
    o The sensorimotor stage is the first stage and lasts from birth to 2 years. In this stage, infants construct an understanding of the world by coordinating sensory experiences.

- _____ is Piaget's term for the crucial developmental accomplishment of understanding that objects and events continue to exist even when they cannot directly be seen, heard, or touched.
  o The second stage of development is the preoperational stage and lasts from 2 to 7 years. Preoperational thought is more symbolic than sensorimotor and children in this stage begin to represent their world with words, images, and drawings.
    - Preoperatinal thought is limited because children in this stage do not grasp the concept of _____, a belief in the permanence of certain attributes of subjects or situations in spite of superficial changes. For example, a child in this stage does not understand that when all the water from a tall, thin beaker is poured into a short, wide beaker, the amount of water is actually the same even though the beakers are different shapes.
    - Preoperational thought is also limited by egocentrism, the inability to distinguish between one's own perspective and someone else's perspective.
  o The _____ operational stage occurs from 7 to 11 years of age. This type of thought involves using operations and replacing intuitive reasoning with logical reasoning. Classification skills are present but abstract thinking has not yet developed at this stage.
  o The formal operational stage occurs from 11 to 15 years of age. Formal thought is more abstract, idealistic, and logical than concrete operational thought.
    - Adolescents in this stage begin to think like a scientist and use hypothetical-deductive reasoning, which means the ability to develop hypotheses and solve problems such as algebra.
  o These stages are perhaps more fluid than Piaget originally proposed. Sometimes these developmental milestones happen earlier or later than this strict stage model suggests.
  o Lev Vygotsky was a Russian psychologist who criticized Piaget's theory on the grounds that cognitive development does not occur in a sociocultural vacuum. The goal of cognitive development is to learn the skills that will allow you to be competent in your culture and, since cultures vary, so do cognitive development milestones.
- Erik Erikson's theory of socioemotional development in childhood:
  1. Trust vs. mistrust occurs during the first 18 months of life. Trust is built when needs (food, shelter, warmth, etc.) are met.
  2. _____ occurs from 1.5 to 3 years. In this stage children either develop a positive sense of independence and autonomy or a negative sense of shame and doubt.
  3. Initiative vs. guilt occurs between 3 to 5 years. When asked to assume more responsibility for themselves, children can develop initiative. When allowed to be irresponsible or made to feel anxious, they can develop too much guilt.
  4. _____ occurs from age 6 to puberty. Children can achieve industry by mastering knowledge and intellectual skills. When they do not, they can feel inferior.
  o Erikson emphasized lifelong development

- Attachment in developmental psychology is the close emotional bond between infant and caregiver.
  - John Bowlby theorized that the infant and mother instinctively form an attachment. The infant's goal is keep the mother nearby.
  - To show the importance of warm contact between infant and caregiver, Harry Harlow conducted an experiment in which infant monkeys were presented with two "mother" options. One was a cold wire "mother" while another was a warm fuzzy "mother." Both "mothers" could provide milk but the infant monkeys showed a clear preference for the warm fuzzy option and ran to that "mother" when scared.
  - Mary Ainsworth developed the notion of secure attachment to describe how some infants use their caregiver as a base from which to explore the surrounding environment. The "strange situation" is a procedure used to identify securely attached children during which a child is in a room with a stranger and the caregiver leaves. A securely attached child will be upset but calm down when the caregiver returns. Insecurely attached children will avoid the caregiver or be ambivalent.
- Temperament is an individual's behavior style and characteristic way of responding. There are 3 types.
  - The easy child is generally in a positive mood, quickly establishes routines, and adapts to changes.
  - The difficult child tends to react negatively, cry frequently, and is slow to accept change.
  - The _____ child has a low activity level, is somewhat negative, shows low adaptability, and displays a low intensity of mood.
- Parenting styles are also important for development and vary from family to family.
  - Authoritarian parenting is a restrictive, punitive style in which the parent exhorts the child to follow the parent's direction and value hard work and effort. Differences of opinion are not tolerated. Children of authoritarian parents often fail to initiate activity, have poor communication skills, and compare themselves to others.
  - Authoritative parenting encourages children to be independent but still places limits and controls on behavior. Children of authoritative parents tend to be socially competent, self-reliant, and socially responsible.
  - _____ parenting is a style in which parents are uninvolved in their child's life. Children of these parents tend to be less competent socially, handle independence poorly, and show poor self-control.
  - _____ parenting is a style in which parents are involved with their children but place few limits on them. These parents let their children do what they want. Children of these parents often fail to learn respect for others, expect to get their own way, and have difficulty controlling their behavior.
- Parenting style is not a product of parents alone. Through the process of reciprocal socialization children socialize their parents just as parents socialize children.

- Many children are highly vulnerable to stress during divorce but factors such as harmony between divorced parents, authoritative parenting, and having an easy rather than difficult temperament can mitigate the vulnerability associated with divorce.
- _____ are parents who monitor their children's emotions, view negative emotions as opportunities for teaching about emotion, and provide guidance in effectively dealing with emotions. These parents tend to reject their children less, praise more, and generally be more nurturant.
- Kohlberg's theory of moral development:
    o The preconventional level is based primarily on punishments or rewards that come from the external world. Children are typically at this level.
    o At the conventional level, the individual abides by standards such as those learned from parents or society's laws. Adolescents are typically at this level.
    o At the _____ level, the individual recognizes alternative moral courses, explores the options, and then develops a personal moral code. This level can be reached in adulthood.
- Bullying behavior in childhood is a serious problem and bullies are likely to show negative consequences such as criminal convictions later in life.
- Gender develops because of hormones. The Y chromosome in the male embryo triggers the secretion of androgens, the main class of male sex hormones, which triggers male sex organs to differentiate from female sex organs.
- Gender roles are the expectations for how males and females should think, act and feel. Culture and peers play important roles in defining gender roles.
- _____ refers to a person's ability to recover from or adapt to difficult times and is key to a person being able to thrive in life. Resilient kids tend to have good intellectual functioning, close, caring relationships with their parents, and supportive adults outside the family.

3. Adolescence
- Puberty is a period of rapid skeletal and sexual maturation that occurs mainly in early adolescence.
- Hormonal changes lie at the core of pubertal development.
    o Testosterone, an androgen, is associated in boys with the development of genitals, an increase in height, and voice change.
    o Estradiol, an estrogen, is associated in girls with breast, uterine, and skeletal development.
- Brain imaging has shown important changes in the adolescent's brain. The amygdala, which involves emotion, develops earlier than the prefrontal cortex, which involves reasoning and logic. Therefore, adolescents experience intense emotions but don't yet have the capacity to control them.
- Adolescent egocentrism involves the belief that others are as preoccupied with you as you are and that you are unique and invincible.
- Erikson's fifth stage of socioemotional development is identity vs. identity confusion and is a challenge faced in adolescence.
    o Adolescents face an identity crisis. Those who explore alternative identities can reach resolution to the crisis but those who do not successfully resolve the crisis become confused leading some to withdraw.

- James Marcia proposed the idea of four identity statuses:
  - Identity _____ is when an individual has not yet explored meaningful alternatives and has not made a commitment.
  - Identity _____ is when a person makes a commitment to an identity before adequately exploring various options.
  - Identity _____ is when a person is exploring alterative paths but has not yet made a commitment
  - Identity _____ is when a person has explored alternative paths and made a commitment.
- Developing an ethnic identity can be challenging for adolescents from minority groups. This is a time when children become aware of how their group is viewed by the majority group. Developing a strong ethnic identity is important because it can serve as a resource that buffers adolescents from the effects of discrimination.
- Adolescence is a time to define one's identity. It is an enormous error to confuse adolescents' enthusiasm for trying out new identities and enjoying moderate amounts of outrageous behavior with hostility towards parents and society.

4. Adult Development and Aging

- Developmental psychologists divide adulthood into three periods: early adulthood (20s and 30s), middle adulthood (40s and 50s), and late adulthood (60s and on).
  - Emerging adulthood is a somewhat new classification that psychologists are interested in and is the period between 18-25 years.
- Emerging adulthood is characterized by experimentation and exploration. Jeffrey Arnett outlined five key features of this period:
  - Identity explorations, especially in love and work
  - Instability
  - Self-focused
  - Feeling in-between
  - The age of possibilities, a time when individuals have an opportunity to transform their lives.
- Life span is the upper boundary of a species' life. _____ is the number of years that will probably be lived by the average person born in a particular year. Life span has not increased in recorded history (it is about 120). Life expectancy has, however, increased dramatically.
- Many theories of aging center around cell decay.
  - _____ theory by Leonard Hayflick, says that cells can divide a maximum of about 100 times and that, as we age, our cells become less capable of dividing.
  - Free radical theory states that people age because inside their cells unstable oxygen molecules known as free radicals are produced. These molecules ricochet around in the cells and damage the DNA.
- Brain imaging research has recently found that brain activity in the prefrontal cortex is lateralized less in older adults than in younger adults when they are engaging in cognitive tasks. In other words, older adults are more likely to use both hemispheres.
- Alzheimer disease is a progressive, irreversible brain disorder that is characterized by gradual deterioration of memory, reasoning, language, and physical functioning. It

involves a deficiency in _____ which is a neurotransmitter associated with memory.

- Crystallized intelligence is an individual's accumulated information and verbal skills. This increases in middle adulthood.

- _____ is one's ability to reason abstractly. This begins to decline in middle adulthood.

- Only two intellectual abilities decline in middle age: numerical ability and perceptual speed. Other abilities, vocabulary, verbal memory, inductive reasoning, and spatial orientation, actually are at their highest levels in middle adulthood.

- Some aspects of cognition improve with age. Wisdom, or expert knowledge about the practical aspects of life, may increase with age.

- In the last 20 years, people have been waiting longer to get married. The after age in 2000 was between 25 and 27. This is probably good news because 59% of marriages in which the wife is younger than 18 end in divorce within 15 years, compared to just 36% when the wife was 20 or older.

- Gottman listed four principles for successful marriages:
  o Nurturing fondness and admiration;
  o Turning toward each other as friends;
  o Giving up some power;
  o And solving conflicts together.

- One of Erikson's challenges during adulthood is _____. Parenting is one way adults meet this challenge.

- Research on middle adulthood has found that relatively few people experience middle age in a tumultuous way or have a "mid life crisis."

5. Developmental Psychology, Health, and Wellness

- The study of adult development is particularly important because such development occurs in the context of a general decline in functioning.

- Victor Frankl emphasized each person's uniqueness and finiteness of life.

- Frankl's ideas fit well with the concept of life themes which involve people's efforts to cultivate meaningful optimal experiences.

Clarifying Tricky Points
Parenting styles
The different types of parenting can be easy to get confused and this confusion is not helped by two drastically different styles bearing similar names (authoritarian and authoritative). Authori*tarian* is generally a bad style whereas authori*tative* is generally good. The authoritarian style is one in which the family operates a lot like a dictatorship. Rules are rules because the parent says so, and there is no discussion. Authoritative, conversely, is one in which parents set clear limits and controls but there is also some give-and-take.

Do early experiences and parents matter in development?
Some psychologists have suggested that unless infants experience warm, nurturant caregiving in the first year of life, they will not develop well. This early-experience doctrine suggests that, after a period of early development, we are relatively fixed and permanent in our makeup. Similarly, some psychologists (Judith Harris and Sandra Scarr) have suggested that what parents

do doesn't really matter because the active genotype is so strong that there is little that can help or harm a child beyond genes. Most psychologists would argue though that behavior is determined by an interaction between genes (the genotype) and environment (parents and peers). One is not necessarily more important than the other. Rather we are products of our nature and our nurturing environment (or lack thereof).

<u>Schemas, assimilation, and accommodation</u>
Jean Piaget proposed the idea that children use schemas to understand their world. Schemas are frameworks that already exist in your mind and provide a structure for interpreting information. In other words, a schema is how you think things should be. Because things aren't always as we think they should be, we must either assimilate or accommodate the information that doesn't fit into our schemas. Assimilation occurs when new information is incorporated into an existing schema. For example, there is a schema that objects can be picked up, but when a child encounters a novel object that has never been picked up before the schema may not apply. But once the child picks up the object successfully, this object is added to or incorporated into the existing schema used for picking up objects. Accommodation, on the other hand, occurs when an existing schema must be changed to accommodate the new information. For example, the schema a child uses for picking things up may only specifically include picking things up with one hand. When the child encounters an object too heavy to lift with one hand but tries lifting with two hands and does so successfully, the schema for picking things up must be edited to include picking things up with both hands, rather than just one.

<u>Developmental psychology is more than just babies</u>
Most people think that when they open a developmental psychology chapter or hear a presentation by a developmental psychologist, they are likely to encounter a sea of pictures of cute babies doing adorable things. Early childhood is certainly an important area of study for developmental psychology. Childhood is, after all, when most of our developmental increases occur. However, the study of adulthood is also important. Increasingly, a great deal of money and effort is being expended to study how adults' physical, cognitive, and socioemotional abilities peak and then, for the most part, begin to decline. The loss of any ability can be discouraging, so it essential for psychology to study this time period and understand ways to cope successfully and continue to lead happy, active lives.

An Appreciative View of Psychology and Your Life
In chapter 4 you learned about successful aging and how development doesn't stop in childhood. We develop in different ways throughout our entire lives. Think of an adult in your life who you consider to be aging successfully, perhaps someone who is particularly wise, mature, active, etc. What types of things does this person do that contributes to their "successful aging"?

_____

_____

_____

_____

_____

_____

Practice Test 1

1. Psychologists define development as
    a.   behavioral changes.
    b.   patterns of movement or change.
    c.   cognitive maturity.
    d.   physical growth.

2. Which of the following is part of the term *development*?
    a.   a pattern of movement or change
    b.   continues throughout the life cycle
    c.   begins at conception
    d.   All of the answers are correct.

3. Which of the following processes are involved in development?
    a.   biological processes
    b.   cognitive processes
    c.   socioemotional processes
    d.   All of the answers are correct.

4. The debate over whether development is primarily a matter of heredity or experience is also known as the
    a.   mechanics versus pragmatics controversy.
    b.   storm and stress view.
    c.   continuity/discontinuity problem.
    d.   nature/nurture issue.

5. In the context of Piaget's theory of cognitive development, the concept *operations* means
    a.   actions of the person.
    b.   how the person feels.
    c.   mental representations.
    d.   accommodation.

6. Preoperational thinkers cannot yet do which of the following?
    a.   think symbolically
    b.   understand words
    c.   reverse mental representations
    d.   participate in "pretend" play

7. Children are able to grasp the principle of conservation in which stage of development?
    a.   sensorimotor thought
    b.   preoperational thought
    c.   concrete operational thought
    d.   None of the answers are correct.

8.   According to Erikson, the first psychosocial stage of development is called
   a.   autonomy versus shame and doubt.
   b.   industry versus inferiority.
   c.   initiative versus guilt.
   d.   trust versus mistrust.

9.   According to Kohlberg, at what level is moral development completely internalized and not based on others' standards?
   a.   preconventional
   b.   conventional
   c.   postconventional
   d.   justice

10.   Kohlberg's theory of moral development has been criticized because
   a.   it does not reflect the care perspective.
   b.   it does not reflect the justice perspective.
   c.   it is culturally biased.
   d.   Kohlberg excluded males in his study.

11.   Nature is to _____ as nurture is to _____.
   a.   genetics; environment
   b.   environment; genetics
   c.   phenotype; genotype
   d.   parenting; heredity

12.   The embryonic period of prenatal development
   a.   runs from months 2 through 9; during this stage the organs mature to the point where life can be sustained outside the womb.
   b.   occurs during weeks 1 and 2 after conception, when the zygote is created.
   c.   is the time between weeks 38 and 40, when the baby is not at risk of being pre-term.
   d.   occurs between weeks 3 and 8; by this time, arms, legs, and spinal cord are already in development.

13.   Which of the following is NOT one of the abnormalities associated with the teratogen alcohol?
   a.   small head
   b.   below-average intelligence
   c.   breathing problems
   d.   defective limbs

14. Which of the following is NOT one of the reflexes that babies are born with?
    a. coughing
    b. sucking
    c. fear of water
    d. startle

15. By egocentrism, Piaget was referring to
    a. the selfish behaviors of some children.
    b. young children's inability to share.
    c. the inability to distinguish between one's own perspective and someone else's perspective.
    d. the psychology of adolescents.

16. Developmental psychologists use the term _____ to describe the close emotional bond between an infant and caregiver.
    a. attachment
    b. parenting
    c. development
    d. imprinting

17. Which of the following is the temperament in which the child has a low activity level, shows low adaptability, and displays a low intensity of mood?
    a. easy child
    b. difficult child
    c. slow-to-warm-up child
    d. sociable child

18. Which of the following statements is consistent with the arguments Judith Harris made in her 1998 book "The Nurture Assumption"?
    a. Parenting is essential in proper development.
    b. Parents do not make a difference in children's behaviors.
    c. Parents are more important than peers in development.
    d. The genes are less important than parenting.

19. Fetal alcohol syndrome is a cluster of abnormalities that occur in children born to mothers who are heavy drinkers. This syndrome supports the notion that alcohol is
    a. bad for the mother.
    b. a teratogen.
    c. unrelated to birth defects.
    d. an appropriate beverage for pregnant women.

20. Maria is in her fifth week of pregnancy. Which prenatal stage is present?
    a. embryonic period
    b. germinal stage
    c. conception
    d. fetal period

21. Little Miranda screams with delight when she sees a horse. She yells to her dad, "See doggie." According to Piaget, what process has occurred?
    a. assimilation
    b. accommodation
    c. object permanence
    d. reversibility

22. Natalie is an infant who usually displays a sunny disposition, follows a regular sleep/wake schedule, and adjusts quickly to new routines and experiences. Natalie would most likely be classified as a(n)
    a. easy child.
    b. difficult child.
    c. slow-to-warm-up child.
    d. withdrawn child.

23. Which of the following is the type of development involved in deciding whether or not to shoplift?
    a. physical development
    b. cognitive development
    c. social development
    d. moral development

Practice Test 2

1. Authoritarian parents often have children who are
    a. overly self-confident.
    b. good communicators.
    c. socially incompetent.
    d. cognitively deficient.

2. A parenting style that encourages children to be independent but still places limits on their behavior is called
    a. authoritative.
    b. authoritarian.
    c. neglecting.
    d. indulgent.

3. Adolescent egocentrism involves all of the following except
   a. the perception of self as unique.
   b. the perception of self as invincible.
   c. the inability to see an issue from another's point of view.
   d. the belief that others are aware of and watching one's every action.

4. Which of the following characterizes adolescent cognitive development?
   a. formal operational thought
   b. hypothetical-deductive reasoning
   c. adolescent egocentrism
   d. All of the answers are correct.

5. Individuals are able to engage in hypothetical-deductive reasoning after they achieve _____ thought.
   a. sensorimotor
   b. preoperational
   c. concrete operational
   d. formal operational

6. Which of the following development processes is the one that involves changes in personality and relationships?
   a. physical processes
   b. socioemotional processes
   c. cognitive processes
   d. developmental processes

7. According to Erikson, adolescents who experience identity confusion
   a. withdraw and isolate themselves from peers and family.
   b. eventually develop thoughts that are concrete and irrational.
   c. develop a sense of inferiority.
   d. develop postconventional level of moral thinking.

8. A parenting style in which parents are highly involved with their children but place few demands on them is called
   a. authoritative.
   b. authoritarian.
   c. neglecting.
   d. indulgent.

9. Which of the following activities is NOT associated with being an "emotion-coaching parent"?
    a. ignoring when the child gets too emotional
    b. monitoring their children's emotions
    c. viewing their children's negative emotions as opportunities for teaching about emotions
    d. providing guidance in how to deal with emotions effectively

10. Carol Gilligan criticized Kohlberg's theory of moral development on the basis that it did not address the role of this aspect of socioemotional development.
    a. personality
    b. emotions
    c. interpersonal relationships
    d. genetics

11. _____ is the period of rapid skeletal and sexual maturation that currently starts at around age 13.
    a. Identity development
    b. Puberty
    c. Adolescence
    d. Formal operational stage

12. According to the identity status approach, which status is the one in which the person has already explored various identities but has not yet committed to any one identity?
    a. identity diffusion
    b. identity foreclosure
    c. identity moratorium
    d. identity achievement

13. In a _____ study, the same participants are studied over a lengthy period, sometimes many years.
    a. cross-sectional
    b. longitudinal
    c. case
    d. cohort

14. What are the long-term consequences of bullying behavior for the victim?
    a. none
    b. more likely to have a criminal conviction
    c. depression
    d. narcissism

15. What are the long-term consequences of bullying behavior for the bully?
    a. none
    b. more likely to have a criminal conviction
    c. depression
    d. narcissism

16. Which of the following is NOT involved in gender identity?
    a. peers
    b. hormones
    c. culture
    d. Erikson's stage of industry versus inferiority

17. Which of the following parenting styles corresponds with a parent who lets his kids smear food all over their faces and clothes in a restaurant, because he doesn't want to stifle the kids' creativity?
    a. authoritarian
    b. neglectful
    c. authoritative
    d. indulgent

18. Which of the following parenting styles corresponds with a parent who expects a 5-year-old child to make the bed very neatly, with corners tucked in every morning before leaving for school; if the child does not comply, punishment is sure to follow.
    a. authoritarian
    b. neglectful
    c. authoritative
    d. indulgent

19. Which of the following social situations is associated with children experiencing stress, aggressiveness, and poor adjustment?
    a. grandparents babysitting
    b. divorce
    c. authoritative parenting
    d. starting school

20. The following are characteristics of positive parenting, EXCEPT
    a. parents are punitive.
    b. parents are supportive.
    c. parents model moral behavior.
    d. parents involve children in decision making.

21. _____ parents assume that if they interfere with their child's actions they would limit their psychological well-being.
    a. Authoritarian
    b. Neglectful
    c. Authoritative
    d. Indulgent

Practice Test 3

1. According to Erikson, the eighth stage that occurs in late adulthood is called
    a. generativity versus stagnation.
    b. intimacy versus isolation.
    c. integrity versus despair.
    d. ageism versus activity theory.

2. People tend to become more concerned about their health status in
    a. early adulthood.
    b. adolescence.
    c. middle adulthood.
    d. late adulthood.

3. According to Erikson, the two stages of early and middle adulthood consist of intimacy versus isolation and
    a. integrity versus despair.
    b. identity versus identity confusion.
    c. generativity versus despair.
    d. generativity versus stagnation.

4. Emerging adulthood occurs during what ages?
    a. 20-30
    b. 15-20
    c. all teenage years
    d. 18-25

5. Which of the following principles is NOT associated with successful marriages?
    a. admiring each other
    b. having someone else as a best friend
    c. giving up some power
    d. solving conflicts together

6. Viktor Frankl highlighted what feature(s) in his book *Man's Search for Meaning?*
    a. each person's uniqueness and finiteness of life
    b. happiness
    c. individual concepts of morality
    d. marriage and family

Answer Key

- There are many ways to age successfully. Here are just a few that were mentioned in your text:
  - Accommodation or willingness to change with circumstances
  - Volunteering, working with young people, or other activities that cultivate meaningful experiences (generativity)
  - Being actively engaged in life
  - Possessing and sharing wisdom

Practice Test 1 Answers

1.   a.   No; development involves more than just behaviorial changes.
     b.   THAT'S RIGHT; development refers to pattern of movement or change.
     c.   No; development involves more than just cognitive maturity.
     d.   No; development involves more than just physical growth.

2.   a.   No; but you're partially correct.
     b.   No; but you're partially correct.
     c.   No; but you're partially correct.
     d.   YES; development involves all the options.

3.   a.   No; but biological processes are involved in development.
     b.   No; but cognitive processes are involved in development.
     c.   No; but socioemotional processes are involved in development.
     d.   THAT'S RIGHT; it involves biological, cognitive, and socioemotional processes.

4.   a.   No
     b.   No
     c.   No; this refers to how the change occurs, suddenly or slowly.
     d.   YES; nature refers to heredity and nurture refers to experience.

5.   a.   No; Piaget's theory is about cognitive development and does not focus on behaviors.
     b.   No; this theory does not focus on emotions.
     c.   YES; operations are mental representations that are reversible.
     d.   No; while this concept is used in Piaget's theory it refers to the process of adjusting to new information.

6.   a.   These children can think symbolically; they can use language and can   draw.
     b.   No; these children understand words.
     c.   RIGHT; preoperational thinkers (ages 2–7 years) cannot reverse their thinking yet.
     d.   No; these children can do "pretend" play.

7. a. These children are not capable of conservation.
    b. No; these children are not yet capable of conservation.
    c. CORRECT; these children (ages 7–11 years) grasp conservation.
    d. No

8. a. No; this is the second stage.
    b. No; this is the fourth stage.
    c. No; this is the third stage.
    d. RIGHT; trust is built when the child's needs are met.

9. a. In this stage there is no internalization of moral values.
    b. This is the intermediate level of internalization.
    c. RIGHT; this is the highest level of moral thinking.
    d. No; this is the type of orientation that Kohlberg takes.

10. a. RIGHT; a care perspective considers people's connectedness.
    b. No; Kohlberg's theory does take a justice perspective.
    c. No; this is a criticism of Kohlberg's theory.
    d. No; most of his research was with males.

11. a. CORRECT; we are born with our genetics but are nurtured and modified   by our environment.
    b. No; the opposite would be true.
    c. No; the phenotype is influenced by the environment while the genotype is not.
    d. No; the opposite would be true.

12. a. No; this is the fetal period.
    b. No; this is the germinal period.
    c. No
    d. YES; also, toward the end of this period the face starts to form and the intestinal tract appears.

13. a. No; microencephaly is one of the effects of fetal alcohol syndrome.
    b. No; this is also one of the effects of alcohol.
    c. YES; this is a problem associated with the use of heroin during pregnancy.
    d. No; this is also one of the effects of alcohol.

14. a. No; this is a reflex that we are born with and that lasts throughout our life span.
    b. No; this is a reflex that we are born with, initiated when the mouth of the infant is touched.
    c. YES; we are not born with such fears, we learn them through experiences.
    d. No; babies do have a reflexive way of responding to startling stimuli.

15.   a.   No; egocentrism according to Piaget meant the inability to distinguish between one's own perspective and someone else's perspective.

         b.   No; young children can learn to share, they just can't think as if they were another person.

         c.   YES; this is the definition of egocentrism according to Piaget.

         d.   No; while adolescents do experience a type of egocentrism, Piaget used the concept to explain the psychology of children in the preoperational cognitive stage.

16.   a.   YES; attachment results in a close emotional bond between the infant and its caregiver.

         b.   No; unfortunately, parenting does not always involve a positive effort to continue the relationship.

         c.   No; this concept is too broad.

         d.   No

17.   a.   No; this child adapts easily.

         b.   No; this child tends to have higher levels of activity and high intensity of mood.

         c.   YES; while somewhat negative in emotions, this child can adapt easier than the difficult child.

         d.   No; this general description is not a temperament category.

18.   a.   No; Harris argued that what parents do is not an essential determinant of adult personality.

         b.   YES; Harris argued that punishing or nurturing a child would not have a major effect on the child's adult personality.

         c.   No; Harris argued that peers had a stronger impact on development.

         d.   No; Harris argued that both genes and peers are stronger determinants of adult personality than parenting.

19.   a.   No; fetal alcohol syndrome is proof that alcohol is very damaging to the child.

         b.   YES; alcohol is an agent that causes birth defect.

         c.   No; alcohol is a teratogen and mother intake is associated with birth defects.

         d.   No; considering the serious effects of this teratogen, it is not an appropriate beverage for pregnant women.

20.   a.   YES; the fifth week is in the embryonic period (three to eight weeks).

         b.   No; the germinal stage is the first two weeks.

         c.   No; conception refers to the union of sperm and ovum.

         d.   No; the fetal period is 2 months to 9 months.

21. a. YES; new information (horse) is adjusted to fit existing knowledge (doggie).
    b. No; the horse is perceived as a doggie.
    c. No; object permanence is an understanding that objects exist even if they aren't seen.
    d. No; this refers to the ability to think in reverse.

22. a. RIGHT; Natalie has an easy child temperament.
    b. A difficult child reacts negatively, cries frequently, and has an irregular routine
    c. This type involves low activity and shows low adaptability.
    d. This is not a temperament type.

23. a. No; this involves the maturation of the body.
    b. No; this involves the development of thinking; while it is associated, it is not the best answer.
    c. No; this involves the development of relationships in the person's life span.
    d. YES; moral development involves changes with age in thoughts, feelings, and behaviors regarding the principles and values that guide what people should do.

Practice Test 2 Answers

1. a. No
   b. No
   c. CORRECT
   d. No

2. a. RIGHT; this style is characterized by limits and control and verbal give-and-take.
   b. No; this style involves a restrictive, punitive style.
   c. No; a neglecting style refers to a parent who is uninvolved in the child's life.
   d. No; indulgent style entails involvement but few demands.

3. a. No; this is part of adolescent egocentrism.
   b. No; this is part of adolescent egocentrism.
   c. CORRECT; this is not the same as egocentrism in childhood.
   d. No; this is part of adolescent egocentrism.

4. a. No; but formal operational thought is part of cognitive development.
   b. No; but this type of reasoning is part of cognitive development.
   c. No; but egocentrism is one characteristic of cognitive development.
   d. RIGHT; all are characteristics of adolescent cognitive development.

5. a. No; this stage refers to nonsymbolic stage.
   b. No; the child in this stage is capable of symbolic thinking.
   c. No; the child in this stage engages in logical thinking about concrete events.
   d. YES; in formal operational thought, people are able to engage in this reasoning.

6. a.   No; these involve changes in biology and physiology.
    b.   YES; personality, relationship, and emotions all pertain to the socioemotional processes.
    c.   No; these involve changes in thinking.
    d.   No; too general.

7. a.   THAT'S CORRECT.
    b.   No; just the opposite occurs; thoughts become more abstract and logical.
    c.   No; inferiority is part of an earlier stage (6 years to puberty).
    d.   This is the highest level of moral thinking.

8. a.   No; this style is characterized by limits and control and verbal give-and-take.
    b.   No; this style involves a restrictive, punitive style.
    c.   No; a neglecting style refers to a parent who is uninvolved in the child's life.
    d.   YES; indulgent style entails involvement but few demands.

9. a.   CORRECT; this is not consistent with good emotion-coaching parenting; they actually view their children's negative emotions as opportunities for teaching about emotions.
    b.   No; this is one of the characteristics of emotion-coaching parenting.
    c.   No; this is one of the characteristics of emotion-coaching parenting.
    d.   No; this is one of the characteristics of emotion-coaching parenting.

10. a.   No; Gilligan did not argue that personality played a role in the development of morality.
    b.   No; Gilligan did not study the role of emotions in morality.
    c.   YES; Carol Gilligan argued that Kohlberg ignored the role of relationships for morality.
    d.   No; genetics are not a socioemotional aspect of development.

11. a.   No; while this is crucial during adolescence, it is not a biological change.
    b.   YES; this is the correct term.
    c.   No; adolescence is the developmental period, thus a more general concept than just the biological processes of the period.
    d.   No; this refers to the cognitive processes during adolescence.

12. a.   No; during this status the person has neither explored nor committed to an identity.
    b.   No; during this status the person makes a commitment to an identity before exploring alternatives.
    c.   YES; as the concept moratorium suggests, the person has explored alternatives but is holding off on making a decision and commitment; this is common during college years.
    d.   No; during this status the person has already explored alternatives and made his or her commitment to an identity.

13.   a.   No; in a cross-sectional study different people, of different ages, are assessed at the same time.
       b.   YES; longitudinal studies follow the same participants and assess them various times across a lengthy period.
       c.   No; the case study focuses only on one person.
       d.   No; cohort studies is another way of referring to cross-sectional studies.

14.   a.   No; there are consequences.
       b.   No; this is more likely for the bully not the victim.
       c.   Yes; those who are bullied are more likely to experience depression.
       d.   No

15.   a.   No; there are consequences.
       b.   YES; bullies are more likely to have criminal convictions later in life.
       c.   No; this is a consequence for the victim, not the bully.
       d.   No

16.   a.   No; peers are very important in developing gender identity.
       b.   No; hormones are important.
       c.   No; culture is important.
       d.   CORRECT; industry vs. inferiority is irrelevant to gender identity.

17.   a.   No; this parent would stop that behavior summarily.
       b.   No; this parent may let the kids do all that, not because of the concern with creativity, but rather because he just doesn't care.
       c.   No; this parent may allow this behavior at home but would probably modify the behavior of the children to be more appropriate in a social setting such as a restaurant.
       d.   YES; this is correct.

18.   a.   YES; the authoritarian parenting style is adult centered, which means that parents expect the children to be able to do behaviors that adults can do and if they don't do them, punishment is used to modify the behavior.
       b.   No; this parent is not very likely to push consistently for an organized bedroom.
       c.   No; authoritative parents may train the child to make the bed every day, but the expectations would be consistent with the age of the child and they may be more likely to use rewards rather than punishment to mold behaviors.
       d.   No; this parent is not very likely to push consistently for an organized bedroom.

19.   a.   No; this chapter reports no negative effects of grandparents babysitting.
       b.   YES; divorce has been associated with these experiences in children; however, the majority of children of divorce adjust properly.
       c.   No; the authoritative parenting style is a positive style.
       d.   No; starting school is not associated with these three experiences.

20. a.   YES; this is not one of the characteristics of positive parenting; punitive refers to the use of punishment to modify behaviors.
     b.   No; this is one of the characteristics of positive parenting.
     c.   No; this is one of the characteristics of positive parenting.
     d.   No; this is one of the characteristics of positive parenting.

21. a.   No; this belief is not consistent with the authoritarian parenting style.
     b.   No; this belief is not consistent with the neglectful parenting style.
     c.   No; authoritative parents interfere when they think it is in the child's best interest.
     d.   YES; the indulgent parent sees total freedom as essential for psychological well-being.

Practice Test 3 Answers

1.   a.   No; this stage occurs in middle adulthood.
     b.   This stage occurs in early adulthood.
     c.   YES; this is the last stage, when people look back on their lives.
     d.   These are theories of aging and are not among Erikson's stages.

2.   a.   No
     b.   No
     c.   THIS IS CORRECT.
     d.   No; the concern starts earlier in middle adulthood.

3.   a.   No; this occurs in late adulthood.
     b.   This stage takes place in adolescence.
     c.   No
     d.   YES; this stage occurs in the 40s and 50s.

4.   a.   No
     b.   No
     c.   No
     d.   YES

5.   a.   No; this is one of the characteristics of successful marriages.
     b.   YES; this is not a good idea, as people in successful marriages tend to turn to each other for friendship.
     c.   No; this is one of the characteristics of successful marriages.
     d.   No; this is one of the characteristics of successful marriages.

6.   a.   YES; Frankl stated each person is unique and life is finite. His book discusses the implications of these facts.
     b.   No
     c.   No; Frankl was more interested life's meaning than morality.
     d.   No

Chapter 5: Sensation and Perception

Learning Goals
1. Discuss basic principles of sensation and perception.
2. Explain how the visual system enables us to see, and by communicating with the brain, perceive the world.
3. Understand how the auditory system registers sound and how it connects with the brain to perceive it.
4. Explain how the skin, chemical, kinesthetic, and vestibular senses work.
5. Discuss the everyday practices associated with protecting vision and hearing.

After studying Chapter 5, you will be able to:
- Appreciate the importance of using your senses to engage with nature;
- List several easy ways to take care of your senses.

Chapter Outline
1. How We Sense and Perceive the World
- Sensation is the process of receiving stimulus energies from the external environment. Stimuli consist of light, sound, heat, etc.
- Receptor cells in the eyes, ears, skin, nose, and tongue detect stimuli and convert it into an electrochemical impulse, a process called transduction.
    - _____ produces an action potential that relays information about the stimulus through the nervous system to the brain.
- Perception is the process of organizing and interpreting sensory information to give it meaning. Finding meaningful patterns in sensory information, such as interpreting the noise a violin makes into the experience of a symphony, is perception.
- There are two types of processing in sensation and perception.
    - _____ processing begins with sensory receptors registering information and sending it to the brain for interpretation. It is initiated by stimulus input.
    - _____ processing starts with cognitive processing at the higher levels of the brain, such as knowledge, beliefs, and expectations. It does not begin with the detections of a stimulus. For example, you can listen to your favorite song in your head right now even though your sensory receptors in your ears are not detecting the sound.
- Synaesthesia is a rare case in which the experience of one sense induces an experience in another sense. For example, in rare cases, some people actually can "taste" a color or "see" music. The cause is unknown but may have to do with the posterior parietal cortex.
- Sense organs and sensory receptors fall into several classes.
    - Photoreception: detection of light; perceived as sight
    - Mechanoreception: detection of pressure, vibration, and movement; perceived as touch, hearing and equilibrium
    - _____: detection of chemical stimuli; detected as smell and taste
- Absolute threshold is the minimum amount of energy a person can detect. The softest sound you can hear, the dimmest light you can see, etc. This threshold is quantified as the point at which an individual can detect a stimulus 50% of the time.

- Noise is irrelevant and competing stimuli or the background noise that interferes with what you are actually trying to see, hear, taste, smell, and feel.
- You are not always aware of what you are perceiving. _____ perception is the perception of information presented below the conscious threshold.
- _____, or differences that are just noticeable, is the smallest difference in stimulation required to discriminate one stimulus from another 50% of the time.
- Weber's law is the principle that two stimuli must differ by a constant minimum percentage, rather than a constant amount, to be perceived as different.
  - o For example, you might be able to perceive the addition of 1 candle to a group of 60 but not the addition of 1 candle to a group of 120. However, in this example, you would be able to perceive the addition of 2 candles to a group of 120 because 1:60 is the same ratio as 2:120.
- _____ theory focuses on decision making about stimuli in the presence of uncertainty.
  - o Factors such as fatigue, expectancy, and urgency can affect detection of stimuli.
  - o Two main components of signal detection theory are information acquisition and criterion (basis for making a judgment about the available information).
- Selective attention involves focusing on a specific aspect of experience while ignoring others. Also known as the "cocktail party effect" because it refers to the ability to focus on one voice in a noisy environment, such as a party.
- The Stroop effect demonstrates how perception can become automated. In the Stroop test, participants are presented with color words in different color fonts.
  - o For example, the word "green" would be written in red ink. When asked what color the ink is, people will often say green because perception of such common stimuli is automated.
- Perceptual sets refer to predispositions, or a readiness, to perceive something in a particular way.
- Sensory adaptation is a change in the responsiveness of the sensory system based on the average level of surrounding simulation. For example, when you turn off the lights in a room, at first it is difficult to see anything, but over the course of the next several minutes your eyes adapt and then you can see reasonably well.

2. The Visual System
- Light is electromagnetic energy characterized by wavelengths, amplitude, and purity.
  - o The _____ of light is distance from the peak of a wave to the peak of the next.
  - o _____ refers to the height of a wave and is linked with the brightness of a visual stimulus.
  - o Purity is the mixture of wavelengths in light and is associated with the saturation, or richness, of a visual stimulus.
- Parts of the eye (see figure 5.10 and the tour in your text for a complete visualization of the eye)
  - o Sclera: the white, outer part. Helps to maintain the shape and protect it from injury

- o _____: the colored part of the eye (blue in blue eyed people, brown in brown eyed people). It contains muscles that control the size of the pupil and thereby control the amount of light that enters the eye.
  - o Pupil: the black part in the center of the eye. It acts like the aperture of a camera, opening to let in more light when needed and closing to let in less light when there is too much.
  - o _____: clear membrane just in front of the eye.
  - o Lens: transparent and somewhat flexible, disk-like entity filled with gelatinous material.
    - ▪ Cornea and lens work together to bend light falling on the surface of the eye in order to focus it at the back of the eye.
  - o _____: located at the back of the eye. Light-sensitive surface that records what we see and converts it to neural impulses for processing in the brain.
    - ▪ Retina is actually the primary mechanism of sight and contains approximately 126 million receptor cells.
      - • _____: a type of receptor cell in the retina that is sensitive to light.
      - • _____: a type of receptor cell in the retina that is sensitive to color.
    - ▪ Fovea: a minute area in the center of the retina at which vision is best. It contains only cones.
    - ▪ Blind spot is one spot on the retina that contains neither rods not cones.
  - o Signals from rods and cones are transmitted to the bipolar cells and ganglion cells. The axons of the ganglion cells make up the optic nerve which carries information to the brain.
- At the optic chiasm, the optic nerve fibers divide. As a result, the visual information originating in the right halves of the two retinas is transmitted to the left side of the occipital lobe in the cerebral cortex, and the visual information from the left halves of the retina is transmitted to the right side of the occipital lobe (see the tour included in this chapter for a visualization that describes how the process works).
- Feature detectors are neurons in the brain's visual system that respond to particular features of a stimulus. Some neurons are specifically designed to notice certain lines or certain angles.
- Parallel processing is the simultaneous distribution of information across different neural pathways. In visual processing there is a *what* pathway, which processes information about what the object is, including color and texture, and a *where* pathway, which processes information about movement and depth of an object.
- _____ theory was proposed by Thomas Young and Hermann von Hemholtz and states that color perception is produced by three types of receptors (cones in the retina). Each type of receptor is particularly sensitive to different ranges of wavelengths. Color is perceived by combining these three wavelengths.
- Color blindness occurs when one of these three types of cones is inoperative and therefore prevents an individual from distinguishing between certain colors.
  - o _____ are people with only two types of cones.
  - o Trichromats are people with all three types of cones and have normal color vision.

- Ewald Hering proposed opponent-process theory, which states that cells in the visual system respond to red-green and blue-yellow colors. A given cell might be excited by red and inhibited by green, whereas another cell might be excited by yellow and inhibited by blue.
- Figure-ground relationship is the principle by which we organize the perceptual field into stimuli that stand out (figure) and those that are left over (background or ground).
    o The figure-ground relationship is related to gestalt psychology. According to gestalt psychology, people naturally organize their perceptions according to certain patterns. One of the main principles of gestalt psychology is that the whole is different from the sum of its parts.
- _____ is the ability to perceive objects three dimensionally. Images appear on our retinas in two-dimensional form, yet we see a three-dimensional world.
    o Binocular cues are depth cues that depend on the combination of the images in the left and right eyes. The disparity between the images in the two eyes is the binocular cues the brain uses to determine depth.
    o Monocular cues are depth cues available from the image in one eye. Examples are:
        ▪ Familiar size
        ▪ Height in the field of view
        ▪ Linear perspective: objects that are farther away take up less space on the retina.
        ▪ Overlap: an object that partially conceals or overlaps another is perceived as closer.
        ▪ Shading: changes in perception due to the position of the light and position of the viewer.
        ▪ Texture gradient: texture becomes denser and finer the farther away it is.
- Apparent movement occurs when an object is stationary but we perceive it as moving. The experience of watching an IMAX movie can create apparent movement.
- Stroboscopic motion is the illusion of movement created when rapid stimulation of different parts of the retina occurs. Motion pictures are examples of stroboscopic movement.
- Perceptual constancy is the recognition that objects are constant and unchanging even though sensory input about them is changing.
- Size, shape, and brightness constancy is the recognition that an object remains the same size, shape, and brightness even though the retinal image of the object changes.
- A visual illusion occurs when there is a discrepancy between reality and the perceptual representation of it. Illusions are incorrect but not abnormal. More than 200 types have been discovered; see figures 5.30, 5.31, and 5.32 in your text for examples of common illusions.

3. The Auditory System
- Just as light is characterized by wavelengths, so is sound. Our auditory system interprets these waves along the following dimensions.
    o Frequency: the number of cycles that pass through a point in a given time.
        ▪ _____: the perceptual interpretation of the frequency of a sound.

- o Amplitude: measured in decibels (dB) and is the amount of pressure produced by a sound wave relative to a standard (typically 0 dB).
  - ■ _____ is the perception of the sound wave's amplitude.
- Most sounds, including speech and music, are complex sounds which means numerous frequencies of sound blend together
  - o Timbre is the tone saturation, or the perceptual quality of a sound. It is responsible for our ability to distinguish between a trombone and a trumpet playing the exact same note and to distinguish between different peoples' voices.
- Structures of the ear (see figure 5.37 and the tour in your text for a visualization of the structures of the ear):
  - o Outer ear
    - ■ Pinna: the outer, visible part of the ear. It collects sounds and channels them into the interior of the ears.
  - o Middle ear
    - ■ Eardrum: membrane that vibrates in response to sound.
    - ■ _____, _____, and _____: the three smallest bones in the body. When they vibrate, they transmit sound waves to the fluid-filled inner ear. They serve to amplify sound.
  - o Inner ear
    - ■ Oval window: transmits sound waves to the cochlea.
    - ■ _____: a tubular, fluid-filled structure that is coiled up like a snail.
    - ■ Basilar membrane: lines the inner wall of the cochlea and runs its entire length.
      - Hair cells line the basilar membrane and are the sensory receptors in the ear. Tinnitus, or ringing in the ears, is the result of damage to the hair cells.
      - Tectorial membrane: a jelly-like flab above the hair cells that, when the hair cells vibrate against it, generates impulses that are interpreted as sound by the brain.
- _____ theory (Georg von Békésy) is a theory of how the auditory system works and posits that each frequency produces vibrations at a particular spot on the basilar membrane.
  - o This theory is good at explaining high-frequency sounds, but because humans can hear low-frequency sounds better than can be predicted by looking as the basilar membrane vibrations, something else must be involved.
- Frequency theory states that the perception of a sound's frequency depends on how often the auditory nerve fires. Higher frequency sounds cause the nerves to fire more than low frequency sounds.
  - o The _____ states that several nerve cells can fire neural impulses in rapid succession. This principle was proposed to account for the fact that neurons have a maximum firing rate of 1,000 times per second, but frequency theory would indicate higher frequency sounds require a neuron to fire faster than possible.

- Information about sound moves from the hair cells of the inner ear to the auditory nerve which carries neural impulses to the brain's auditory areas (located in the cerebral cortex).

4. Other Senses

- Skin is the largest sensory system and contains receptors for touch, temperature, and pain, known as the cutaneous senses.
  - o Sensory fibers arising from the receptors in the skin enter the spinal cord, then travel through the brain stem and into the thalamus which projects a map of the body's surface onto the somatosensory areas of the parietal lobes in the cerebral cortex.
- Thermoreceptors provide input to keep the body's temperature normal and are located under the skin.
- Sensation of pain is the sensation that warns us of damage to our bodies.
  - o Inflamed joints of sore muscles produce prostaglandins which stimulate the receptors and cause the experience of pain. Aspirin reduces the body's production of prostaglandins.
- _____ theory of pain states that the spinal column contains a neural gate that can be opened (allowing for the perception of pain) or closed (preventing the perception of pain). The brain sends signals to open or close these gates.
  - o It is thought that acupuncture may work by closing pain gates.
  - o This theory has largely been abandoned, because although some pain originates in signals coming through the spinal cord gate, it is now clear that ultimately the brain is responsible for generating the experience of pain.
- Turning pain signals on or off is a chemical process that most likely involves endorphins (a neurotransmitter studied in chapter 3).
- Strategies to reduce acute pain include:
  - o Distraction: focusing on pain magnifies the sensation so distraction works to reduce the experience of pain.
  - o Focused breathing: short, fast breaths can diminish pain.
  - o Counterstimulation: pinch yourself in an area away from your injury and the experience of pain will be reduced.
- Smell and taste are considered the chemical senses because they involve the detection of chemicals in the air and saliva.
- Taste is detected by bumps above the surface of your tongue called papillae, which contain taste buds (about 10,000 in total).
- Smell is detected by receptor cells contained in the olfactory epithelium, which lines the roof of the nasal cavity. Millions of tiny hair-like antennae project through this lining and make contact with air as it passes.
  - o The neural pathway for smell goes through the limbic system which is also responsible for memory and emotion. This is why smells are often strongly associated with memories or emotions.
  - o Smell is adaptive in mating because research has found that women actually prefer the scent of males who have differing sets of genes (known as the major histocompatibility complex, or MHC) which produces healthier offspring with the broadest immune systems.

- _____ senses provide information about movement, posture, and orientation.
  - o No specific organ contains these senses. They are embedded in muscle fibers and joints.
- The _____ sense provides information about balance and movement.
  - o This sense works with the kinesthetic senses to coordinate proprioceptive feedback, which is information about the position of our limbs and body parts in relation to other body parts.
  - o Semicircular canals, located in the inner ear, contain sensory receptors for motion. They consist of fluid-filled, circular tubes that lie in three planes of the body (right-left, front-back, and up-down).
  - o The vestibular nerve is connected mostly to the medulla but a little to the cerebellum, and some may even connect to the cerebral cortex which could explain motion sickness.

5. Sensation, Perception, and Health and Wellness
- Taking care of our senses is important, so here are some ways to keep your senses in good working order:
  - o For your eyes: avoid fatty foods, don't smoke, and consume plenty of vitamins A, E, C, zinc, and beta carotene. Also read with plenty of light and wear sunglasses when outdoors.
  - o For your ears: wear ear plugs when attending concerts (as many musicians do these days) and working with loud equipment.
- Nature has an amazing capacity to engage all our senses in a way that improves physical and psychological well-being. For example:
  - o Hospital patients recover more quickly with a window in the room.
  - o Flowers are a natural mood booster.

Intersection
- Factors such as ethnicity can affect the perception of stimuli. For example, when research participants are forced to act quickly, they are more likely to misperceive innocuous tools as guns, if they see an image of an African American man first rather than a picture of a white man.

Critical Controversy
- Cochlear implants are small electronic devices that are surgically implanted into a person's ear and head that allow deaf people to detect sounds. Their use is controversial because such implants imply that deafness is a problem that needs to be fixed and they undermine the rich deaf culture that has developed.

Clarifying Tricky Points
The difference between sensation and perception
Simply put, sensation is what your senses do and perception is what your brain does. Through a process called transduction, specialized cells in your eyes, ears, nose, and on your tongue and skin work to convert light, sound, chemicals in the air, and temperature into electrochemical energy. This electrochemical energy is transmitted to the brain through your nervous system and then your brain *perceives* these electrochemical transmissions. The perception that occurs in your

brain gives meaning to information from your senses. For example, your senses don't actually see trees. Your eyes simply capture light waves as they are reflected off the braches and leaves of the tree. Your brain finds a meaningful pattern in the information from the eyes which causes you to perceive a tree.

Top-down and bottom-up processing

When it comes to processing information, psychologists typically describe such processing as either top-down or bottom-up. These are two distinct ways of thinking. One is not better than the other, just different. Top-down processing starts at the top with a concept, for example a song, and then works down to the details, such as stimuli from the environment, in this case sound waves detected by sensory receptors in your ear. Bottom-up processing starts at the bottom, the sound waves, and works its way to the top, a song. If you "hear" a song in your head but the stereo is not on, you are using top-down information because your brain already knows the concept of a song. If you turn on the stereo and hear a new song, your brain is using bottom-up processing because your sensory receptors are detecting sound waves, converting them to electrochemical messages, and your brain perceives those messages as a song.

Eyes and ears

Our eyes and ears are enormously complex organs and it can be difficult to remember all the parts and understand the different roles each part plays in sensing stimuli. Just like in chapter 3, use the figures and the tour in your book to visualize how the eyes and ears work (figures 5.10 – 5.12 for eyes; figure 5.37 for ears). Based on the last "tricky point" discussion, in order to learn the parts of the eyes and ears you will probably need to use bottom-up processing. Start with each individual part and build up to the concept of the eye (or ear). But once you are able to visualize the figures, and in your head, understand where the rods and cones are in relation to the retina, for example, you will be able to use top-down processing when you have describe these organs on a test. You will just start with the concept of an eye (or ear) and work your way down all the way to the point where you can describe what each individual component does.

Composition of light and sound

The idea that light and sound travel in waves can seem confusing but is crucial to understanding how the body, mainly our senses, interprets light and sound. Light waves differ in two ways: length (different colors operate at different wavelengths) and height (technically called amplitude, but it really just determines brightness). The only other factor that matters for light is how different wavelengths mix. When different wavelengths mix, color and richness change just like mixing colors on an artist's palate.

Sound operates similarly in the sense that it travels in waves that vary by length (called frequency when talking about sound) and height (called amplitude just like with light waves, but here amplitude determines the loudness of sound). Just like light waves, sound waves can mix creating different timbre (which is the quality or richness of a sound and allows you to perceive the difference between a trumpet playing the music note C and a piano playing the same note).

An Appreciative View of Psychology and Your Life

It's no secret that taking a walk in the middle of a busy work day or study session can be relaxing and refreshing. In this chapter, you learned why a walk outdoors is so refreshing. Simply put, being outdoors engages our senses, which makes us feel good. If the weather is nice right now where you are, go outside and take a break; if the weather is not nice where you are, go to window and take a minute to appreciate what you see outside.

How is engagement with nature, either while walking outdoors or looking out the window, good for us?

_____

_____

_____

_____

_____

_____

_____

Practice Test 1

1.   The process of detecting and encoding stimuli is called
   a.   sensation.
   b.   perception.
   c.   gestalt psychology.
   d.   accommodation.

2.   The minimum amount of energy that we can detect is called
   a.   the absolute threshold.
   b.   minimal threshold.
   c.   the difference threshold.
   d.   subliminal perception.

3.   Psychologists call the presence of competing and irrelevant stimuli
   a.   noise.
   b.   accommodation.
   c.   saturation.
   d.   subliminal perception.

4.   Wavelength is defined as the distance between
   a.   peak and valley of a light wave.
   b.   peak and peak of a light wave.
   c.   valley and amplitude of a light wave.
   d.   amplitude and peak of a light wave.

5.   In order to do its job, the pupil depends most on which other part of the eye?
   a.   lens
   b.   iris
   c.   cornea
   d.   retina

6.   The rods and cones are found in what part of the eye?
   a.   the sclera
   b.   the retina
   c.   the cornea
   d.   the fovea

7.   Why is vision sharpest in the fovea?
   a.   because it contains only cones
   b.   because it contains more cones than rods
   c.   because it contains both rods and cones
   d.   because it is located in the center of the retina

8.   What allows you to focus on this question while ignoring all the other stimulation in your environment?
   a.   perception
   b.   hue
   c.   selective attention
   d.   selective adaptation

9.   A change in the wavelength of light would result in a change in our perception of
   a.   hue.
   b.   saturation.
   c.   brightness.
   d.   timbre.

10.   Which of the following is the name for the process of sending sensory information to the brain for analysis and interpretation?
   a.   bottom-up
   b.   top-down
   c.   cognition to motor
   d.   brain to motor

11.   The cells that are dedicated to the reception and transmission of stimulus information are the
   a.   glial cells.
   b.   eyes.
   c.   ears.
   d.   sensory receptors.

12.   The sensory receptors in the eye are
   a.   photoreceptors.
   b.   mechanoreceptors.
   c.   chemoreceptors.
   d.   in the cornea.

13.   Which of the following is NOT associated with the reduction of pain?
        a.   focused breathing
        b.   counterstimulation
        c.   distraction
        d.   overstimulation

14.   The retina is to the visual sense as the _____ are to the detection of head motion.
        a.   rods
        b.   eardrums
        c.   semicircular canals
        d.   cones

15.   All sensation begins with
        a.   sensory receptors.
        b.   the brain.
        c.   perception.
        d.   chemoreceptors

16.   The eye is to sensation as the brain is to
        a.   feeling.
        b.   perception.
        c.   impression.
        d.   hearing.

17.   The simultaneous distribution of information across different neural pathways that is
        responsible for, among other things, processing the what and where of visual objects is
        called
        a.   subliminal processing.
        b.   parallel processing.
        c.   linear perspective.
        d.   binocular vision.

18.   When you turn out the lights, at first you can't see much, but over the course of a few
        minutes you can begin to see things in the darkened room. This is an example of
        a.   sensory adaptation.
        b.   perceptual set.
        c.   selective attention.
        d.   subliminal perception.

Practice Test 2

1. After information passes the optic chiasm, images from the left side of our visual field end up
    a. being reflected back to the blind spot.
    b. being reflected back to the optic nerve.
    c. on the right side of the brain.
    d. on the left side of the brain.

2. The visual cortex, which is responsible for processing visual information, is located in the _____ lobe.
    a. occipital
    b. parietal
    c. temporal
    d. frontal

3. Which theory of color vision does the best job of explaining afterimages?
    a. trichromatic theory
    b. the opponent-process theory
    c. the additive-subtractive theory
    d. No theory currently explains afterimages.

4. Which of the following is NOT true regarding color blindness?
    a. Complete color blindness is rare.
    b. Color blindness has to do with cones.
    c. Most people who are color blind are men.
    d. Most color blind people can only see in black and white.

5. The principle by which we organize perception into those stimuli that stand out and those that are left over is called
    a. figure-ground.
    b. closure.
    c. similarity.
    d. proximity.

6. The tendency to mentally "fill in the spaces" in order to see figures as complete refers to the gestalt principle of
    a. closure.
    b. figure-ground.
    c. proximity.
    d. similarity.

7.   When an object is partially concealed, the concealing object is perceived as being closer. This monocular cue of depth is referred to as
    a.   linear perspective.
    b.   texture gradient.
    c.   shading.
    d.   overlap.

8.   Which of the following monocular cues of depth is the one in which the cue involves how dense and fine are the images?
    a.   linear perspective
    b.   texture gradient
    c.   overlap
    d.   shading

9.   The _____ is the part of the forebrain that contributes to the perception of touch by relaying sensory information to the appropriate spot on the somatosensory areas of the parietal lobes.
    a.   hippocampus
    b.   hypothalamus
    c.   pons
    d.   thalamus

10.   What we sense in our left eye first goes to the right side of our brain and vice versa; however, the information is integrated in the
    a.   temporal lobe.
    b.   parietal lobe.
    c.   frontal lobe.
    d.   occipital lobe.

11.   _____ perception is the ability to detect information below the level of conscious awareness.
    a.   Movement
    b.   Depth
    c.   Subliminal
    d.   Unconscious

12.   A painter who is able to tell the difference between two similar shades of paint is demonstrating
    a.   the absolute threshold.
    b.   the difference threshold.
    c.   Weber's law.
    d.   sensory adaptation.

13. An object that partially conceals another object is perceived as being closer, according to the monocular cue of
    a. shadowing.
    b. overlap.
    c. texture gradient.
    d. linear perspective.

14. Which of the following is NOT true about color blindness?
    a. Complete color blindness is rare.
    b. There are different types of color blindness.
    c. People with color blindness see in black and white.
    d. Color blindness typically involves a malfunction of the green cone system.

15. The gestalt principles of visual perception may be applied to social perception. Which of the perceptual principles would explain the tendency to assume that a man and a woman walking together are a romantic couple?
    a. similarity
    b. closure
    c. proximity
    d. depth perception

Practice Test 3

1. Pitch is to frequency as loudness is to
    a. amplitude.
    b. Hertz.
    c. wavelength.
    d. pulsation.

2. Which structures comprise the inner ear?
    a. eardrum, oval window, and stirrup
    b. pinna, external auditory canal, and eardrum
    c. hammer, anvil, stirrup
    d. oval window, cochlea, and the basilar membrane

3. Which part of the ear is most important in the translation of sound?
    a. the auditory nerve
    b. the outer ear
    c. the middle ear
    d. the inner ear

4. Which theory of hearing suggests that high-frequency tones are explained by cells firing in rapid succession?
    a. place theory
    b. frequency theory
    c. volley theory
    d. similarity theory

5.   What is the main difference between touch receptors and thermoreceptors?
a.   sensitivity and speed
b.   location and function
c.   number and location
d.   function and speed

6.   The semicircular canals are found in
a.   Venice.
b.   the inner ear.
c.   the outer ear.
d.   the middle ear.

7.   What do the sense of taste and the sense of smell have in common?
a.   They are both mechanical senses.
b.   They are both chemical senses.
c.   They are both electromagnetic senses.
d.   They are both electric senses.

8.   Which of the following is NOT one of the categories of taste detected by our taste buds?
a.   salty
b.   sour
c.   pasty
d.   bitter

9.   Feedback about the position of our limbs and body parts in relation to other body parts relies on the collaboration of these two senses.
a.   kinesthetic and vestibular
b.   vestibular and visual
c.   kinesthetic and visual
d.   visual and olfactory

10.   The olfactory epithelium is to the sense of smell as the _____ are to the sense of taste.
a.   retinas
b.   papillae
c.   semicircular canals
d.   rods

11.   Which of the following is NOT necessary for all people in order to take care of your eyes?
a.   reading with plenty of light
b.   wearing sunglasses outdoors
c.   wearing glasses indoors
d.   eating foods high in beta carotene

12. Which of the following is important for ALL your senses?
    a. active engagement with nature
    b. protective lenses
    c. vitamin A
    d. zinc

13. Perceptual quality of sound is to _____ as a sound wave's amplitude is to _____.
    a. timbre; loudness
    b. pitch; timbre
    c. loudness; pitch
    d. pitch; loudness

14. Place theory and frequency theory are two approaches to explaining
    a. how the outer ear collects sound waves.
    b. how the middle ear registers the amplitude of sound.
    c. how the inner ear registers the frequency of sound.
    d. why children get ear infections.

Answer Key

- Engaging with nature broadens attention, improves well-being, aids in the management of stress, helps recovery from illness, and generally serves as a positive mood booster.

Practice Test 1 Answers

1. a. RIGHT; this is sensation.
    b. No; perception refers to organizing and interpreting sensory information.
    c. Gestalt psychology refers to the notion that perception follows certain patterns.
    d. Accommodation is the lens changing its curvature.

2. a. YES
    b. No
    c. The difference threshold refers to the smallest difference required to discriminate two stimuli.
    d. Subliminal perception is the ability to detect information below the level of conscious awareness.

3. a. THAT'S RIGHT
    b. Accommodation refers to the ability of the lens to change its curvature.
    c. Saturation is based on the color's purity.
    d. Subliminal perception is the ability to detect information below the level of conscious awareness.

4. a. No; this is not the correct definition.
    b. CORRECT
    c. No
    d. No

5. a. The lens focuses.
    b. RIGHT; the iris is a muscle that controls the size of the pupil.
    c. The cornea is clear membrane in front of the eye.
    d. The retina contains the rods and cones and is located in the back of the eye.

6. a. No; the sclera is outer white part of the eye.
    b. YES; the rods and cones are found in the retina.
    c. No; the cornea is the clear membrane in the front of the eye.
    d. No; the fovea is the area of the retina where vision is the most sensitive.

7. a. YES; cones are the receptors that provide us with fine detail.
    b. No; it contains only cones.
    c. No; the fovea contains only cones.
    d. While the fovea is located in the center of the retina, the presence of cones is responsible for the sharp vision.

8. a. Although you are perceiving this question, perception does not allow you to focus on the question.
    b. No
    c. CORRECT; selective attention allows you to attend to one thing while ignoring other things.
    d. No

9. a. YES; hue is based on the color's wavelength.
    b. Saturation is based on the color's purity.
    c. Brightness refers to the intensity of light.
    d. Timbre is the perceptual quality of sound.

10. a. YES; the bottom-up process is the one through which the senses send information up to the brain.
    b. No; this is the process of sending commands from the brain down to the rest of the body.
    c. No; this is not the name of a process, and in any case, the concepts are backward.
    d. No; this is not the name of a process, and in any case, the concepts are backward.

11. a. No
    b. No; the eyes contain sensory receptors, but they are not "a cell."
    c. No; the ears contain sensory receptors, but they are not "a cell."
    d. YES; this is the name of those cells.

12.   a.   YES; the sensory receptors in the eye detect light.
       b.   No; mechanoreceptors are involved in the touch, hearing, kinesthetic, and vestibular senses.
       c.   No; mechanoreceptors are involved in smell and taste.
       d.   No; photoreceptors are in the retina.

13.   a.   No; this is a good technique practiced in Lamaze child birth.
       b.   No; this works for pain, because causing another pain mutes the original pain.
       c.   No; this works for pain, because focusing on something other than the source and place of pain mutes the original pain.
       d.   YES; overstimulation will not reduce pain, it may contribute to more experience of pain as pain receptors continue to be stimulated.

14.   a.   No; these are sensory receptors found in the retina.
       b.   No; the eardrum is in the ear, but is not involved in the detection of head motion.
       c.   YES; this structure is found in the inner ear.
       d.   No; these are sensory receptors found in the retina.

15.   a.   YES; there are three types of sensory receptors: photoreceptors, mechanoreceptors, and chemoreceptors.
       b.   No; sensations start with the activation of sensory receptors by stimulations from the environment.
       c.   No; perception follows sensation.
       d.   No; chemoreceptors are just one type of sensory receptors; for this question, item a is the better answer.

16.   a.   No
       b.   RIGHT; perception refers to the brain's process of organizing and interpreting sensory information.
       c.   No
       d.   No

17.   a.   No
       b.   YES; parallel processing is the simultaneous distribution of information across different neural pathways.
       c.   No
       d.   No

18.   a.   YES
       b.   No
       c.   No
       d.   No

Practice Test 2 Answers

1. a. No
    b. No
    c. RIGHT; information crosses over to the other side.
    d. No; information crosses over to the other side.

2. a. YES; the occipital lobe contains the visual cortex.
    b. No
    c. No
    d. No

3. a. No; the trichromatic theory says that there are three types of color receptors.
    b. YES; the opponent-process theory suggests that if one member of the pair fatigues, the other member rebounds and gives an afterimage.
    c. No
    d. No

4. a. No; this statement is correct.
    b. No; this statement is correct.
    c. No; this statement is correct.
    d. YES; this statement is not true.

5. a. CORRECT
    b. No; closure refers to seeing incomplete figures as complete.
    c. No; we tend to perceive objects together that are similar to each other.
    d. No; we tend to group objects together that are near each other.

6. a. YES
    b. No; figure-ground illustrates how we divide our visual world.
    c. No; we tend to group objects together that are near each other.
    d. No; we tend to perceive objects together that are similar to each other.

7. a. No; linear perspective is when two parallel lines appear to converge in the distance.
    b. No; texture gradient refers to how the texture changes as distance changes.
    c. No; shading involves changes in perception due to the position of the light and the position of the viewer.
    d. CORRECT; this refers to one object partially blocking another object.

8. a. No; this monocular cue relies on the amount of space the image takes on the retina.
    b. YES; the finer the texture, the farther away the object is perceived.
    c. No; this monocular cue relies on the partial covering of an object to figure out which object is closer.
    d. No; this monocular cue relies on the position of the light and the creation of shades to determine the depth.

9. a.   No; the hippocampus is linked to memory.
    b.   No; the hypothalamus is associated with pleasure.
    c.   No; the pons is a part of the hindbrain.
    d.   YES; the thalamus projects the map of the body's surface onto the somatosensory areas of the parietal lobes, and sends information to the appropriate spot.

10. a.   No; this lobe is associated with the integration of auditory information.
    b.   No; this lobe is associated with the integration of tactile information.
    c.   No; this lobe is associated with higher level processing.
    d.   YES; this lobe is associated with the processing of visual information.

11. a.   No; we are aware of movement perception.
    b.   No; we are aware of depth perception.
    c.   YES; quickly flashing visual stimuli can result in a subliminal perception.
    d.   No; there is no unconscious perception.

12. a.   This is the minimum amount of energy that can be detected.
    b.   CORRECT; the difference threshold refers to the smallest difference required to discriminate two stimuli, in this case two shades of paint.
    c.   No
    d.   Sensory adaptation is the change of responsiveness to stimulation

13. a.   No; the shadow of the objects provides information to its depth.
    b.   YES
    c.   No; texture gradient refers to how the texture changes as distance changes.
    d.   No; linear perspective is when two parallel lines appear to converge in the distance.

14. a.   No; this is correct about color blindness.
    b.   No; this is correct about color blindness.
    c.   YES; this is incorrect; people with color blindness have problems sensing some color but not all colors.
    d.   No; this is correct about color blindness.

15. a.   No; the man and the woman may be very different.
    b.   No; we are not adding/assuming another figure/person to the situation.
    c.   YES; we perceive the two individuals as a whole, a couple.
    d.   No; this is not one of the gestalt principles of perception.

Practice Test 3 Answers

1. a.   EXACTLY; loudness is determined by the sound's amplitude.
    b.   Hertz is a measurement of sound.
    c.   Wavelength refers to the physical characteristic of sound.
    d.   No

2. a. No
    b. No
    c. No; these structures make up middle ear.
    d. CORRECT; the inner is made up of these structures.

3. a. This is important, but not in the actual translation of sound.
    b. No
    c. No
    d. RIGHT

4. a. No; each frequency stimulates cells at particular places on the basilar membrane.
    b. Frequency theory says that how often cells fire is important.
    c. YES, THAT'S RIGHT; the volley theory says that neural cells produce a volley of impulses.
    d. No

5. a. No
    b. CORRECT
    c. No
    d. No

6. a. No
    b. YES
    c. No
    d. No

7. a. No
    b. CORRECT
    c. No
    d. No

8. a. No; this is one of the dimensions of taste.
    b. No; this is one of the dimensions of taste.
    c. YES; pasty may refer more to texture than to actual taste.
    d. No; this is one of the dimensions of taste.

9. a. YES
    b. No
    c. No
    d. No

10.   a.   No; these correspond to the visual sense.

          b.   YES; the papillae, like the olfactory epithelium, hold the sensory receptors.

          c.   No; the sensory receptors in the semicircular canals determine the position of the head.

          d.   No; the rods are sensory receptors in the retina.

11.   a.   No; reading with plenty of light is VERY important to protect your eyes.

          b.   No; sunglasses are necessary in order to protect your eyes from UV rays.

          c.   YES; while wearing glasses indoors is good if you have prescription lenses, it is not necessary for all people to protect their eyes.

          d.   No; beta carotene is good for your eyes.

12.   a.   YES; active engagement with nature helps, not only your senses, but your overall health and well-being.

          b.   No; protective lenses is good for eyes but irrelevant for other senses.

          c.   No; vitamin A is good for your eyes but not necessary for other senses.

          d.   No; zinc is good for your eyes but not necessary for other senses.

13.   a.   YES; timbre is perceptual quality (or tone saturation), and loudness is determined by the amplitude of the sound wave.

          b.   No; pitch is determined by the frequency of the sound wave.

          c.   No

          d.   No

14.   a.   No; the pinna and external auditory canal, which compose the outer ear, channel the sounds into the interior ear.

          b.   No; the parts and functions of the middle ear have been clearly studied, and these theories are not addressing this.

          c.   YES; place theory says that each frequency of sound waves produces vibrations at specific spots on the basilar membrane, while frequency theory says that it all depends on how often the auditory nerve fires and sends information to the brain.

          d.   No; these theories don't address this.

Chapter 6: States of Consciousness

Learning Goals
1. Discuss the nature of consciousness.
2. Explain the nature of sleep and dreams.
3. Describe hypnosis.
4. Evaluate the uses and types of psychoactive drugs.
5. Discuss the role of the conscious mind in constructing a happy and healthy life.

After studying chapter 6, you will be able to:
- Appreciate the role of sleep in maintaining a healthy way of life;
- Describe how hypnosis can be used to reduce recovery time after surgery;
- Explain how mindfulness meditation can help increase well-being and boost your immune system.

Chapter Outline
1. The Nature of Consciousness
- _____ refers to thinking about thinking.
- Consciousness refers to:
  - _____ of external events and internal sensations. The _____ (part of the brain) is typically involved in this.
  - _____ is the act of being engaged with the environment. The _____ (part of the brain) is responsible for this.
- _____ (name) described the mind as a _____ or a continuous flow of changing sensations, images, thoughts and feelings.
- There is not one specific location in the brain that takes incoming information and converts it into the conscious world we are aware of. Rather, it is likely that a number of separately distributed processing systems connect to produce consciousness.
- _____ represent the most alert states of human consciousness, in which individuals actively focus their efforts toward a goal.
- _____ are states of consciousness that require minimal attention and do not interfere with other ongoing activities.
- _____ is a low level state of consciousness somewhere in between active consciousness and actual dreaming.
- _____ are mental states that are noticeably different from normal awareness. Such states can be produced by drugs, trauma, fatigue, hypnosis, or sensory depravation.
- Subconscious information occurs along with conscious processing. For example, it is conscious awareness that sees something running down the street, but it is due to subconscious processing that you know the object is a dog and that it is black.

2. Sleep and Dreams
- Sleep and dreams are not the absence of consciousness but rather are _____ of consciousness.

- _____ are periodic physiological fluctuations such as hormones in the body that, for the most part, we are unaware of. These are controlled by biological clocks which include:
    o _____or seasonal cycles such as migration of birds and seasonal fluctuations in human eating habits.
    o _____ cycles such as the female menstrual cycle.
    o _____ cycles such as the sleep/wake cycle.
- A _____ rhythm is a daily behavioral or physiological cycle such as the sleep/wake cycle, body temperature, blood pressure, and blood sugar.
- The change in the body from night to day is monitored by the _____ which is a small structure in the brain that synchronizes its rhythm with the daily schedule of light/dark.
- Jet lag is an example of when biological clocks become _____, because time zone changes alter the natural light/dark schedule you experience, but your body's sense of time is unchanged and therefore out of sync.
- Sleep is important because of benefits such as _____, _____, _____, and _____.
    o _____ occurs because during sleep cells show increased production and reduced breakdown of proteins.
    o Sleep is _____ because the search for food and water is less dangerous during the day and night provides time to save energy.
    o Deep sleep coincides with the release of _____ in children.
    o Sleep, particularly REM sleep, plays a role in the _____ of long-term memory.
- Sleep expert _____ (name) argues that the _____ of our lives is jeopardized due to sleep depravation. Most experts agree that we need at least _____ of sleep each night.
- Sleep depravation is associated with _____brain activity and declines in _____ and cognitive performance.
- The biological clocks of _____ shift as they get older.
- Sleep patterns adjust as people get older such that _____ to bed for adolescents and _____ to bed for middle age adults.
- Stages of sleep correspond to the massive _____ changes that occur throughout the brain.
    o When we are relaxed but awake, our brain waves slow down, _____ in amplitude, and become more _____. These waves are called _____ waves.
    o Stage 1 sleep is characterized by _____ waves. (See figure 6.4 in your text).
    o Stage 2 sleep is characterized by sleep _____ which involve a sudden increase in _____.
    o Stages 3 and 4 are characterized by _____ waves. These stages represent out deepest sleep.
    o _____ is an active stage of sleep during which dreaming occurs.
- Why do infants get almost 8 hours of REM sleep, while older adults get less than 1 hour of REM sleep?

_____

_____.

- The three neurotransmitters involved in sleep are _____, _____, and _____.
- Neurons that control sleep interact closely with the _____ system. The reason for this connection is because of chemicals called _____.
- Depression affects sleep because those with depression spend less time in _____ wave sleep.
- The inability to sleep is called _____.
- _____ is the formal term for sleepwalking. This occurs during sleep stages ____ and ____.
- An increase in nightmares is often associated with an increase in _____.
- A _____ is characterized by sudden arousal from sleep and intense fear.
- The overpowering urge to sleep is called _____. People suffering from this enter _____ sleep immediately.
- _____ is a disorder in which individuals stop breathing.
- The _____proposes that dreaming can be understood by applying the same cognitive concepts used to study the waking mind. In this theory there is little or no search for hidden or symbolic content.
- _____ theory states that dreaming occurs when the _____ (part of the brain) synthesizes neural signals generated from activity in the lower part of the brain.

3. Hypnosis
- Hypnosis is a psychological state or possibly altered attention and awareness in which a person is unusually receptive to _____.
- Hypnosis is recognized as a _____ process in psychology and medicine.
- Individuals in a hypnotic state show a predominance of _____ and _____ waves which are associated with a _____ state.
- Some people can be hypnotized while other cannot. Approximately ____% are highly susceptible to hypnosis, ____% are moderately hypnotizable, and ____% cannot be hypnotized.
- It is _____ that somebody who is hypnotized will do anything that violates his or her morals or that is dangerous.
- _____ (name) proposed that hypnosis involves a special divided state of consciousness, a sort of _____ into separate parts.
- In the _____ view of hypnosis, hypnosis is a normal state in which the hypnotized person behaves in a way he or she feels that a hypnotized person should behave.
- Those who are hypnotized to experience less pain do indeed report the experience of electrical shocks as less painful than those who are not hypnotized. Explain how this could be based on the brain scanning results reported in your text.

_____

_____

_____

_____

4. Psychoactive Drugs

- During the first part of the 21st century, the proportion of secondary school students reporting the use of illicit drugs has _____.
- _____ drugs are substances that act on the _____ to alter states of consciousness, modify perceptions, and change moods.
- Continued use of psychoactive drugs leads to _____, which is the need to take increasing amounts of the drug to get the same effect.
- _____ describes either physical or psychological dependence.
- Withdrawal symptoms are associated with _____ dependence.
- The strong desire to use a drug for emotional reasons is _____dependence.
- Psychoactive drugs increase _____ (neurotransmitter) levels in the brain's reward pathways which are located in the _____ and _____ (areas of the brain).
- _____ are psychoactive drugs that slow down mental and physical activity. The following are the most widely used of this type of drug: _____.
- Alcohol _____ the brain's activities and increases levels of _____ (neurotransmitter).
- Binge drinking is defined as _____.
- People who begin drinking before the age of 14 are more likely to become _____ than those who begin drinking at 21.
- The long-term, repeated, uncontrolled, compulsive, and excessive use of alcohol is a disorder called _____.
- _____ are depressant drugs that decrease central nervous system activity and were once prescribed as sleep aids.
- Drugs that reduce anxiety and induce relaxation are called _____.
- Morphine and heroin are examples of _____.
- _____ are psychoactive drugs that increase the central nervous system's activity.
- _____ is the world's most widely used psychoactive drug.
- _____ is the main psychoactive ingredient in all forms of smoking.
- In adolescents, the number of people smoking is _____ (increasing or decreasing).
- _____ are stimulant drugs that are often prescribed as diet pills.
- The Drug Enforcement Agency is so concerned about the use of _____ (a highly addictive synthetic stimulant) that they created the web site www.justthinktwice.com to share the horrifying effects of this drug.
- _____ is a drug derived from the coca plant.
- Drugs that are intentionally breathed in to produce psychoactive effects are called _____.
- _____ are drugs that modify a person's perceptual experiences.
- The active ingredient in marijuana, a mild hallucinogen, is _____.
- The technical name for the drug commonly referred to as Ecstasy is _____. This substance has adverse effects on _____ and cognitive processing.

- _____ is a strong hallucinogen once advocated by Timothy Leary and acts primarily on _____ (neurotransmitter) in the brain.

5. Consciousness, Health, and Wellness

- _____ meditation can be used as pain management by focusing attention on the pain and isolating it from an emotional response.

- Depression, panic attacks, anxiety, chronic pain, and stress can all be helped by

_____.

- Describe what brain scan research has revealed regarding meditation.

_____

_____

_____

- _____ is an overwhelming feeling of wellness experienced right before you fall asleep. Mediation has been compared to this state.

- List three examples of meditation like practices that, while not explicitly mentioning meditation, involve several of the same processes.

    o _____
    o _____
    o _____

Intersection

- Describe one example of how the behavior of children can help us understand *theory of mind*.

Critical Controversy

- Psychoactive drugs are powerful substances that are often abused. However, some substances may have therapeutic or medicinal purposes. Describe the potential therapeutic or medicinal benefits of one psychoactive drug.

Clarifying Tricky Points

What exactly is consciousness?

This is a difficult question and one that has puzzled psychologists, philosophers, theologians, and many other scholars for centuries. For the purposes of modern psychological research, consciousness is your awareness of external and internal events and occurs under a condition of arousal, or engagement in the environment. Sleep is not consciousness in the same way as when you are awake because your level of arousal is drastically lower when you are sleeping. Sleep is not, however, the absence of consciousness, just a very low level of it. For a person to be truly not conscious, it typically requires a severe blow the head or anesthesia.

Subconscious vs. low level consciousness

Subconscious processing occurs while you are wide awake but you are not aware of it. Subconscious processing can be thought of as how your brain fills in the blanks when perceiving the world. For example, it would be a waste of time and energy for your mind to thoroughly and consciously process all information associated with an object moving off in the distance. You are consciously aware of the object, but it is subconscious processing that filled in all the blanks and has identified it as a black dog. Low levels of consciousness, on the other hand, are very different than subconscious. Sleep and daydreaming are examples of low levels of consciousness because our awareness and arousal are decreased and, obviously, sleep and daydreaming do not occur when we are wide awake as subconscious processing does.

<u>Hypnosis</u>

If you've been a part of a lot of clubs and organizations or attended a lot of campus events, chances are you've seen your classmates be "hypnotized" and cluck like a chicken while hopping up and down on one leg. Were your classmates really hypnotized? Possibly. Hypnosis is a state of altered attention and awareness in which a person is particularly susceptible to suggestion and it is very much a real phenomenon. At its lower reaches, hypnosis is responsible for people clucking like a chicken, but at its higher reaches hypnosis can be a powerful technique to reduce pain during surgery without anesthesia. A hypnotic state is not a sleep like state. Rather it is more like a very relaxed waking state in which a person's consciousness has been divided into one component that follows commands and another that acts as a hidden observer making sure you don't do anything that violates your morals or puts you in danger.

An Appreciative View of Psychology and Your Life

In your text you read about meditation and how it can help people of all sorts, not just Zen masters or Buddhist monks. Think about one thing you do relatively often (or maybe something you *should* do more often than you do) that closely resembles the processes involved in meditation (see your book for some examples). Now write down how that behavior can affect you in the following ways:

Brain activity:

_____

_____

Conscious awareness and arousal:

_____

_____

Immune functioning:

_____

_____

Overall well-being:

_____

_____

Practice Test 1

1.   If you are aware of both external and internal stimuli, you are in a(n)

    a.   altered state.
    b.   conscious state.
    c.   REM state.
    d.   narcoleptic state.

2.   A form of consciousness that requires minimal attention is

    a.   controlled processes.
    b.   automatic processes.
    c.   stream of consciousness.
    d.   unconscious thought.

3. Which of the following would be least likely to induce an altered state of consciousness?
    a. meditation
    b. hypnosis
    c. caffeine
    d. cocaine

4. William James described the mind as a
    a. blank slate.
    b. confusing aspect that should not be studied by psychologists.
    c. stream of consciousness.
    d. lack of awareness

5. A person who is daydreaming about an upcoming job interview is engaged in
    a. higher-level awareness.
    b. lower-level awareness.
    c. an altered state of consciousness.
    d. subconscious awareness.

6. Most experts argue that consciousness is
    a. located and processed in a very small area of the frontal lobe.
    b. located and processed in the hypothalamus.
    c. processed in numerous areas distributed across the whole nervous system.
    d. processed in numerous areas distributed across the brain.

7. At the beginning of his lecture class, Mike, a student, finds that he is alert, attentive, and focused on the lecture. In which state of consciousness is Mike?
    a. controlled processes
    b. automatic processes
    c. hypnotized
    d. stream of consciousness

8. You can talk, eat a sandwich, or listen to music while driving an automobile (but probably shouldn't because, as you will learn in chapter 8, multitasking is bad) because
    a. driving an automobile has become an automatic process.
    b. you have developed an altered state of consciousness.
    c. you have the special ability to concentrate on several things at one time.
    d. driving an automobile has become a controlled process.

Practice Test 2

1. Circadian rhythm refers to
    a. a popular Latin dance.
    b. a daily cycle.
    c. the brain's level of activity when taking a psychoactive drug.
    d. an abnormal biological rhythm associated with jet lag.

2.   Which of the following is a circadian rhythm?
a.   the stream of consciousness
b.   the four stages of sleep
c.   hypnosis
d.   the sleep/wake cycle

3.   Delta waves are produced in which stage of sleep?
a.   REM sleep
b.   Stage 1 sleep
c.   Stage 2 sleep
d.   Stage 4 sleep

4.   A person who usually sleeps 8 hours completes an average of how many sleep cycles per night?
a.   2
b.   3
c.   4
d.   5

5.   Another name for somnambulism is
a.   sleepwalking.
b.   hallucination.
c.   insomnia.
d.   bed-wetting.

6.   The cognitive view of dreaming asserts that dreams
a.   help dissipate problematic sexual and aggressive energy.
b.   are the conscious equivalent of innate instincts.
c.   are the conscious interpretation of relatively random neural activity.
d.   are used to review daily events and orient toward future goals.

7.   According to the activation-synthesis view,
a.   dreams represent wish fulfillment.
b.   dreams have no inherent meaning.
c.   dreams are a way to solve problems and think creatively.
d.   dreams have manifest and latent content.

8.   The part of the brain that keeps the biological clocks synchronized is the
a.   suprachiasmic nucleus.
b.   thalamus.
c.   hindbrain.
d.   frontal lobe.

9.   Which of the following is NOT one of the reasons we need sleep?
   a.   restoration
   b.   dreams
   c.   adaptation
   d.   growth

10.   Which of the following neurotransmitters is not decreased as the sleep cycles progress from stages 1 to 4?
   a.   epinephrine
   b.   serotonin
   c.   GABA
   d.   acetylcholine

11.   Which of the following is NOT TRUE about the relationship between sleep and disease?
   a.   People with depression tend to have sleep problems.
   b.   When we have an infectious disease, we have a harder time falling asleep.
   c.   Asthma attacks are more likely during the night, probably because of biological changes associated with sleep.
   d.   People with Alzheimer's disease tend to experience sleep problems.

12.   The theory of dreams that says dreams provide alternative ways for solving problems is called the
   a.   cognitive theory of dreams.
   b.   I-got-it dream approach.
   c.   activation-synthesis theory.
   d.   manifest content theory.

13.   During what age are nightmares more frequent?
   a.   newborns
   b.   late adulthood
   c.   childhood
   d.   early adulthood

14.   The following are characteristics of the sleep stages, EXCEPT
   a.   The stages of sleep correspond to electrophysiological changes in the brain.
   b.   When a person is sleeping he/she shows beta waves in an EEG.
   c.   The first stage of sleep is characterized by the presence of electrical waves that are slow in frequency and great in amplitude.
   d.   Sleep spindles show up in stage two of sleep.

15.   Which of the following waves of electrical brain activity is the one consistent with the deepest sleep?
  a.   theta
  b.   beta
  c.   delta
  d.   alpha

16.   Which of the following is NOT true about REM sleep?
  a.   It does not take a long time in REM sleep for the person to report a long and complex dream.
  b.   Infants spend most of their sleeping time in REM sleep.
  c.   There is rapid eye movement during REM sleep.
  d.   During REM sleep, the brain waves are similar to alpha waves.

17.   The activation-synthesis theory proposed that dreams are
  a.   symbolic expressions of what we wish would happen in our lives.
  b.   predictions of the future.
  c.   a result of brain activity.
  d.   based on our childhood troubles.

Practice Test 3

1.   Which brain waves are most common in the brain of a hypnotized person?
  a.   alpha and delta
  b.   theta and beta
  c.   delta and beta
  d.   alpha and beta

2.   When hypnosis is induced, the hypnotist
  a.   tries to keep the subject distracted.
  b.   discourages the subject from concentrating on anything specific.
  c.   suggests to the subject what will be experienced in the hypnotic state.
  d.   is careful to prevent posthypnotic amnesia.

3.   What do caffeine and cocaine have in common?
  a.   They are stimulants.
  b.   They are depressants.
  c.   They are hallucinogens.
  d.   They are opiates.

4.   Which of the following is a stimulant?
  a.   marijuana
  b.   alcohol
  c.   cocaine
  d.   LSD

5.	Which of the following is NOT one of the areas in which hypnosis has been applied?
	a.	medicine
	b.	studies of controlled processing
	c.	psychotherapy
	d.	dentistry

6.	The difference between physical dependence and psychological dependence is that
	a.	psychological dependence does not cause addiction.
	b.	physical dependence does not cause addiction.
	c.	physical dependence is associated with the direct cause of withdrawal symptoms.
	d.	psychological dependence is not related to stress.

7.	Psychoactive drugs increase the neurotransmitter, _____ in the brain's reward pathways.
	a.	serotonin
	b.	acetylcholine
	c.	GABA
	d.	dopamine

8.	The reason a person "loosens up" after a few drinks is because
	a.	alcohol is a stimulant that makes people feel happy.
	b.	alcohol is a hallucinogen that makes things look different.
	c.	alcohol slows down the areas of the brain involved in inhibition.
	d.	alcohol, like cocaine, is a depressant.

9.	The following are characteristics of alcoholism, EXCEPT
	a.	uncontrolled use of alcoholic beverages.
	b.	compulsive use of alcoholic beverages.
	c.	short-term use of alcoholic beverages.
	d.	repeated use of alcoholic beverages.

10	Which of the following are psychoactive drugs associated with increased energy?
	a.	opiates
	b.	marijuana
	c.	amphetamines
	d.	alcoholic beverages

11.	Which percentage of alcoholics is expected to have a genetic predisposition for the disorder?
	a.	10%
	b.	25%
	c.	50%
	d.	90%

12.   Which of the following statements presents correctly one of the differences between barbiturates and tranquilizers?

    a.   Barbiturates are more likely to be addictive than tranquilizers.

    b.   Tranquilizers are given to induce sleep.

    c.   Barbiturates are more likely to be prescribed than tranquilizers.

    d.   An overdose of barbiturates is unlike to be dangerous or lethal.

13.   Which of the following is NOT true about Ecstasy?

    a.   It is a stimulant.

    b.   It is a hallucinogenic.

    c.   It is an illegal drug that comes from a bean.

    d.   It causes brain damage.

14.   Marijuana is a

    a.   barbiturate.

    b.   hallucinogen.

    c.   stimulant.

    d.   depressant.

15.   Daily prayer is similar to

    a.   a high level of consciousness.

    b.   a sleep like state.

    c.   a meditative state.

    d.   an altered state of consciousness.

Answer Key

Mediation and related activities:

- Increase activity in the basal ganglia and prefrontal cortex (the area responsible for consciousness) and decrease activity in the anterior cingulated (the area responsible for acts of will).
- Increase awareness
- Are associated with heightened immune functioning.
- Create an overall sense of well-being including lowered anxiety and fewer negative emotions.

Practice Test 1 Answers

1.   a.   No; this state refers to a state that is noticeably different from normal awareness.

    b.   YES; this is the definition of consciousness.

    c.   No; REM is rapid eye movement that occurs in sleep.

    d.   No

2. a. No; controlled processes require much attention and focus.
    b. CORRECT; automatic processes require minimal attention.
    c. No; this refers to the continuous flow of sensations and thoughts.
    d. No; unconscious thought refers to the reservoir of unconscious wishes and feelings.

3. a. No; this is very likely to cause an altered state of consciousness.
    b. No; this is very likely to cause an altered state of consciousness.
    c. YES; caffeine is a stimulant and will not likely induce an altered state.
    d. No; this is very likely to cause an altered state of consciousness.

4. a. No; James did not see the mind as a static blank slate.
    b. No; James did consider the study of the mind a worthy topic for psychologists.
    c. YES; James thought of the mind as a dynamic continuous flow of sensations, images, thoughts, and feelings.
    d. No; James understood the mind as conscious.

5. a. No; this occurs when we are engaged in controlled processing, and we are very alert of what we are doing and thinking.
    b. YES; daydreaming is a type of lower-level awareness, in which we may be in automatic processing.
    c. No; daydreaming is not an altered state of consciousness, such as those induced by drugs, trauma, fatigue, and other factors.
    d. No; sleeping and dreaming are examples of subconscious awareness.

6. a. No; consciousness is not processed in any specific or small area of the brain.
    b. No; consciousness is not processed in any specific or small area of the brain.
    c. No; remember that the nervous system runs throughout our body; only areas inside the brain are engaged in the production of consciousness.
    d. CORRECT; experts agree that consciousness is produced through the integrated and coordinated processing of many areas in the brain.

7. a. THAT'S RIGHT; Mike is experiencing a controlled process with   attention.
    b. No, automatic processes require minimal attention.
    c. No; hypnosis involves heighten suggestibility.
    d. No; this refers to the continuous flow of sensations and thoughts

8. a. YES; driving requires minimal attention and doesn't interfere with ongoing activities.
    b. No; altered states refer to a state that differs from normal awareness.
    c. No; this is not a special ability.
    d. No; driving is not a controlled process, since it doesn't interfere with ongoing activities.

Practice Text 2 Answers

1. a. No;
   b. YES; a circadian rhythm is a daily behavioral or physiological cycle.
   c. No; circadian rhythm is not related to drug use.
   d. No; jet lag is the result of rhythms being out of sync

2. a. No; the stream refers to the ever-changing thoughts, sensations, and images.
   b. No; the four stages of sleep are not necessarily a daily cycle.
   c. o; hypnosis is a change in consciousness.
   d. YES; this is an example of a circadian rhythm.

3. a. No; in REM we experience fast waves.
   b. No
   c. No; in stage 2 sleep there are sleep spindles.
   d. YES

4. a. No
   b. No
   c. No
   d. RIGHT; the cycles of sleep last about 90 minutes.

5. a. CORRECT; somnambulism is the formal term for sleepwalking.
   b. No
   c. No
   d. No

6. a. No; this option sounds Freudian.
   b. No
   c. No; this answer summarizes the activation-synthesis theory.
   d. YES; it focuses on information processing, memory, and problem solving.

7. a. No; Freud would argue this option.
   b. YEP; dreams are the brain's effort to make sense of neural activity.
   c. No; the cognitive theory is consistent with this option.
   d. No; Freud's theory includes manifest and latent content.

8. a. YES; this little structure in the hypothalamus registers light and uses it to synchronize our biological clocks; this is why blind people tend to have problems with their biological clocks, because they cannot perceive light and the information does not get to the suprachiasmatic nucleus.
   b. No; the thalamus is not involved in this function.
   c. Incorrect; the hindbrain is not involved in this function; the suprachiasmatic nucleus is in the hypothalamus, which in turn is in the forebrain.
   d. Incorrect

9. a. No; this is one of the most important functions of sleep.
    b. YES; while there are various theories of dreams, no one argues that dreaming is the reason we sleep; however, the type of deep sleep we are in when we dream is very important.
    c. No; adaptation seems to be an important reason to sleep; after all, we need the rest to face the challenges presented by our environment.
    d. No; growth also is enhanced by sleep

10. a. No; levels of epinephrine decrease as sleep progresses from stages 1 to 4.
    b. No; levels of serotonin do decrease as sleep progresses from stages 1 to 4.
    c. YES; a decrease in GABA is not observed as the sleep stages progress from 1 to 4.
    d. No; levels of acetylcholine do decrease from stages 1 to 4 and begin increasing when REM starts.

11. a. No; this statement is correct.
    b. YES; this statement is incorrect, when we are fighting an infectious disease we tend to get sleepy, probably due to the work of the chemicals called cytokines.
    c. No; this statement is true.
    d. No; this statement is true.

12. a. YES; this theory argues that while dreaming we are engaging in the same cognitive processes as when we are awake and among those processes features problem solving.
    b. No; while this may seem like a trick item it is not; first of all, there is no theory called the *I-got-it dream approach*, but more importantly, theories in psychology are usually named with meaningful concepts, such as "cognitive"; remember that theories are broad and the names of theories are expected to carry a lot of meaning.
    c. No; this theory focuses on the role of brain activity in the generation of dreams.
    d. No; while manifest content is a concept relevant in the study of dreams, it is not a theory.

13. a. No; a newborn is unlikely to have specific images to symbolize danger, the usual topic of nightmares.
    b. No
    c. YES; nightmares peak at 3 to 6 years of age and then decline.
    d. No; college students tend to have only 4 to 8 nightmares a year.

14. a. No; this is correct about sleep stages.
    b. YES; beta waves are characteristic of wakefulness and are highest in frequency and lowest in amplitude.
    c. No; this is correct about sleep stages.
    d. No; this is correct about sleep stages.

15. a. No; these are characteristic of the first stage.
     b. No; these are characteristic of being awake.
     c. YES; these are the waves that are characteristic of our deepest sleep; they are the slowest and the highest in amplitude.
     d. No; these are characteristic of being relaxed but awake.

16. a. YES; this is incorrect because the longer the period of REM sleep, the more likely the person will report dreaming.
     b. No; this is correct about REM sleep; older adults spend about one-eighth of the time in REM sleep that an infant spends in REM sleep.
     c. No; this is correct about REM sleep.
     d. No; this is correct about REM sleep.

17. a. No; this would be more consistent with the psychoanalytic view of Freud.
     b. No; psychologists do not believe that dreams are predictions of actual future events.
     c. YES; according to this view, dreams are generated when the cerebral cortex synthesizes neural signals resulting from activity in the lower part of the brain.
     d. No; this is not consistent with the activation-synthesis theory.

Practice Test 3 Answers
1.   a. No
     b. No
     c. No
     d. YES; this suggests that hypnosis, in terms of brain activity, is no different from being deeply relaxed, yet awake.

2.   a. No; in fact, concentration and focus are very important.
     b. No; concentrating and focusing on something specific are very important.
     c. CORRECT; when the experience occurs, the person will believe it was suggested.
     d. No; the hypnotist may actually desire posthypnotic amnesia to occur.

3.   a. YES, THAT'S RIGHT; both caffeine and cocaine are stimulants.
     b. No
     c. No
     d. No

4.   a   No; marijuana is a hallucinogenic drug.
     b. No; alcohol is a depressant.
     c. YES; cocaine is classified as a stimulant.
     d. No; LSD is a hallucinogenic drug.

5. a.   No; hypnosis has been used in medicine.
    b.   YES; hypnosis would not be useful in studying the higher-level consciousness of controlled processing.
    c.   No; hypnosis is used in psychotherapy.
    d.   No; hypnosis has been used in dentistry.

6. a.   No; this statement is false.
    b.   No; this statement is false.
    c.   YES; physical dependence is associated with the experience of withdrawal symptoms.
    d.   No; this statement is incorrect, as some people may become psychologically dependent, because the drug reduces stress.

7. a.   No
    b.   No
    c.   No
    d.   YES; while different drugs have different mechanisms of action, each drug increases the activity of the reward pathway by increasing dopamine transmission.

8. a.   No; alcohol is a depressant.
    b.   No; alcohol is not a hallucinogenic.
    c.   YES; alcohol is a depressant that slows down brain activity in various areas, including the one involving inhibition.
    d.   No; while alcohol is depressant, cocaine is not; it is a stimulant.

9. a.   No; this is one of the characteristics of alcoholism.
    b.   No; this is one of the characteristics of alcoholism.
    c.   YES; alcoholism involves a long-term use of alcoholic beverages.
    d.   No; this is one of the characteristics of alcoholism.

10. a.   No; these are depressants, not stimulants.
    b.   No; marijuana is a hallucinogen; it does not provide a boost in energy.
    c.   YES; amphetamines are stimulants that are used to boost energy, stay awake, and lose weight.
    d.   No; alcohol is a depressant.

11. a.   No; while environmental factors are important, they do not account for 90% of the cases of alcoholism.
    b.   No; while environmental factors, such as friends and culture are important, they do not account for 75% of the cases of alcoholism.
    c.   YES; an estimated 50–60% of those who become alcoholics are believed to have a genetic predisposition.
    d.   No; genetics are important factors, but they do not account for 90% of the cases of alcoholism.

12.   a.   YES; this is true, and it is one of the main reasons why tranquilizers have largely replaced barbiturates in the treatment of insomnia.

       b.   No; barbiturates are given to induce sleep, while tranquilizers are usually given to calm an anxious and nervous individual.

       c.   No; the opposite is true.

       d.   No; this is grossly incorrect; barbiturates are the most common drug used in suicide attempts because of the lethal effects of overdoses.

13.   a.   No; this is true about Ecstasy.

       b.   No; this is also true about Ecstasy, it is a stimulant and a hallucinogenic.

       c.   YES; this is incorrect because Ecstasy is a synthetic drug; it does not come from a bean or a plant.

       d.   No; Ecstasy can cause brain damage, especially to neurons that use serotonin to communicate with other neurons.

14.   a.   No

       b.   YES; marijuana has a mild hallucinogenic effect.

       c.   No

       d.   No

15.   a.   No

       b.   No

       c.   Yes, daily prayer is similar to meditation.

       d.   No

Chapter 7: Learning

Learning Goals
1. Explain what learning is.
2. Describe classical conditioning.
3. Discuss operant conditioning.
4. Understand observational learning.
5. Discuss the role of cognition in learning.
6. Identify biological, cultural, and psychological factors in learning.
7. Describe how principles of learning apply to health and wellness.

After studying chapter 7, you will be able to:
- Describe the most effective ways to reinforce good behavior in people;
- Understand how the way you think of intelligence can affect how you respond to failures;
- Create strategies to improve self-control.

Chapter Outline
1. Types of Learning
- _____ is a relatively permanent change in behavior that occurs through experience.
- Behaviorism is a theory of learning that focuses on _____
  _____.
- Associative learning is when a _____ is made between two events.
  - Conditioning is _____.
  - The two types of conditioning are_____ and _____.
- _____ learning takes place when a person observes and imitates another's behavior.
2. Classical Conditioning
- Classical conditioning is a process by which a _____ becomes associated with a _____ and acquires the capacity to elicit a similar response.

> **Classical Conditioning Abbreviations**
> **UCS** = Unconditioned Stimulus
> **UCR** = Unconditioned Response
> **CS** = Conditioned Stimulus
> **CR** = Conditioned Response

- _____ is the person who, through an informal study of dogs, came up with classical conditioning.
- An unconditioned stimulus (UCS) is _____
  _____.
- An unconditioned response (UCR) is _____
  _____.
- A conditioned stimulus (CS) is _____
  _____.
- A conditioned response (CR) is _____
  _____.

- In Pavlov's studies, the bell became a _____ and salivation became a _____.
- Acquisition is the _____.
- The _____ between the CS and UCS is one of the most important aspects of classical conditioning.
- Contingency is also important is the _____.
- Generalization is the tendency of a new stimulus that is similar to the original CS to _____.
- Generalization is not always beneficial. It is also important to discriminate, which is the process of _____.
- _____ is the weakening of the CR in the absence of the UCS.
- Spontaneous recovery is the process by which _____
  _____.
- Phobias are _____.
  - o Classical conditioning can explain phobias through the example of Albert and a white rat.
- Counterconditioning is a procedure for weakening a CR by _____
  _____.
- Classical conditioning can explain drug habituation, because if a drug is taken in an unusual situation, no _____ have been built up for the new setting and therefore the body is not prepared to handle the drug, making the effect of the drug much greater.

3. Operant Conditioning

- Operant conditioning was developed by _____ (name) and is a form of _____.
- The law of effect was developed by _____ (name) and states that
  _____.
  - o A hungry cat inside a box with a piece of fish outside is an example of the law of effect.
- S-R theory, by Thorndike, states that _____
  _____.
- Skinner's approach to operant conditioning is exhibited in his book _____
  _____ about his vision for a utopian society based on the principles of operant conditioning.
- Shaping is a form of learning where _____
  _____.
- Reinforcement is the process by which a stimulus or event _____
  _____.
  - o In positive reinforcement, the frequency of a behavior _____,
    because it is followed by a rewarding stimulus.
  - o In negative reinforcement, the frequency of a behavior _____
    because it is followed by the_____.
- Primary reinforcement involves the use of reinforces that are _____
  _____. For example, _____.

- Secondary reinforcers are _____ reinforcers. For example, _____.
- Gift certificates are examples of token reinforcers because they can be _____ _____.
- In continuous reinforcement, a behavior is reinforced _____ _____.
- Most of life's behaviors follow _____ which is reinforcement that follows a behavior only some of the time.
- There are four schedules for reinforcement (see figure 7.8 in your text for help).
  - fixed-ratio: _____.
  - variable ratio: _____.
  - fixed-interval: _____.
  - variable-interval: _____.
- Generalization in operant conditioning is different than generalization in classical conditioning. In operant conditioning, generalization means _____ _____.
- In operant conditioning, _____ means responding to stimuli that signal that a behavior will or will not be reinforced.
- In operant conditions, extinction occurs when _____ _____.
- Punishment is a consequence that decreases the likelihood that a behavior will occur and is different from reinforcement because _____ _____.
  - In positive punishment, a behavior decreases when _____ _____. An example is _____.
  - In negative punishment, a behavior decreases when _____ _____. An example is _____.
- When the delayed consequences of behavior are punishing and the immediate consequences are rewarding, the _____ usually wins.
  - Smoking and drinking are examples of this.
- The Premack principle states that _____ _____.
  - An example is when a teacher lets a student play a video game only after completing a less desirable writing assignment.

4. Observational Learning

- Observational learning is also called _____ and is learning that occurs when a person _____.
- _____ is the person typically associated with observational learning and described four main processes that are involved in such learning. (see figure 7.13 in your text for help)
  - Attention: _____.
  - Retention: _____.

- o Motor reproduction: _____.
- o Reinforcement: _____.

5. Cognitive Factors in Learning

- An example of selective disobedience is when a service dog _____
  _____.
- The purposiveness of behavior is the idea that _____
  _____.
- Expectancies are acquired from _____.
- A cognitive map is an organism's mental representation of the structure of physical space.
- Latent learning, or implicit learning, is _____
  _____.
- _____ is a form of problem solving in which the organism develops a sudden insight into the solution to a problem.
  - o Kohler used apes to demonstrate this effect.

6. Biological, Cultural, and Psychological Factors in Learning

- _____ is the tendency of animals to revert to instinctive behavior that interferes with learning.
- Preparedness is the species-specific biological predisposition to _____
  _____.
- Taste aversion to food that has made you ill can last for 30 days or more. Such long-term effects cannot be explained by _____ so perhaps taste aversion is adaptive in an evolutionary sense.
- Classical conditioning, operant conditioning, and observational learning are powerful learning processes in every culture. But culture can influence the degree to which these processes are used.
- In 1928, John Watson took the principles of _____ too far in his book that became the official government guidebook for parents. One example of where he went too far is _____.
- Carol Dweck describes two beliefs about intelligence.
  - o Entity theory: _____
    _____.
  - o Incremental theory: _____
    _____.
  - o From the perspective of entity theory, failure means _____. Whereas from the perspective of incremental theory, failure means _____
    _____.
- Based on Dweck's research, when a child does well at school, parents should direct their praise towards _____ rather than the good grade itself.

7. Learning and Health and Wellness

- _____ (form of learning) can produce immunosupression (a decrease in the production of antibodies that your body needs to fight illnesses).

- Predictable events are less stressful than unpredictable events.
- _____ means that, through experience, one has learned that outcomes are not controllable. This has been used to explain aspects of depression.
- The perception of improvement, even in a situation that is objectively worse, is related to _____ stress.
- Having outlets for frustration such as exercise can reduce the experience of stress.
- Applied behavior analysis (or behavior modification) is the application of

  _____.

  o Advocates of behavior modification contend that many emotional and behavior problems are caused by _____

     _____.

- These five steps can help you improve your self-control:
  1. _____
  2. _____
  3. _____
  4. _____
  5. _____

Intersection
- Neuroscience researchers have found that _____ (a neurotransmitter) plays a crucial role in the reinforcement of behavior.

Critical Controversy
- Research has found that spanking can increase immediate compliance but lead to lower levels of _____.

Clarifying Tricky Points
CS, CR, UCS, UCR: What does it all mean?
Classical conditioning is essentially a way of describing the relationships between stimuli and responses, some of which are intended and some of which are not. UCS and UCR are acronyms for *unconditioned* stimuli and responses, respectively. Unconditioned means no learning is required. If you hear a loud noise, you will probably jump a little and feel startled. You did not need to learn this response, it just happens, and is therefore an unconditioned response (UCR; the loud noise in this example is a UCS). Since this chapter is about learning, it is mostly about conditioned stimuli and responses (CS and CR respectively). Conditioned means the relationship must be learned. When a phone rings you don't necessarily jump and feel startled. But, if every time you heard a loud noise that made you jump, you also heard a phone ring, then the phone ringing would be a CS and now jumping, rather than being a UCR, is a CR because you had to learn that jumping (the CR) is associated with a phone ringing (the CS).

Positive and negative reinforcement
Negative reinforcement is not administering punishment. Spanking, for example, is not a form of negative reinforcement. Negative reinforcement is the *removal* of something aversive. For example, "twisting your arm" is a form of negative reinforcement. Someone

holds your arm in an uncomfortable position until you do something and, once you do it, they let go or "remove and aversive stimulus." This example obviously applies to when someone is literally twisting your arm, but metaphorical arm twisting is also negative reinforcement in the sense that if you agree to do something, the person "twisting your arm" will stop nagging and thereby remove an aversive stimulus (nagging). Positive reinforcement, by contrast, is when you give somebody something good once he or she has done what you want. Giving a child candy for good behavior is positive reinforcement.

Reinforcement vs. punishment
In reinforcement, the goal is to *increase* a behavior. In punishment, the goal is to *reduce* a behavior. See figure 7.10 in your text for examples on how reinforcement and punishment differ. Just like reinforcement, punishment comes in a positive and negative form. And, just like in reinforcement, positive refers to giving something whereas negative means taking something away. In punishment, however, positive means giving an unpleasant stimulus (such as spanking). Negative punishment is the act of removing something positive, like taking away video game privileges when a child misbehaves. See figure 7.11 in your text for examples of positive punishment, negative punishment, positive reinforcement, and negative reinforcement.

An Appreciative View of Psychology and Your Life
Carol Dweck outlined two ways of thinking about intelligence: entity and incremental. An entity approach to intelligence means some people are smart, some people are not, and there's not much that can be done about that. An incremental approach means, with hard work, intelligence can increase. So just because someone isn't smart now, doesn't mean that, if they work hard enough, they can't be smart later. Which approach to intelligence you have can affect the way you react to failure.

Think back to a time when you did not do well on an exam.
- How did you react to your poor performance? _____
  _____
- Does your reaction indicate you have an incremental or an entity approach to intelligence? _____
- Explain why taking an incremental approach to intelligence will serve you better in school. _____
  _____
  _____
  _____

Practice Test 1
1.   Each of the following is a part of the definition of learning except
     a.   relatively permanent.
     b.   change in behavior.
     c.   maturation.
     d.   experience.

2.   As the term has been used in traditional psychology, learning refers to
 a.   any relatively permanent change in behavior brought about by experience.
 b.   changes in behavior, including those associated with fatigue and maturation.
 c.   most changes in behavior, except those caused by brain damage.
 d.   all permanent changes in behavior, including those caused by heredity.

3.   In Pavlov's experiment, the bell was a previously neutral stimulus that became a(n)
 a.   conditioned stimulus.
 b.   conditioned response.
 c.   unconditioned response.
 d.   unconditioned stimulus.

4.   The classical conditioning process by which a conditioned response can recur after a time delay without further conditioning is called
 a.   extinction.
 b.   generalization.
 c.   spontaneous recovery.
 d.   discrimination.

5.   In Watson and Rayner's study, little Albert was conditioned to fear a white rat. Later, Albert showed a fear of similar objects, such as a white rabbit, balls of cotton, and a white stuffed animal. This is an example of stimulus
 a.   generalization.
 b.   substitution.
 c.   discrimination.
 d.   inhibition.

6.   The term *counterconditioning* best describes which of the following procedures?
 a.   presenting the conditioned stimulus by itself
 b.   reintroducing the conditioned stimulus after extinction has occurred
 c.   pairing a fear-provoking stimulus with a new response incompatible with fear
 d.   reinforcing successive approximations of the goal response

7.   Shaping is defined as the process of
 a.   reinforcing every avoidance response an organism makes.
 b.   reinforcing successive approximations of the target behavior.
 c.   directing an organism toward a specific stimulus target.
 d.   changing a primary reinforcer into a secondary reinforcer.

8. When an animal responds only to stimuli associated with reinforcement, it shows that it has the ability to
   a. discriminate.
   b. extinguish.
   c. generalize.
   d. modify.

9. Little Noelle has learned to throw a temper tantrum in front of Dad (who often gives in). Noelle has learned, however, that this same behavior is not effective with Mom. Noelle has demonstrated
   a. discrimination.
   b. instinctive drift.
   c. generalization.
   d. superstitious behavior.

10. Observational learning can occur
    a. in less time than operant conditioning.
    b. whether or not a model is reinforced.
    c. only if a model is reinforced.
    d. only with young children.

11. In Pavlov's classical conditioning studies, the bell before the conditioning is referred to as the
    a. unconditioned stimulus.
    b. neutral stimulus.
    c. conditioned stimulus.
    d. conditioned response.

12. Unconditioned is to conditioned as _____ is to _____.
    a. learned; reflex
    b. classical; operant
    c. reflex; learned
    d. operant; classical

13. _____ in classical conditioning occurs when a person learns to be afraid of being in a pool but not afraid of being in a bathtub full of water.
    a. Generalization
    b. Spontaneous recovery
    c. Extinction
    d. Discrimination

14. _____ occurs when a baby learns to get stressed when approached by all blond women, because once a blond woman who was holding her screamed and made her cry.
   a.   Generalization
   b.   Spontaneous recovery
   c.   Extinction
   d.   Discrimination

15. Which of the following is NOT one of the health issues associated with classical conditioning?
   a.   Classical conditioning can be involved in the proper working of the immune system.
   b.   Classical conditioning explains why people repeat risky health behaviors, such as smoking, because they are immediately rewarding.
   c.   Classical conditioning can cause the body to react in anticipation to receiving a drug when the person is exposed to stimuli that have become associated with the use of the drug.
   d.   Classical conditioning can contribute to asthma through the association with certain stimuli that cause stress and thus make the person more vulnerable to asthma attacks.

16. According to Tolman, in classical conditioning, the conditioned stimulus has informational value because it signals the upcoming
   a.   conditioned response.
   b.   unconditioned stimulus.
   c.   unconditioned response.
   d.   neutral stimulus.

Practice Test 2

1. Which approach to learning represents the view that people learn from the consequences of their actions?
   a.   response cost theory
   b.   operant conditioning
   c.   observational learning
   d.   classical conditioning

2. In operant conditioning, the association is between a _____ and its _____.
   a.   reinforcer; stimulus
   b.   behavior; response
   c.   consequence; punisher
   d.   behavior; consequences

3. Which schedule of reinforcement is most resistant to extinction?
   a. fixed-interval
   b. fixed-ratio
   c. variable-ratio
   d. variable-interval

4. If you wanted to encourage a child to work hard in order to get good grades, which would be your best choice of reinforcement schedule?
   a. variable-interval
   b. variable-ratio
   c. fixed-interval
   d. fixed-ratio

5. Which of the following sets of terms best describes the difference between secondary and primary reinforcers?
   a. learned; unlearned
   b. hidden; observable
   c. positive; negative
   d. psychological; physical

6. According to Thorndike's law of effect,
   a. a conditioned stimulus ultimately produces a conditioned response.
   b. behaviors followed by positive outcomes are strengthened.
   c. behavior learned on variable-interval schedules is difficult to extinguish.
   d. reinforcers should be given immediately after a desired response.

7. _____ learning involves watching what other people do, whereas _____ learning involves making connections between two events.
   a. Operant; classical
   b. Classical; operant
   c. Associative; observational
   d. Observational; associative

8. Which of the following pairs of concepts presents two concepts that mean virtually the same?
   a. conditioning/learning
   b. operant/observational
   c. behavior/mental process
   d. unconditioned stimulus/conditioned stimulus

9. _____ is a form of associative learning in which the consequences of behavior produce changes in the probability of a behavior's occurrence.
   a. Operant conditioning
   b. Classical conditioning
   c. Observational learning
   d. Insight learning

10. Which of the following is NOT one of the predictions of Thorndike's law of effect?
   a. If a behavior is followed by a bad consequence, then it is less likely that it will be repeated.
   b. If an unconditioned stimulus is associated with a neutral stimulus, after a number of associations, the neutral stimulus will become a conditioned stimulus.
   c. If a behavior is followed by a good consequence, then it is less likely that it will be repeated.
   d. If a behavior is followed by a good consequence, then it is more likely that it will be repeated.

11. In his book, *Walden Two*, Skinner presented
   a. the basic principles of classical conditioning.
   b. the role of cognition in operant conditioning.
   c. a utopia created on the principles of operant conditioning.
   d. a utopia created on the principles of observational learning.

12. Sandi is trying to potty train her toddler. She plans to give her five M&Ms when the child first sits at the potty. After the child dominates this behavior, Sandi plans to give her the five M&Ms only when she sits and goes at the potty. What process of learning is Sandi planning to use?
   a. shaping
   b. observational learning
   c. classical conditioning
   d. extinction

13. Which of the following is an example of a primary reinforcer?
   a. sexual pleasure
   b. money
   c. a pat on the back
   d. an award

14. Thomas has a one-year contract, and he gets paid every two weeks. What is Thomas's schedule of reinforcement?
    a.   fixed-ratio
    b.   variable-ratio
    c.   fixed-interval
    d.   variable-interval

15. _____ in operant conditioning occurs when a previously reinforced behavior is no longer reinforced.
    a.   Discrimination
    b.   Generalization
    c.   Punishment
    d.   Extinction

16. Which of the following is an example of a negative punishment?
    a.   removing an undesired chore, such as folding clothes
    b.   giving a desired stimulus, such as candy
    c.   removing a desired object, such as a favorite toy
    d.   giving an undesired task, such as mowing the lawn

17. Which of the following issues is NOT associated with the positive punishment of spanking?
    a.   Spanking by parents is associated with children's antisocial behaviors.
    b.   When spanking, the adult is presenting a model of a person dealing with anger in a controlled manner.
    c.   Children who are spanked are more likely to become bullies in school.
    d.   Children who are spanked tend to be more disobedient than children who are not spanked.

18. Lisa was very shy and would not play with her fellow first-graders. If the teacher praised her only when Lisa was interacting with her classmates, the teacher would be attempting to use
    a.   positive reinforcement.
    b.   shaping.
    c.   negative reinforcement.
    d.   extinction.

19. Which reinforcement schedule helps explain the popularity of gambling?
    a.   fixed-ratio
    b.   variable-ratio
    c.   fixed-interval
    d.   variable-interval

20. Learning is more efficient in operant conditioning if the reward is _____ and not
    _____.
    a. delayed; immediate
    b. negative; positive
    c. immediate; delayed
    d. positive; negative

Practice Test 3

1. Wolfgang Köhler did experiments with apes on the issue of
   a. classical conditioning.
   b. insight learning.
   c. latent learning.
   d. learned helplessness.

2. The frequency of little Johnny's temper tantrums decreased sharply after his
   parents began to ignore the behavior. In the language of operant conditioning,
   Johnny's behavior was undergoing
   a. generalization.
   b. extinction.
   c. discrimination.
   d. All of the answers are correct.

3. If you wanted a group of kids to learn from your example or modeling of
   behavior, you would first have to make sure of which of the following?
   a. that they can imitate the behavior
   b. that they remember what you tell them
   c. that they are paying attention
   d. that they get reinforced

4. How can culture influence learning?
   a. Classical and operant conditioning are not used in some cultures.
   b. Culture can influence the degree to which operant and classical
       conditioning are used.
   c. Culture often determines the content of learning.
   d. Both b and c are correct.

5. Shawna and Wayne are very unhappy with the latest school grades of their
   teenage son. In response, they have taken away their son's driving privileges.
   Which of the following are Shawna and Wayne using?
   a. positive punishment
   b. negative reinforcement
   c. positive reinforcement
   d. negative punishment

6. Which of the following learning methods is the one that makes reference to the person using the behavior as an instrument to obtain the consequence?
    a. classical conditioning
    b. observational learning
    c. latent learning
    d. operant conditioning

7. Which of the following is NOT one of the steps of an operant conditioning behavior modification program?
    a. determining the neutral stimuli that will be used to associate with the unconditioned stimuli
    b. creating an operational definition of the behavior that will be changed and what it will be changed to
    c. measuring the behavior as it is at the beginning and throughout the behavior modification program
    d. determining the reinforcements that will be used to make the program last

8. _____ occurs when the reinforcement offered for behavior A is not as strong as the innate urge to do behavior B, and thus behavior B is performed and behavior A is not performed.
    a. Instinctive drift
    b. Preparedness
    c. Classical conditioning
    d. Insight learning

9. During the early 20th century, an expert in child development would have suggested that
    a. if children behave badly they should not be punished.
    b. positive behaviors will automatically develop in good children and are not learned.
    c. an infant could be shaped into any child the parents wanted.
    d. children should not be allowed to cry themselves out.

10. In observational learning, the learner acquires a behavior by imitating the behavior of a model. Which of the following is NOT one of the characteristics of a model that would promote observational learning?
    a. The model is different from others.
    b. The model is a powerful figure.
    c. The model is intimidating and cold.
    d. The model is nice and warm.

Answer Key

An Appreciative View of Psychology and Your Life
When taking an incremental approach to intelligence, failure is seen as an indication of what you still need to learn, not a lack of ability. Also, when faced with a challenging task, an incremental approach is associated with feeling energized by challenges and perseverance.

Practice Test 1 Answers

1.
   a. No; this is part of the definition of learning.
   b. No; this is part of the definition of learning.
   c. YES; the change in observable behavior is due to experience, not maturation.
   d. No; this is part of the definition of learning.

2.
   a. CORRECT; this is the definition of learning.
   b. No; in fact, changes in behavior owing to fatigue and maturation is not learning.
   c. No; this is not the definition of learning.
   d. No; the behavior change is relatively permanent and is due to experience.

3.
   a. CORRECT; the neutral stimulus becomes the conditioned stimulus since it can elicit the conditioned response.
   b. No; a stimulus never becomes a response.
   c. No; a stimulus never becomes a response.
   d. No; a UCS is never a previously neutral stimulus.

4.
   a. No; extinction in classical conditioning involves the weakening of the association.
   b. No; generalization involves stimuli similar to the original stimulus eliciting the same response.
   c. YES; spontaneous recovery occurs after extinction.
   d. No; discrimination in classical conditioning is the process of learning to respond to certain stimuli and not to others.

5.
   a. GOOD; his fear was generalized from a white rat to other similar objects.
   b. No; the CS is not substituting for the UCS.
   c. No; in discrimination, the response is seen only for specific stimuli.
   d. No

6.
   a. No; this would cause extinction, but the CS is associated with fear.
   b. No; this would have little effect on the fear.
   c. GOOD; the CS is paired with a new response that is pleasant.
   d. No; this describes shaping.

7.   a.   No
     b.   YES, THAT'S CORRECT; this is the definition of shaping.
     c.   No
     d.   No

8.   a.   RIGHT; this occurs when there is response to stimuli that signal reinforcement.
     b.   No; this is not extinction.
     c.   No; there is no responding to a similar stimulus.
     d.   No

9.   a.   YES; she has learned that Dad reinforces her behavior, while Mom does not.
     b.   No; this refers to the biological influences on learning.
     c.   No; this means that the same response is given to similar stimuli.
     d.   No

10. a.   No
     b.   YES; the model does not have to be reinforced for observational learning to occur.
     c.   No; the model does not have to be reinforced for observational learning to occur.
     d.   No; observational learning takes place in people of different ages.

11. a.   No; the bell is never unconditioned, because dogs don't have a reflex associated with the sounding of a bell.
     b.   YES; before conditioning, the bell is neutral, which means that it does not have any particular effect.
     c.   No; the bell will be the conditioned stimulus, but only after conditioning has occurred.
     d.   No; the bell is never a response, only a stimulus.

12. a.   No; the opposite is true.
     b.   No; classical and operant are different types of associative learning and would not fit in this analogy.
     c.   YES; something that is unconditioned is not learned; therefore, it is a reflex, an instinct, or some other process that is innate.
     d.   No; the order does not matter; classical and operant are different types of associative learning and would not fit in this analogy.

13.   a.   No; generalization would occur if the person did not distinguish from being in a pool versus being in a bathtub.
       b.   No; this example does not address the issue of a learned behavior reappearing.
       c.   No; this example does not address the issue of a learned behavior disappearing.
       d.   YES; this is the process of learning to respond to certain stimuli and not to others.

14.   a.   YES; the baby has generalized to fear other stimuli that are similar to the one that caused the original fear.
       b.   No; this example does not address the issue of a learned behavior reappearing.
       c.   No; this example does not address the issue of a learned behavior disappearing.
       d.   No; the opposite is true.

15.   a.   No; this is one of the ways in which classical conditioning contributes to health problems.
       b.   YES, this item corresponds to how operant conditioning can contribute to health problems.
       c.   No; this is one of the ways in which classical conditioning contributes to health problems.
       d.   No; this is one of the ways in which classical conditioning contributes to health problems.

16.   a.   No
       b.   YES; in classical conditioning the learner associates the conditioned stimulus with the unconditioned stimulus; Tolman argued that the association created an expectation; therefore, classical conditioning involves cognition.
       c.   No
       d.   No

Practice Test 2 Answers

1.   a.   No
       b.   CORRECT; consequences that follow behavior affect the probability of it repeating.
       c.   No; observational learning involves modeling the behaviors of others.
       d.   No; two stimuli are paired in classical conditioning.

2.   a.   No; although a reinforcer could be a consequence.
       b.   No; these terms refer to the same thing.
       c.   No; these terms refer to the same thing.
       d.   RIGHT; in operant conditioning the learning involves associating the behavior with its consequence.

3. a. No; this schedule leads to behavior that is less resistant to extinction.
    b. No; when this schedule leads to behavior that is less resistant to extinction.
    c. YES; variable-ratio scheduling results in behavior that is very resistant to extinction.
    d. No; this schedule leads to behavior that is less resistant to extinction.

4. a. No
    b. YES; when the reward *is given is unpredictable.
    c. No.
    d. No

5. a. YES; primary reinforcers are unlearned and secondary reinforcers are learned.
    b. No
    c. No; reinforcers are considered to be positive (or pleasant).
    d. No; both primary and secondary reinforcers can be psychological or physical.

6. a. No; this option refers to classical conditioning.
    b. YES; the law of effect includes this option.
    c. No; while the law of effect does involve behavior, it does not involve schedules.
    d. No; the law of effect does not refer to timing of consequences.

7. a. No; both are types of associative learning.
    b. No; both are types of associative learning.
    c. No; the opposite is true.
    d. YES; observational learning happens through seeing others behave, while associative learning involves associations between stimuli or events.

8. a. YES; conditioning is another way of referring to learning, particularly associative learning.
    b. No; operant refers to acting on the environment and being directly influenced by the environment, while observational refers to a vicarious experience.
    c. No; these are basic concepts to psychology that are different in meaning.
    d. No; these concepts are clearly different.

9. a. YES; this is the definition of operant conditioning.
    b. No; classical conditioning is based on associations between stimuli.
    c. No; observational learning is not a form of associative learning.
    d. No; insight learning is not dependent on consequences of behavior, as it is spontaneous.

10. a.   No; this is one of the predictions of Thorndike's law of effect.
     b.   YES; while this statement is true, it pertains to classical conditioning, and Thorndike's law of effect refers to operant conditioning.
     c.   No; this is one of the predictions of Thorndike's law of effect.
     d.   No; this is one of the predictions of Thorndike's law of effect.

11. a.   No; Skinner did not work on classical conditioning.
     b.   No; Skinner did not study cognition.
     c.   YES; the book is a novel in which the principles of operant conditioning are used to shape and design a utopian society.
     d.   No; Skinner did not work on observational learning.

12. a.   YES; Sandi plans to reward approximations of the desired behavior.
     b.   No; Sandi is not planning on modeling to her toddler how to go to the potty.
     c.   No; potty training is a complex behavior and it would be hard to use classical conditioning; however, you do want the child to associate being in the potty with a positive emotion, not with stress and anger from the parent.
     d.   No; Sandi is trying to foster a new behavior, not eliminate one.

13. a.   YES; we do not need to learn to like sexual pleasure; it is innately a good experience.
     b.   No; money is a secondary reinforcer.
     c.   No; a pat on the back is a secondary reinforcer.
     d.   No; an award is a secondary reinforcer.

14. a.   No; this is a schedule in which the person gets rewarded based on a fixed amount
          of responses.
     b.   No; this is a schedule in which the person gets rewarded based on a variable amount of responses.
     c.   YES; Thomas gets paid every 2 weeks, therefore his reinforcer is given after a fixed amount of time has elapsed (2 weeks).
     d.   No; this a schedule in which the person gets rewarded based on a variable amount of elapsed time.

15. a.   No; discrimination refers to responding to stimuli which signal that a behavior will be reinforced or will not be reinforced.
     b.   No; this means giving the same response to similar stimuli.
     c.   No; the absence of reinforcement does not imply punishment.
     d.   YES; this is the definition of extinction.

16. a. No; this is a negative reinforcement.
    b. No; this is a positive reinforcement.
    c. YES; this is an example of a negative punishment.
    d. No; this is a positive punishment.

17. a. No; this is true.
    b. YES; this is incorrect, as it is more likely than not that the parent is presenting a model of a person dealing with stress in an uncontrolled manner.
    c. No; this is one of the findings of a correlational study.
    d. No; this is one of the findings of a correlational study.

18. a. RIGHT; the teacher was presenting something pleasant (i.e., praise).
    b. No; there is nothing in the question that refers to rewarding approximations.
    c. No; negative reinforcement refers to withdrawing something unpleasant.
    d. No; in extinction, a previously reinforced behavior is no longer reinforced.

19. a. No; this refers to an unchanging number of responses to get reinforced.
    b. YES; the number of responses necessary to obtain reinforcement keeps changing.
    c. No; this refers to reinforcement given after passage of an unchanging amount of time.
    d. No; this refers to reinforcement given after passage of a changing amount of time.

20. a. No; the opposite is true.
    b. No; negative and positive reinforcers can be equally effective.
    c. YES; a reward that immediately follows a behavior is more effective than a reward that is delayed.
    d. No; negative and positive reinforcers can be equally effective.

Practice Test 3 Answers

1. a. No
    b. YES; Köhler used the stick problem and box problem to study insight learning.
    c. No
    d. No

2. a. No; there is no response being made to similar stimuli.
    b. YES; the previously reinforced behavior is no longer reinforced.
    c. No; Johnny is not responding to a stimulus that signals availability of reinforcement.
    d. No

3.   a.   No; important, but not of primary importance.
          b.   No; important, but not of primary importance.
          c.   CORRECT; the first step in observational learning is for the model to pay attention.
          d.   No; important, but not of primary importance.

4.   a.   No; classical and operant conditioning are universal.
          b.   No; but you are half right.
          c.   No; but you are half right.
          d.   YES; both degree and content of learning are influenced by culture.

5.   a.   No; while this is a punishment, it is not a positive punishment.
          b.   No
          c.   No
          d.   YES; Shawna and Wayne have taken away something that their teenage son enjoys (driving privileges).

6.   a.   No; this is learning associations between stimuli.
          b.   No; in this learning, the learner sees somebody else use behavior as an instrument to obtain a consequence.
          c.   No
          d.   YES; operant conditioning is learning by acting on the environment to obtain a desired consequence.

7.   a.   YES; this would be appropriate if the behavior modification program was going
              to use classical conditioning.
          b.   No; this corresponds to step 1 of a behavior modification program.
          c.   No; this corresponds to step 3 of a behavior modification program.
          d.   No; this corresponds to step 5 of a behavior modification program.

8.   a.   YES; instinctive drift is the tendency of animals to revert to instinctive behavior that interferes with learning.
          b.   No; preparedness refers to a biological predisposition to learn in certain ways and not others.
          c.   No
          d.   No

9.   a.   No; the opposite was recommended.
          b.   No; during this period the conditioning approaches were very popular and the general idea was that parents should teach their children to be however they wanted them to be.
          c.   YES; experts in child development proposed that genetics were not that important and that learning and the environment were really the most important determinants of behavior.
          d.   No; the opposite was recommended.

10.   a.   No; this promotes observational learning.
        b.   No; this promotes observational learning.
        c.   YES; this is not a characteristic of a model that would contribute to or facilitate observational learning.
        d.   No; this promotes observational learning.

Chapter 8: Memory

Learning Goals
1. Articulate the three processes of memory: encoding, retention, and retrieval.
2. Understand the different types of memory.
3. Describe how people forget things.
4. Put the psychological research from this chapter to use in your own study habits.
5. Explain why autobiographical memories are important.

After studying Chapter 8, you will be able to:
- Develop your own study strategies based on a scientific understanding of memory;
- Understand how your autobiographical memories have played a role in forming your identity and social bonds with friends and family;
- Describe how to keep your brain in good shape to help lessen the effects of aging on memory.

Chapter Outline
1. The Nature of Memory
- Memory occurs through three processes: _____, _____, and
_____.

2. Memory Encoding
- Encoding is _____.
- To begin the encoding process, we must pay attention to things in the environment.
    - Selective attention involves _____
    _____.
    - _____ attention occurs when a person must attend to several things at once and it is not as good for memory as selective attention.
- Levels of processing is a principle that states that encoding occurs on a continuum from shallow to deep, with _____ producing better memory.
    - Shallow level: _____.
    - Intermediate level: _____.
    - Deepest level: _____.
- _____ is the extensiveness of processing at any given level.
- Mental imagery is one of the best ways to make memories distinctive.
- Allan Paivio's _____ claims that memory for pictures is better than memory for words because _____.

3. Memory Storage
- The Atkinson-Shiffrin theory states that memory storage involves three separate systems:
    - Sensory memory: _____.
    - Short-term memory: _____.
    - Long-term memory: _____.
- _____ is rich and detailed and includes all the sights and sounds you encounter while engaging in daily life.
    - Echoic memory is memory from the _____ and can be retained for several seconds.

- o Iconic memory is memory from the _____ and is retained for only a fraction of a second.
  - ▪ Sperling's classic study on iconic memory found that _____

  _____

  _____.

- Short-term memory lasts longer than sensory memory but also has limited capacity.
  - o George Miller found that people can usually hold _____ (plus or minus _____) items in short term memory.
  - o Chunking is a technique to enhance short-term memory and involves

  _____. For example, you can probably remember 30 or more letters if you group them into about 7 words.
  - o Rehearsal is the _____.
  - o _____, or photographic memory, is a way to retain information through visualization.

- Working memory is another way to think about short-term memory and is a kind of mental "work bench" on which information is manipulated and assembled. Working memory has three components:
  - o Phonological loop: _____.
  - o Visuospatial working memory: _____

  _____. For example,_____.
  - o Central executive: _____

  _____.

- _____ is relatively permanent and almost limitless. It can be divided into explicit and implicit forms (see figure 8.8 in your text).
  - o Explicit memory, or declarative memory, is the _____

  _____.

    - ▪ Permastore content is information that _____

    _____.

    - ▪ Gradual learning of information (as is done in most college courses) over the course of several sessions (or class periods) is best.
    - ▪ Episodic memory is the _____

    _____.

    - ▪ _____ memory is a person's knowledge about the world including expertise, general knowledge learned in school, and everyday knowledge such as famous people or places.
  - o _____ memory, or _____ memory, is memory that affects behavior by previous experience but is done so without conscious awareness.
    - ▪ Procedural memory involves memory for skills. For example,

    _____.

    - ▪ _____ is the automatic leaning of associations between stimuli and is another type of implicit memory.
    - ▪ Priming is the _____

    _____.

- _____ is when priming unconsciously affects behavior as demonstrated in your text by the example of students behaving rudely when they were exposed to words like *rude* and *aggressive.*
- Semantic networks are _____
_____. See figure 8.12 in your text for a visualization of how semantic networks are organized. The more connections each memory has, the more likely it is it can be recalled in the future.
- Schemas are _____
_____.
   - A script is a schema for a specific event. For example, _____
_____
_____.
- Connectionism, or parallel distributed processing (PDP), is the theory that _____
_____.
- Long-term potentiation is a concept that explains how memory functions at the _____ level and is similar to connectionism.
   - If two neurons are activated at the same time, the connection between them and therefore the memory, may be _____.
- There is no one memory center in the brain. Rather, specific brain structures are involved in particular aspects of memory.
   - The amygdala plays a role in _____.
   - The _____ is/are associated with explicit memory.
   - The cerebellum is involved in _____ memory.

4. Memory Retrieval
- The _____ is the tendency to recall certain items in a list more than others.
   - Primacy effect refers to _____
_____.
   - Recency effect refers to better recall for items at the _____
_____ and occurs because, when it comes time for recall, these items may still be in _____ memory.
- Retrieval is also affected by:
   - The nature of the cues that prompt your memory.
   - The retrieval task you set for yourself. For example, deciding whether or not something is familiar is called _____ and is typically easier than _____, which involves remembering specific details.
- Encoding specificity principle states that _____
_____.
- _____ means you are more likely to successfully recall information in the context in which you learned it. For example, it would be more difficult to take an exam in a room other than your regular classroom, because the classroom itself can serve as a cue for retrieval.

- State-dependent memory is similar to context-dependent memory but refers to _____. For example, when in a good mood, you are more likely to remember _____ events.
- Autobiographical memory, a special form of episodic memory, is a _____ _____. There are three levels of autobiographical memory that vary in specificity. Below are examples of each level.
    o Life time periods: _____.
    o General events: _____.
    o Event specific knowledge: _____.
- Dan McAdams has argued that autobiographical memories are more about _____ and less about _____.
- _____ are memories of emotionally significant events that people often recall with more accuracy and vivid imagery than everyday events.
    o The vast majority of these memories are personal, though the most famous examples are national events like September 11th, 2001.
    o People are often very confident about the details contained in flashbulb memories, but research has found that _____ _____.
- The existence of repressed memories is somewhat controversial. Repression is a defense mechanism by which _____ _____. Repression does not erase a memory but it does make conscious remembering difficult.
    o If repressed memories do exist, they are probably examples of _____ _____, which occurs when an individual forgets something because it is so painful that remembering is intolerable.
- Research on memory is especially important when it comes to eyewitness testimony. Such research focuses on the distortion, bias, and inaccuracy of memory.
    o Distortion: _____.
    o Bias is a factor because, for example, studies have shown that _____ _____ _____.
    o Inaccuracy can occur when _____ _____. For example, _____ _____.
    o To correct for distortion, bias, and inaccuracy, police encourage eyewitnesses to write down what they saw immediately after witnessing the event.

5. Forgetting
- Ebbinghaus was the first person to research forgetting when he _____ _____. He concluded that most forgetting occurs _____.
- More recent research has disputed Ebbinghaus' claim somewhat because when we memorize _____, forgetting is neither so rapid nor so extensive.
- Encoding failure is when _____ _____.

- Retrieval failure includes problems with _____,
_____, _____, and
_____.
- _____ states that people forget not because memories are actually lost from storage, but because other information gets in the way.
  - Proactive interferences in when _____
  _____
  _____.
  - Retroactive interference is when _____
  _____
  _____.
- Decay theory states that when something new is learned, a _____
_____is formed but over time the trace disintegrates. Therefore, the passage of time will always increase forgetting.
  - Transience refers to forgetting that occurs with the passage of time.
- _____ is a type of effortful retrieval that occurs when people know they know something but can't quite pull it out of memory.
- Retrospective memory is _____.
- Prospective memory is remembering _____ and contains information about _____ and _____.
  - Time-based prospective memory is _____
  _____.
  - _____ is a memory that tells you to engage in a specific behavior when it is elicited by an external event (ex., give a message to your roommate when he or she gets home).
- Amnesia is the _____.
  - _____ is a memory disorder that affects the retention of new information and events.
  - Retrograde amnesia involves memory loss for_____
  _____.
  - Retrograde amnesia is much more common than anterograde and is caused by
  _____.

6. Study Tips from the Science of Memory
- Much of what you learned in Chapter 8 about memory can be applied to your very own study habits. Here are some study tips based on the psychological research presented in this chapter:
  - Make sure the information you are studying is accurate.
  - Organize the material in a sensible way, perhaps hierarchically.
  - To enhance your ability to encode information, pay attention during class and while studying.
  - Elaborate on the information you've learned and use imagery.
  - Create associations between topics.
  - Rehearsal of information after class will help it to solidify in memory. Rehearsal can be quietly going over your notes yourself but can also be talking with friends about what you learned in class today.

- o Don't just look at your notes and say "Yeah, I know this." *Recognition* of information is easier than *recall* of information and on your test you will have to recall the information. Cover up the definitions of concepts, write what you think they mean, and then check your answers.
- o Your brain functions better when you are well rested and well nourished.
- o Use retrieval cues during the test. The test question provides your first cue, but if that's not enough, try to think of related material or even look ahead to other questions which likely contain other cues that might trigger the information you are looking for.

7. Memory and Health and Wellness
- In autobiographical memories, we store the lessons we've learned from life. Such memories also provide us with a source of _____.
  - o Autobiographical memories can also be sources of social bonding because

  _____

  _____.

- When it comes to memory, the saying "use it or lose it" is true. Individuals who lead active intellectual lives seem to be protected against the mental decline typically associated with age.

Intersection
- The sense of _____ is most closely associated with memory.

Critical Controversy
- Elizabeth Loftus is a famous memory researcher who conducted an experiment on false memories. Loftus was able to convince people that they saw Bugs Bunny at Disney Land (which is impossible). Her results have implications for _____

  _____

  _____.

Clarifying Tricky Points
Where are memories stored?
In chapter 8 you learned that various parts of the brain play an important role in certain types of memory. For example, the amygdala is associated with emotional memories, the hippocampus is associated with explicit memory, and the cerebellum is associated with implicit memory (see figure 8.14 in your text for more information about the areas of the brain associated with long-term memory). But are there parts of the brain you can point to and say "this is where all my childhood memories are, this is where all the information I learned in high school is, etc.?" The answer to that question is a resounding "No." The way the brain stores memories is very complex. One memory alone can involve around 1,000 neurons spread out over large areas of the cerebral cortex. Also, as you learned in chapter 3, if one part of the brain begins to deteriorate, another part can take over. So, while generally speaking the right frontal lobe is associated with memory retrieval, as we age, the left fontal lobe steps in to help out in memory retrieval. It would be fun to point to a specific part of your brain and say, "This is where I remember everything about Grandma," but the brain is just too complex and integrated for such pinpoint accuracy.

Elaboration is the key to encoding successfully

According to chapter 8, the human memory is nearly limitless. So it should be easy to ace every exam in school as long as you read the material. Right? The answer of course is no. It is not easy to ace every exam because, unfortunately, our ability to recall information depends in large part on how well the information was initially encoded. To recall a memory, there must be a cue and any given memory can be associated with multiple cues. For example, the guy that sits in front of you in class is Will. Class is one cue associated with Will's name. But say when you were first introduced to Will he mentioned that he works at the local coffee shop, which is where you study with Maria because Maria's friend Sarah gives you both free muffins when she's working. Now, providing you processed all this information deeply (see "Levels of Processing" in your text), "Will" is associated with many cues: coffee, studying, Maria, free food, and Sarah. This is an example of elaboration and, the more elaborate your memories are, the more cues there are available, and the more likely you are to remember things (for example, Will's name when you see him at a party). Elaboration is also useful because it leads to more distinctive memory codes which can be recalled more easily. For example, there are probably far fewer people in your memory associated with the memory code "free food" than are associated with the rather generic memory code of "class." See figure 8.3 in your text for more examples of elaborate encoding.

Repressed memories: Fact or fiction?

If you've ever spent time watching a soap opera, odds are you've probably seen an important memory repressed and then recalled at a pivotal moment creating a plot twist that keeps you watching for weeks to come. But can memories really be repressed, or are they simply a tool for script writers? This question is actually highly controversial and the answer has major implications (see the Critical Controversy in your text for a discussion on how repressed memories have been used as key evidence in courts of law). Repression is the act of forgetting, and then forgetting forgetting and is typically associated with very traumatic memories such as abuse. The general consensus in psychological research is that memories of true events can be repressed for long periods of time and then resurface, but exactly how this happens is not fully understood yet. It is also possible, however, to unknowingly create false memories that appear to be repressed memories of actual events but are, in fact, false. So the answer to the above question of "Fact or fiction?" is: it depends on the memory. Some repressed memories are probably true, others however are probably false. Telling the difference is a provocative area of research in psychology.

The accuracy of eyewitness accounts

If you witness a crime (or anything else for that matter), you have unique knowledge about that event that is not shared by the thousands or even millions of people that will eventually hear about the crime on the news. That unique knowledge you possess should be the most accurate information available because, after all, you were there. However, memory is imperfect and eyewitness accounts are surprisingly inconsistent and flawed, because they are plagued by distortion, bias, and inaccuracy. Memory, even of important events, fades over time creating distortion. Bias in memory can occur because people tend to have better memory for faces of people in their own ethnic group. Your memory can also be affected by the memory of others. If you talk to another person about a shared event, there may be subtle discrepancies between the two memories of the same event, and your memory may be altered to reflect that of the other person. Eyewitness testimony is particularly tricky in a court of law because eyewitnesses are often very confident of what they saw. Although, as a psychologically savvy consumer of information, you now know that, regardless of confidence, eyewitness accounts are plagued by inaccuracy and typically need to be corroborated with other evidence.

An Appreciative View of Psychology and Your Life
In chapter 8, you learned that memory is more than just random bits of information stored all over the brain. Some types of memories provide us with facts like who sailed across the ocean to discover America or the name of your high school biology teacher, but other memories, such as autobiographical memories, are special memories that contain a person's recollections of his or her life experiences. Autobiographical memories provide us with a sense of meaning and identity. Take a few minutes to write down one of your own autobiographical memories. Then compare your memory to the research by Dan McAdams, Laura King, and others described in chapter 8.

Now, to help you further understand the aspects of memory described in chapter 8, think about how this memory was encoded, stored, and, just now, retrieved.
1. Did it contain elaboration and imagery? Using the definitions of these different forms of encoding, describe how your memory was encoded.
2. Did the encoding you used for the memory affect your ability to recall it just now?
3. Unless this important autobiographical memory happened 30 seconds ago, it was probably recalled from long-term memory, but was it an implicit or explicit memory?
4. Describe one way you can make sure you don't forget this and other memories as you get older.

Practice Test 1
1. Which of the following is the correct definition of memory?
   a. the retention of information over time
   b. the retention of time through conditioning
   c. the conditioning of thoughts via observation
   d. the neural processing of subconscious material

2. The encoding of memory refers to how information is
   a. retained.
   b. retrieved.
   c. placed into memory.
   d. All of the answers are correct.

3. Thinking of examples of a concept is a good way to understand the concept. This approach is referred to as
   a. deep processing.
   b. storage.
   c. imagery.
   d. elaboration.

4.   Early semantic network theories of memory were primarily criticized for

   a.   underestimating the complexity of human memory.
   b.   being too abstract.
   c.   including too many hierarchical levels.
   d.   focusing exclusively on semantic memory.

5.   Which of the following theories is most consistent with reconstructive memory?

   a.   network theories
   b.   schema theories
   c.   script theories
   d.   None of the answers are correct.

6.   A schema for an event, such as the checkout procedure at your local supermarket, is referred to as

   a.   implicit memory.
   b.   nondeclarative memory.
   c.   working memory.
   d.   script.

7.   _____ is a type of nondeclarative memory that involves information that is already in memory aiding in the retrieval of new information.

   a.   Priming
   b.   Procedural memory
   c.   Prospective memory
   d.   Semantic memory

8.   Remembering that you have a doctor's appointment later today required the activity of

   a.   semantic memory.
   b.   implicit memory.
   c.   retrospective memory.
   d.   prospective memory.

9.   Being able to recite the last 5 US presidents involves

   a.   priming.
   b.   explicit memory.
   c.   nondeclarative memory.
   d.   procedural memory.

10.   The component of working memory that is involved in the storage of the sounds of language is the

   a.   central executive.
   b.   visuospatial working memory.
   c.   phonological loop.
   d.   sensory memory.

11.   Chunking is used to improve which memory time frame?
    a.   sensory memory
    b.   short-term memory
    c.   working memory
    d.   long-term memory

12.   Which of the following factors does not affect encoding?
    a.   priming
    b.   selective attention
    c.   level of processing
    d.   divided attention

13.   A person who repeats 20 times the definition of psychology, until the exact words in the definition are memorized, is engaging in elaboration at the
    a.   shallow processing level.
    b.   intermediate processing level.
    c.   definition processing level.
    d.   deepest processing level

14.   Which of the following statements is NOT true about elaboration?
    a.   Elaboration makes memory codes more unique or distinctive.
    b.   Elaboration is associated with brain activity in the occipital lobe.
    c.   Greater elaboration is linked with neural activity.
    d.   The more information is stored, the more distinguishable is the code; thus, the information is easier to retrieve.

15.   Based on the dual-code hypothesis, which of the following would produce a better memory?
    a.   a drawn map of directions from school to your new job
    b.   a verbal description of the route from school to your new job
    c.   the definition of psychology
    d.   the rhythm of salsa music

16.   The following are examples that involve implicit memory, EXCEPT
    a.   making an egg omelet.
    b.   feeling good after smelling the perfume used by someone you love.
    c.   giving someone your phone number.
    d.   playing your favorite sport.

17.   First impressions tend to be very important. It seems that we more clearly remember details we learn about a person during that first encounter. This tendency is explained by the
   a.   encoding specificity principle.
   b.   recency effect.
   c.   recognition memory task.
   d.   primacy effect.

18.   When you meet an acquaintance in a school hall and can't remember his name, but you remember that he is a friend of your roommate, you are experiencing the
   a.   recency effect.
   b.   primacy effect.
   c.   tip-of-the-tongue phenomenon.
   d.   dual-code effect.

19.   Which of the following is an example of an encoding failure?
   a.   failing to recall your old cell phone number
   b.   failing to recognize that B. F. Skinner is associated with operant conditioning, because you were not paying attention the day that was covered in class
   c.   recalling the old cell phone number but failing to recall the new number
   d.   failing the recall the details of a traumatic car accident

Practice Test 2

1.   Storage is the memory process primarily concerned with
   a.   getting information into memory.
   b.   retaining information over time.
   c.   taking information out of storage.
   d.   registering information with our senses.

2.   A teacher who wants to help students with long-term retention should present information in which manner?
   a.   organized randomly
   b.   without any specific order
   c.   organized alphabetically
   d.   organized logically or hierarchically

3.   The capacity of working memory can be expanded by grouping information into higher-order units. This technique is called
   a.   rehearsal.
   b.   eidetic imagery.
   c.   chunking.
   d.   the phonological loop.

4. Which memory system can retain information in its original form for only an instant?
    a. sensory memory
    b. working memory
    c. long-term memory
    d. short-term memory

5. According to the Atkinson-Shiffrin theory of memory, the best way to move information into long-term memory is to
    a. rehearse the information and keep it in short-term memory as long as possible.
    b. move the information directly from sensory memory into long-term memory.
    c. rehearse the information in sensory memory as long as possible.
    d. move complex information directly to long-term memory.

6. Which of the following statements about sensory memory is incorrect?
    a. Information does not stay in sensory memory for very long.
    b. Sensory memory processes more information than we may realize.
    c. Sensory memory retains information from our senses.
    d. Information in sensory memory is resistant to decay.

7. Visual images that are stored in the sensory registers are called _____ memory.
    a. iconic
    b. echoic
    c. semantic
    d. nondeclarative

8. Auditory information that is stored in the sensory memory is referred to as
    a. iconic memory.
    b. echoic memory.
    c. nondeclarative memory.
    d. memory span.

9. You are reading a book, and your friend Rachel asks you a question.
    By the time you say, "Sorry, what did you say?" you "hear" her question in your head. This is due to
    a. echoic memory.
    b. long-term sensory memory.
    c. working memory.
    d. iconic memory.

10. Which of the following can store information for up to 30 seconds?
    a. sensory memory
    b. working memory
    c. long-term memory
    d. iconic memory

11.   The storage capacity of working memory is _____ units of information.
        a.   12
        b. 7 ± 2
        c. 2.8×10^{20}
        d.   .45

12.   Declarative memory is subdivided into
        a.   procedural and virtual memory.
        b.   episodic and semantic memory.
        c.   echoic and iconic memory.
        d.   automatic and deliberate memory.

13.   Experiments with sea slugs led to the speculation that memories are related to activity of
        a.   the hippocampus.
        b.   the amygdala.
        c.   brain chemicals.
        d.   the cell nucleus.

14.   The idea that memories are stored throughout the brain in connections between neurons is referred to as the
        a.   serial position effect.
        b.   interference theory.
        c.   parallel distributed processing theory.
        d.   dual-code hypothesis.

15.   Which of the following theories is the one that considers the biological basis of memory?
        a.   schema theory
        b.   hierarchies theories
        c.   connectionism
        d.   semantic networks theories

16.   Which of the following brain structures is involved in procedural memory?
        a.   hippocampus
        b.   amygdala
        c.   cerebellum
        d.   limbic system

17.   Which of the following is the way of improving short-term memory that involves the conscious repetition of information?
        a.   chunking
        b.   recall
        c.   recognition
        d.   rehearsal

18. People who claim they can memorize whole pages of text by just looking briefly at the pages are said to have
    a. episodic memory.
    b. implicit memory.
    c. echoic memory.
    d. eidetic memory.

19. Activity in the hippocampus may occur when experiencing the following memories, EXCEPT
    a. remembering how to swing a golf club.
    b. remembering the date of your birthday.
    c. remembering your address.
    d. remembering where you left the keys.

Practice Test 3

1. The typical serial position effect pattern shows which of the following?
   a. stronger recency effect than primacy effect
   b. stronger primacy than recency effect
   c. equal strength for primacy and recency effect
   d. weaker recency effect than primacy effect

2. Essay questions measure which type of memory?
   a. recognition
   b. recall
   c. serial position
   d. None of the answers are correct.

3. An essay examination is to recall as a multiple-choice test is to
   a. recognition.
   b. reconstruction.
   c. reorganization.
   d. restructuring.

4. According to _____, associations formed at the time of encoding tend to be effective retrieval cues.
   a. recall
   b. the serial position effect
   c. anterograde encoding
   d. the encoding specificity principle

5.   Adam took a Spanish course during his first semester at college; during his second semester, he took a French course. Retroactive interference would suggest that Adam
   a.   should now consider taking German.
   b.   is going to have a difficult time learning French.
   c.   is not going to remember his Spanish very well.
   d.   is going to have a difficult time with both Spanish and French.

6.   Which theory suggests that forgetting is caused by a fading memory trace?
   a.   reconstruction theory
   b.   repression
   c.   decay
   d.   interference theory

7.   In retrograde amnesia, there is memory loss
   a.   only for new information.
   b.   only for segments of new information.
   c.   for the complete past.
   d.   only for a segment of the past.

8.   Which of the following is not an effective study strategy?
   a.   rehearsing and memorizing information by repetition
   b.   paying attention and minimizing distraction
   c.   organizing what you put into memory
   d.   using mnemonic strategies

9.   There are three levels of autobiographical memories. Which of the following would be the one involved in your memory of what you did last summer?
   a.   life time periods
   b.   general events
   c.   event-specific knowledge
   d.   flashbulb memories

10.   When an eyewitness to a crime is asked to pick the suspect from a lineup, he or she will engage in which of the following memory tasks?
   a.   recall
   b.   encoding
   c.   storage
   d.   recognition

11. Which of the following theories of memory storage would argue that people will notice and thus remember better things that are consistent with the information they already have stored in memory?
    a. hierarchies
    b. semantic networks
    c. schemas
    d. connectionist networks

12. These are all good studying strategies, EXCEPT
    a. creating your own study guide.
    b. eating a snack before studying.
    c. studying at least five straight hours the day before the test.
    d. studying five hours across two weeks, dedicating approximately 20 minutes a day.

Answer Key

An Appreciative View of Psychology and Your Life

1. Elaboration is the extensiveness of encoding. If your memory contained a lot of details and connections to other things, it was likely quite elaborate. Imagery is a visual representation in your mind of the event. If you could really see yourself back there, then the memory was likely encoded with imagery.

2. If your memory was elaborate and contained imagery, it was probably easier to recall.

3. Since the memory was in your conscious awareness and probably contained people, places, and events, it was stored in explicit memory, specifically episodic memory.

4. Maintaining an active intellectual life in which you continually engage in new and challenging tasks is the key to maintaining memory.

Practice Test 1 Answers

1. a. RIGHT
    b. No; this is not the correct definition of memory.
    c. No; this is incorrect.
    d. No; memory is not defined in this way.

2. a. No; how information is retained refers to storage.
    b. No; this sounds like retrieval.
    c. YES; encoding refers to how information gets into memory.
    d. No

3. a. No; although at deep processing the stimulus' meaning is processed.
    b. No; storage refers to retaining information over time.
    c. No; imagery is the use of mental images and may or may not involve examples.
    d. RIGHT; thinking of examples increases the extensiveness of processing information.

4. a. THAT'S RIGHT; hierarchical networks are too simple.
    b. No; if anything, network theories are too concrete.
    c. No; that is not a primary criticism.
    d. No; this is not a primary criticism.

5. a. No; network theories are not consistent with reconstructive memory.
    b. YES; schema are used when we reconstruct information.
    c. No; there are script theories, but a script is a schema for an event.
    d. No

6. a. No; you could explain verbally the procedure to check out at a supermarket.
    b. No; same as item a.
    c. No; working memory is a temporary memory site.
    d. YES; a script is the framework of expectations we have about events; you know what to expect at the checkout in a supermarket.

7. a. YES; priming occurs when information in memory is activated to help in the retrieval of new information.
    b. No; while this is also an implicit memory, it refers to memory for skills.
    c. No; this refers to remembering information about doing something in the future.
    d. No; this refers to the conceptual knowledge we have about the world.

8. a. No; this refers to remembering concepts and their meaning.
    b. No; nondeclarative memory is not involved here.
    c. No; this refers to remembering the past.
    d. YES; prospective memory involves remembering things that have to do with expected future activities.

9. a. No; reciting is a conscious verbal behavior and requires declarative memory.
    b. YES; explicit or declarative memory would be involved in the recitation.
    c. No; reciting is a conscious verbal behavior and requires explicit memory.
    d. No; reciting the last 5 presidents requires the recollection of the words in the appropriate order, and not any particular procedure or set of actions.

10. a. No; this component integrates the information stored in the phonological loop and the visuospatial working memory.
    b. No; this component stores images.
    c. YES; this component involves an acoustic code and rehearsal.
    d. No; this is not one of the components of working memory.

11.   a.   No; sensory memory lasts from only fractions of a second to a few seconds.
       b.   YES; chunking can improve short-term memory by packing down extensive information into chucks that fit the 7 ± 2 items limit of this time frame.
       c.   No; this concept was not applied in the theories of working memory.
       d.   No; long-term memory does not require chunking for improvement.

12.   a.   YES; priming does not take place until after the information has been encoded and stored.
       b.   No; selective attention, which involves focusing on some stimuli and not others, does affect encoding, since we will encode what we attend to.
       c.   No; the level at which we process the information does have an effect on encoding.
       d.   No; divided attention also affects encoding; this happens when we have to pay attention to various things at the same time.

13.   a.   No; shallow processing would involve merely reading over the words without even tying then together as a definition.
       b.   YES; elaboration can occur at any level of processing; in this case, elaboration is taking place at the intermediate level, in which the person is focusing on the look and sound of the words in the definition and recalling how the words go together in the sentence.
       c.   No; this is not one of the levels of processing.
       d.   No; the elaboration presented in the question is not characteristic of the deepest level of processing.

14.   a.   No; this is correct.
       b.   YES; this is incorrect, elaboration is associated with neural activity in the brain's left frontal lobe; as we learned in Chapter 3. The occipital lobe is mainly associated with the processing of visual information.
       c.   No; studies with MRI have demonstrated this relationship.
       d.   No; this is correct about elaboration.

15.   a.   YES; images, such as maps, are stored as both an image and a verbal code, thus they produce a better memory.
       b.   No; a verbal description would be stored only in a verbal code.
       c.   No; a definition is no different from a verbal description.
       d.   No; the dual-code hypothesis does not address the memorizing of auditory stimuli.

16. a. No; the procedure of making an omelet would involve nondeclarative memory.
     b. No; the good feeling resulting from perceiving the familiar perfume is also implicit since the association is likely to have been established through classical conditioning.
     c. YES; this involves declarative or explicit memory.
     d. No; playing sports you have experience with involves procedural memory, a type of implicit memory.

17. a. No; the encoding specificity principle states that information present at the time of encoding tends to be effective as a retrieval cue.
     b. No; this is the tendency for the latest information we have experienced to be remembered better.
     c. No; this memory task is a process not an effect.
     d. YES; the primacy effect states that information learned at the beginning of a series of information will be remembered better; the same principle that applies to remembering early items in a list applies to remembering better information from early in a relationship, such as the first impression.

18. a. No; this is the tendency for information learned later in a list to be remembered better.
     b. No; this is the tendency for information learned earlier in a list to be remembered better.
     c. YES; you remember some aspects of the stimuli but not others.
     d. No; actually, it is called the dual-code hypothesis, and it refers to the tendency for images to be remembered easier than conceptual information.

19. a. No; this is an example of retroactive interference, which is a retrieval failure.
     b. YES; this example demonstrates an encoding failure because the information was never stored in memory.
     c. No; this is an example of proactive interference, which is a retrieval failure.
     d. No; this is motivated forgetting, which is a retrieval failure.

Practice Test 2 Answers

1. a. No; this option defines encoding.
    b. YES; storage consists of retention of information over time.
    c. No; this describes retrieval.
    d. No; this option best relates to encoding.

2. a. No; this would also reduce long-term retention since it lacks organization.
    b. No; in fact, this would decrease long-term retention.
    c. No; but only if there is a more logical organization.
    d. YES; when information is presented in a logically organized way, memory is helped.

3. a. No; rehearsal is the conscious repetition of information.
    b. No; this is a type of photographic memory.
    c. CORRECT; chunking packs information into higher-order units.
    d. No; the phonological loop is a subsystem of working memory.

4. a. THAT'S RIGHT; sensory memory holds information for only a short time.
    b. No
    c. No
    d. No

5. a. YES; this is correct, according to the Atkinson-Shiffrin theory.
    b. No; the model includes short-term memory located between sensory and long-term.
    c. No; information lasts for only a short time in sensory memory.
    d. No; complex memory must first go through sensory and short-term memory.

6. a. No; this statement is correct.
    b. No; this statement is correct.
    c. No; this statement is correct.
    d. YES; information in sensory memory decays very rapidly.

7. a. CORRECT; iconic memory refers to visual images.
    b. No; echoic memory refers to auditory stimuli.
    c. No; semantic memory is memory of the meanings of words.
    d. No; nondeclarative memory refers to implicit memory.

8. a. No; iconic memory refers to visual images.
    b. YES; the word echoic includes the word echo.
    c. No; this term refers to memory that cannot be verbalized or consciously recalled.
    d. No; memory span describes the storage capacity of working or short-term memory.

9. a. YES; this demonstrates echoic memory or auditory information in sensory memory.
    b. No; this is not long-term sensory memory.
    c. No; working memory would not cause this experience.
    d. No; iconic memory refers to visual images, not auditory information.

10. a. No; in fact, information in sensory memory lasts for a very short time.
    b. YES; working memory (short-term) stores information for up to 30 seconds.
    c. No; information in long-term memory can be stored for a lifetime.
    d. No; iconic memory is visual information in sensory memory.

11. a. No; but that is close.
    b. THAT'S CORRECT.
    c. No; this is the estimated storage capacity of long-term memory.
    d. No

12.   a.   No
      b.   RIGHT
      c.   No; these refer to the types of information found in sensory memory.
      d.   No

13.   a.   No; the hippocampus is involved in human memory.
      b.   No; the amygdala is involved in human memory.
      c.   CORRECT; in particular, serotonin may play a role in memory.
      d.   No

14.   a.   No; this refers to the tendency to remember items at the beginning and the end of lists better.
      b.   No; this refers to proactive and retroactive interference.
      c.   YES, this theory also says that several neurons may work together to process or produce a single memory.
      d.   No; this refers to the better recall of images over words.

15.   a.   No; schema theory looks at the cognitive basis and reconstructive nature of memory.
      b.   No; hierarchies' theories argue that information is highly organized in memory.
      c.   YES; connectionism, connectionist networks, or parallel distributed processing theories consider the role of neurons and parts of the brain in memory.
      d.   No; these are also cognitive approaches to memory.

16.   a.   No; this part is involved in explicit memory.
      b.   No; this part is involved in emotions such as fear and anger.
      c.   YES; the cerebellum is involved in the implicit memory required to perform skills.
      d.   No; the limbic system is involved in explicit memory.

17.   a.   No; while chunking does improve short-term memory, it involves the grouping of information to fit the 5–9 items limit.
      b.   No; this is a memory task, not a way of improving short-term memory.
      c.   No; this is a memory task, not a way of improving short-term memory.
      d.   YES; rehearsal is basically repeating the information to keep it in short-term memory.

18.   a.   No; episodic memory refers to memory of events.
      b.   No; implicit memory cannot be described verbally.
      c.   No; echoic memory involves the memories of auditory stimuli.
      d.   YES; eidetic memory is also known as photographic memory; this phenomenon is very rare and some psychologists doubt it even exists.

19.   a.   YES; this is an example of implicit memory, which is associated with   activity in the cerebellum.
       b.   No; this is an example of explicit memory, which involves the hippocampus.
       c.   No; this is an example of declarative memory, which involves the hippocampus.
       d.   No; this is an example of explicit memory, which involves the hippocampus.

Practice Test 3 Answers

1.   a.   YES; this describes the typical serial position effect pattern.
     b.   No; this does not describes the typical serial position effect.
     c.   No; the typical pattern is stronger recency effect than primacy effect.
     d.   No; this is just the opposite of the typical serial position effect.

2.   a.   No; multiple-choice questions involve recognition.
     b.   CORRECT; in recall, the study must retrieve learned information.
     c.   No; serial position refers to the pattern of information remembered.
     d.   No

3.   a.   YES; multiple-choice tests require the learner to recognize learned items.
     b.   No; recognition is the type of retrieval used in multiple-choice tests.
     c.   No; reorganization is not involved in multiple-choice tests.
     d.   No; this is not correct.

4.   a.   No; recall is a type of retrieval in which information must be retrieved from previously learned information.
     b.   No; this describes how retrieval is affected by the position of information in a list.
     c.   No; anterograde refers to a type of amnesia and is not a form of encoding.
     d.   CORRECT; this describes the encoding specificity principle.

5.   a.   No; the question makes no reference to taking German.
     b.   No; this would describe proactive interference of old information disrupting new.
     c.   YES; retroactive interference occurs when new information disrupts old.
     d.   No; retroactive interference would predict problems remembering Spanish.

6.   a.   No; reconstruction describes how we remember information.
     b.   No; repression blocks memories from the conscious.
     c.   YES; decay theory says that the neurochemical memory trace disintegrates.
     d.   No; interference theory says memories are forgotten because of other information.

7.   a.   No; this more accurately describes anterograde amnesia.
     b.   No; this more accurately describes anterograde amnesia.
     c.   No; only segments of the past are forgotten in retrograde amnesia.
     d.   THAT'S RIGHT; this is the definition of retrograde amnesia.

8.   a.   YES; instead, you should try to understand the material.
     b.   No; this is an effective strategy.
     c.   No; this is an effective strategy.
     d.   No; this is an effective strategy.

9.   a.   No; this is the most abstract and general level and it refers to general periods of your life, such as childhood.
     b.   YES; what you did last summer would classify under this level of autobiographical memories.
     c.   No; this level is much more specific; remembering how crowded it was at that lawn concert you went to, for example, would classify at this level.
     d.   No; this is not one of the levels of autobiographical memories.

10.   a.   No; recall would be involved if the eyewitness is asked to describe the offender to a sketch artist.
     b.   No; at the time of picking out the suspect from a lineup, the encoding of the suspect's information will have occurred previously.
     c.   No; at the time of picking out the suspect from a lineup, the storage of the suspect's information will have occurred previously.
     d.   YES; the eyewitness will have to recognize the suspect from various options, much like in a multiple-choice test.

11.   a.   No; the hierarchies approach assumes that all information may be attended to and added to the hierarchy at the appropriate spot.
     b.   No; semantic networks theories propose that information is organized based on their meaning, but it does not suggest that if something is not consistent with the nodes already in memory that it will not be encoded.
     c.   YES; according to this approach, schemas are frameworks that influence how we encode, make inferences, and retrieve information; previous schemas may influence what we pay attention to and thus what gets stored in memory.
     d.   No; the connectionist networks approach considers the biological basis of memory.

12.   a.   No; this is a good strategy, discussed in the textbook as "as yourself questions."
     b.   No; this is a good strategy, discussed in the textbook under "storage strategies."
     c.   YES; while this is fairly common, cramming before a test tends to produce short-term memory that is processed in a shallow rather than a deep manner.
     d.   No; this is a good strategy; while 20 minutes might seem brief, spreading out the study sessions contributes to the consolidation of the memories, making them better for future retrieval.

Chapter 9: Thinking, Intelligence, and Language

Learning Goals
1. Describe cognitive psychology and discuss the role of the computer in the development of the field.
2. Explain the processes involved in thinking and describe capacities related to superior thinking.
3. Describe intelligence and its measurement and discuss influences on and types of intelligence.
4. Identify the possible connections between language and thought, and summarize how language is acquired and develops.
5. Discuss the importance of cognitive appraisal with respect to stress and describe various types of coping.

After studying chapter 9, you will be able to:
- Think critically and creatively and be able to overcome functional fixation;
- Understand how intelligence tests are biased towards people of a certain race, ethnicity, or economic status;
- Describe multiple strategies that can help you cope with stressful life events.

Chapter Outline
1. The Cognitive Revolution in Psychology
- Cognitive psychologists often compare the brain and cognition to a computer because

  _____

  _____

  _____.

- Artificial intelligence is _____

  _____.

- The cognitive revolution began in _____ and reached its peak in

  _____.

- Cognitive psychology describes approaches to psychology that _____

  _____.

- Cognition is _____

  _____.

2. Thinking
- Thinking involves _____.
- Concepts are _____

  _____ and occur for four reasons.
    - _____
    - _____
    - _____
    - _____
- In the classical model to explain the structure of concepts _____

  _____.

    - One weakness of this model is _____

      _____.

- The prototype model _____
  _____.

- Problem solving is an attempt to _____
  _____. The steps are:
  1. _____
     - Example: _____
       _____.

  2. _____
     - Example: _____
       _____.

     - Subgoaling involves _____
       _____.

     - Algorithms are strategies that guarantee a solution to a problem.
     - Heuristics are _____
       _____.

  3. _____
     - Example: _____
       _____.

  4. _____
     - Example: _____
       _____.

- Fixation involves _____.
  o Functional fixedness occurs when_____
    _____.
    - Example: _____.

- Reasoning is _____.
  o Inductive reasoning is _____
    _____.
  o Deductive reasoning is _____
    _____.

- Decision making involves _____.
- Confirmation bias is the tendency to _____
  _____.

- Hindsight bias is to _____
  _____.

- Availability heuristic _____.
  o Example: _____
    _____.

- Critical thinking involves grasping the deeper meaning of ideas, keeping an open mind,
  and _____.
  o The cultivation of _____ and _____ is
    essential to critical thinking.
  o Mindfulness means being alert and _____.
  o Open mindedness means _____
    _____.

- Creativity is the ability to _____ _____.
  - o Divergent thinking:_____ _____.
  - o In contrast, conventional intelligence tests require _____ _____.

- Creative people tend to exhibit the following characteristics:
  - o _____
  - o _____
  - o _____
  - o _____
- Csikszentmihalyi believes that the creative process requires _____, _____, _____, _____, and _____.

- Experts differ from novices in that experts _____ _____.

3. Intelligence
- Intelligence refers to _____.
  - o Cultures vary in how they define intelligence. For example _____ _____.

- When measuring intelligence, validity _____ _____, whereas reliability is _____ _____.

- Standardization involves _____ _____.
- _____ (name) developed the concept of mental age (MA), which _____.
- Intelligence quotient (IQ) was devised by _____ (name) which is an individual's MA divided by _____.
- Cultural bias in intelligence tests is exhibited by _____ _____.

- Intelligence measured by the Binet test represents a normal distribution which is _____.

- The WISC and WAIS were developed by _____ (name) and are widely used today to measure intelligence in children and adults respectively.
  - o See figure 9.10 for the subscales of these tests.
- Culture fair tests are tests that _____ _____ and correct for the problem of _____.
- Genes influence intelligence.
- Heritability is _____.
  Correlations of _____ suggest a strong genetic influence.
- _____ also plays an important role in intelligence.

- The Flynn effect is _____
  _____.
- Gifted people are those who have an IQ of at least _____ and/or have
  _____.
- _____ (name) is famous for his study of gifted children.
- Mental retardation is defined as a condition of _____
  _____ and an IQ below _____.
  - These characteristics must have been demonstrated by the age of _____.
- Organic retardation is caused by _____.
- Cultural-familial retardation is _____
  _____.
- Sternberg's triarchic theory of intelligence states that intelligence comes in three forms:
  - _____
  - _____
  - _____
- Gardner's eight frames of mind include _____
  _____
  _____.
- Doubts about multiple intelligences such as that proposed by Sternberg and Gardner is
  controversial because _____
  _____
  _____.

4. Language
- Language is _____.
- All human languages possess infinite generativity which is the ability to
  _____.
- Languages are characterized by four main rule systems:
  - Phonology: _____.
  - Morphology: _____.
  - Syntax: _____.
  - Semantics: _____.
- Benjamin Whorf argued _____
  _____.
  - Critics of this view argue _____
    _____.
- According to Noam Chomsky, language has a _____ basis, the
  strongest evidence being that _____
  _____.
- The brain contains particular regions that are predisposed to be used for language.
- In contrast to Chomsky's view, behaviorists argue that language is _____
  _____.
  - For example, _____.
  - Problems with the behaviorist view include _____
    _____.

- Socioeconomic status matters for language development. For example, children from middle-income families hear about _____ words an hour, whereas _____.

- Strategies for parents in talking to their babies include:
  - o _____
  - o _____
  - o _____

- Most individuals develop a clear understanding of language structure during _____ (period of life).

- A child's first words occur at _____ (age) and by _____ (age) they can grasp the importance of expressing concepts.

- The whole-language approach stresses that _____ _____.

- The phonics approach stresses that _____ _____.
  - o Children benefit from both approaches but the _____ approach is essential.

5. Thinking, Problem Solving, and Health and Wellness

- Cognitive appraisal is _____ _____.

- Coping is _____ and involves _____ _____.

- Primary appraisal: _____ _____.

- Secondary appraisal: _____ _____.

- Problem focused coping: _____ _____.

- Emotion focused coping: _____ _____.

- Most people use _____ when adjusting to stressful circumstances.

- Approach coping means _____.

- Avoidant coping means _____.

- _____ coping is more effective than _____.

- Successful coping is associated with the following positive factors: _____ _____ _____.

Critical Controversy

- One advantage to bilingual education is _____ _____.

  However, a disadvantage is _____ _____.

Intersection

- Positive mood is associated with _____ type of thinking, whereas negative mood is associated with _____ _____ type of thinking.

Clarifying Tricky Points

Inductive vs. deductive reasoning

The differences between inductive and deductive forms of reasoning can be difficult to keep straight. Both are ways of processing information and reaching conclusions, but they differ in their approaches. To use inductive reasoning is to start at the bottom with specific facts and then generalizing to a broader idea. Therefore inductive reasoning is driven solely by incoming data without regard to a predetermined general idea. Deductive reasoning is essentially the inverse. To use deductive reasoning is to start at the top with a general idea and then uncover specific facts. A scientific theory is a form of deductive reasoning, because you begin with a broad idea and then test specific hypotheses to draw conclusions. Basically, to induct is to have no preconceived notion, whereas to deduce is to have a preconceived notion (ex., theory).

Not all tests are created equally

Intelligence tests (like the WAIS and WISC) and other tests (such as the SAT and ACT) should be unbiased and, as long as you study hard, everybody should have an equal shot at doing well. Right? They are, after all, standardized, which means these types of tests have uniform procedures that are based on norms. Unfortunately, this is not the case. Most tests have some bias in them. Language comprehension is one obvious issue that leads to bias. Understanding nuances of a question is essential to answering correctly but if English is your second language, it is difficult if not impossible to understand such nuances. Tests are hard enough in your native language; imagine taking them in a foreign language. Another, more subtle, form of bias has to do with where people come from. Kids from the suburbs, inner cities, rural communities, and other countries all take the same tests but have very different backgrounds and perspectives. These different perspectives cause people to approach problems differently and sometimes arrive at different conclusions, which is a good thing. The right answer to a problem in an inner city is probably different than the right answer to a problem in a rural community with limited access to common modern conveniences such as high-speed internet and rapid response police. Unfortunately, standardized tests have one and only one right answer so if the test was written by a person from a middle-class suburban family, the right answer likely reflects that perspective, not other, equally valid perspectives. Culture-fair tests try to overcome the bias in standardized tests of intelligence. but it is a difficult task because what is classified as intelligent behavior in one culture or community may not be in another.

Life can be stressful. How to cope?

Approach coping, avoidance coping, problem focused coping, emotion focused coping – it can be overwhelming just to decide how to cope with a problem that was overwhelming in the first place. Fortunately, a lot of research as been done to find out what works best when life challenges us. Approach vs. avoid: deciding between these two options is easy. Is it better to approach a problem and tackle it head on or is it better to avoid the problem and run away and pretend like it doesn't exist? Approaching head on is best and is actually associated with more positive emotional experiences. Now, is it better to take a problem-focused coping style, where you identify the problem and develop a smart strategy to handle it, or an emotion-focused style where you try to manage your own emotional reaction to the problem? In this case the answer is both but with an emphasis on problem-focused. Emotions are important and should not be neglected but strategies for success are essential. So to deal with most challenges you should address your emotions, calmly develop a strategy to approach the problem head-on, and not run away. Successful coping can lead to increased control over your life, a healthier body, and more positive emotions.

An Appreciative View of Psychology and Your Life
Lisa Aspinwall, a prominent psychologist, has found that optimism is associated with having a more positive and constructive approach to problems and life in general. Some people are just naturally more optimistic than others, but that doesn't mean we can't all try to be just a little more optimistic and maybe, as Dr. Aspinwall has found, we can deal more constructively with frightening situations. Think back to a time in your life in which you were faced with a potentially frightening and challenging situation. Maybe this was a time when you or a loved one fell ill, maybe a time when you had to take a really important test, or maybe something completely different.

- Did you take an optimistic or pessimistic approach? _____

- Did you use problem-focused coping, emotion-focused coping, or both?
  _____
  - In what was your coping strategy problem-focused or emotion-focused?
    _____
    _____
    _____

- Did you use approach or avoidance coping? _____
  - In what way was your strategy approach or avoidance? _____
    _____
    _____

- If you encounter a problem like this in the future, how might you use what you learned in this chapter to engage in effective coping?

Practice Test 1
1. When comparing the computer to the human brain, which statement is incorrect?
   a. Computers perform complex numerical calculations faster than the human brain.
   b. Computers apply rules more consistently than the human brain.
   c. Computers can develop more sophisticated learning goals than the human brain.
   d. Computers can represent complex mathematical patterns better than the human brain.

2.   Which of the following was the most important in stimulating the growth of cognitive psychology?
   a.   the development of MRI scan
   b.   the development of the computer
   c.   a study done by B. F. Skinner supporting cognitive psychology
   d.   the case of Genie

3.   The ability to form concepts helps us with all of the following cognitive activities except which one?
   a.   generalizing experiences
   b.   relating experience and objects
   c.   feeling tired after a workout
   d.   remembering associations

4.   The use of concepts allows us to
   a.   avoid the hindsight bias.
   b.   extend the critical learning period for language.
   c.   make memory less efficient.
   d.   make generalizations.

5.   A good strategy for subgoaling is to
   a.   work without a specific plan.
   b.   work backward in establishing subgoals.
   c.   set no more than three subgoals.
   d.   work randomly in establishing subgoals.

6.   An algorithm is
   a.   a rule of thumb that does not a guarantee a solution.
   b.   a rule of thumb that guarantees a problem.
   c.   a strategy that guarantees a solution.
   d.   a strategy for framing problems.

7.   "A paper clip is used for attaching papers together and nothing more." This person is most likely experiencing
   a.   inductive reasoning.
   b.   mindfulness.
   c.   functional fixedness.
   d.   hindsight bias.

8.   A person who has just used a penny to tighten a screw has
   a.   solved an anagram.
   b.   overcome functional fixedness.
   c.   learned that heuristics can be ill defined.
   d.   demonstrated proper use of language.

9.   Inductive reasoning may be related to
   a.   confirmation bias.
   b.   analogies.
   c.   overconfidence bias.
   d.   belief perseverance.

10.   A specific conclusion derived from general information involves
   a.   representative heuristics.
   b.   simulation heuristics.
   c.   inductive reasoning.
   d.   deductive reasoning.

11.   "I knew it all along" is an example of
   a.   the availability heuristic.
   b.   the simulation heuristic.
   c.   the representativeness heuristic.
   d.   hindsight bias.

12.   The heuristic that involves judging the probability of an event by how well it matches a prototype is the
   a.   availability heuristic.
   b.   similarity heuristic.
   c.   representativeness heuristic.
   d.   subgoaling strategy.

13.   The _____ model of the structure of concepts proposes that concepts are categories of objects that share all the defining properties.
   a.   classical
   b.   prototype
   c.   exemplar
   d.   biased

14.   There are various steps involved in optimal problem solving. Which of the following is the step in which we explain what the problem actually is?
   a.   developing strategies
   b.   evaluating solutions
   c.   framing the problem
   d.   subgoaling

15.   A(n) _____ is a problem-solving strategy that involves extensive trial-and-error sessions; all possible strategies are tested until the right one is found.
   a.   heuristic
   b.   algorithm
   c.   mnemonic
   d.   mental set

16. The following factors facilitate problem solving, EXCEPT
    a. being internally motivated to solve the problem.
    b. being an expert in the domain of the problem.
    c. having a mental set.
    d. being a critical thinker when it comes to the framing of the problem.

17. Which of the following is NOT one of the questions we would expect of psychology students who engage in critical thinking of psychological issues?
    a. I wonder why that person did that.
    b. Is there another way of explaining that behavior?
    c. What is the evidence to back up your explanation of that behavior?
    d. Which theory of thinking is the correct one?

18. Ashley claims that she knew beforehand who was going to win an election; she is engaging in the
    a. confirmation bias.
    b. availability heuristic.
    c. representativeness heuristic.
    d. hindsight bias.

19. According to the _____ model of concept structure, we would have a hard time concluding that a penguin is a bird, because penguins don't fly.
    a. classical
    b. prototype
    c. exemplar
    d. cognitive

20. Which of the following is an illustration of mindfulness?
    a. the office administrator who always communicates with the boss with handwritten messages
    b. the individual who resides in a nursing home and does not make any decisions during the course of a day, since all instructions come from the staff (This person does not have a physical or psychological condition that would impede decision making.)
    c. the person who plans to stop at the supermarket before getting home but finds himself in his driveway, having completely forgotten the planned stop
    d. the student who has always used a PC but tries a Mac to see if it fits her better

Practice Test 2

1. Which of the following represents the least comprehensive definition of intelligence?
    a. being original
    b. having problem-solving skills and the ability to adapt to and learn from everyday experiences
    c. becoming immersed in one's domain
    d. having verbal ability

2. If a person was given an intelligence test, and later given the same test again, the scores on the two test administrations should be close to identical if the test is
    a. reliable.
    b. standardized.
    c. normalized.
    d. valid.

3. When a test measures what it is intended to measure, it is
    a. valid.
    b. reliable.
    c. standard.
    d. psychometric.

4. In terms of intelligence testing, chronological age (CA) means
    a. years in school.
    b. actual age of the child in years.
    c. number of years until school is finished.
    d. predicted mental age of the child.

6. According to the IQ test score calculation developed by Stern, a child with a mental age of 8 and a chronological age of 10 would have an IQ of
    a. 80.
    b. 125.
    c. 100.
    d. 95.

6. If IQ scores form a normal distribution, it means that
    a. the scores are symmetrical.
    b. most scores fall at the extremes.
    c. most scores fall in the middle range.
    d. all scores are below average.

7.   According to Sternberg, a person who is street smart and gets along well with other people most likely has high
        a.   creative intelligence.
        b.   practical intelligence.
        c.   analytical intelligence.
        d.   visuo-spatial intelligence.

8.   The finding that African-American schoolchildren score, on average, 10 to 15 points lower on standardized intelligence tests than do white American schoolchildren indicates
        a.   poor standardization of intelligence tests.
        b.   cultural bias of intelligence tests.
        c.   poor reliability of intelligence tests.
        d.   inconsistency of intelligence tests.

9.   What do the Raven Progressive Matrices Test and the SOMPA have in common?
        a.   Both are entirely nonverbal.
        b.   Both represent efforts to develop culture-fair intelligence tests.
        c.   Both are designed for children from low-income families.
        d.   Both have strict time limits.

10.   Which of the following is NOT consistent with culture-fair testing?
        a.   including questions that address aspects of everyday life that children should know, such as what time of the year do we rake leaves; the answer: fall
        b.   including questions that are familiar to people from all socioeconomic backgrounds
        c.   including nonverbal questions
        d.   including questions that are familiar to people from all ethnic backgrounds

11.   These are descriptions of each of the three intelligences proposed by Sternberg, EXCEPT:
        a.   scoring high in the IQ test.
        b.   being creative.
        c.   having musical ability.
        d.   getting along with people.

12.   Mental retardation is likely to be diagnosed in which of the following individuals?
        a.   James: 14 years of age; IQ of 120; no apparent cognitive deficits
        b.   Barbara: 16 years of age; IQ of 100; has a reading disability
        c.   Andrew: 18 years of age; IQ of 80; has difficulty when several instructions are given at once
        d.   Julia: 8 years old; IQ below 70; has difficulty adapting to changes in everyday situations.

13. Children with cultural-familial retardation have a mental deficit without an organic foundation. Which of the following situations is NOT consistent with this type of mental retardation?
    a. A child with cultural-familial retardation tends to become an adult who is unable to function in society.
    b. Cultural-familial retardation may be initially detected by a teacher during the grade school years.
    c. Giving money to a child with cultural-familial retardation is more effective to motivate him to do something than giving him a hug.
    d. A child with cultural-familial retardation can get very upset if the teacher does not recognize his efforts in the same way that he recognizes the efforts of others in the classroom.

14. People who are gifted are
    a. highly creative.
    b. more likely to have mental problems than people with lower intelligence.
    c. socially well adjusted.
    d. able to consider many things at the same time, which also makes them less likely to be able to focus effectively.

15. Csikszentmihalyi recommends a number of activities that lead to a more creative life. Which of the following activities is NOT consistent with his recommendations?
    a. Keep a diary to make sure that you do all the things that you are supposed to do.
    b. Bring flowers to your secretary for no particular reason (Secretary's Day excluded).
    c. Spend time in places in which you feel creative.
    d. Follow your interests.

16. Which of the following environmental factors has not been associated with intelligence assessments?
    a. ethnicity
    b. workplace
    c. socioeconomic class
    d. gender

Practice Test 3

1. According to advocates of bilingual education,
    a. teaching immigrants in their native language leaves them behind in the workplace.
    b. teaching immigrants in their native language increases their self-esteem.
    c. the whole-language approach is flawed.
    d. the whole-language approach is the best strategy to teach immigrants English.

2.   All human languages have the capacity to create an endless number of meaningful sentences using a finite set of words and rules. This is called
   a.   functional fixedness
   b.   heuristics.
   c.   semantics.
   d.   infinite generativity.

3.   Language is made up of basic sounds called
   a.   morphemes.
   b.   syntax.
   c.   semantics.
   d.   phonemes.

4.   The meaning of words and sentences is called
   a.   morphology.
   b.   semantics.
   c.   syntax.
   d.   infinitive generativity.

5.   According to the Whorf's view of language,
   a.   language determines our thoughts.
   b.   thinking determines our language.
   c.   language influences but does not determine thought.
   d.   language can create an endless number of sentences.

6.   Which statement best describes reading experts' consensus on the most effective   method of reading instruction?
   a.   The whole language approach works best for most children.
   b.   Reading instruction should focus exclusively on the basic-skills-and-phonetics approach.
   c.   The best approach is to combine the whole language and the basic-skills-and-phonetics approach.
   d.   The basic-skills-and-phonetics approach works better with younger readers.

7.   Skinner is to _____ as Chomsky is to _____.
   a.   imitation; reinforcement
   b.   reinforcement; biology
   c.   biology; reinforcement
   d.   reinforcement; imitation

8. The observation by Edward Sapir that the Inuit of Alaska have over a dozen words to describe snow has been used to support the view that _____ determines _____.
   a. thinking; language
   b. language; thinking
   c. thinking; cognition
   d. cognition; language

9. Damage to a certain area of the brain can result in speech impairments; the person may be able to think what he or she wants to say but may be unable to speak. Which area of the brain does this statement refer to?
   a. Wernicke's area
   b. the occipital lobe
   c. the right hemisphere
   d. Broca's area

Answer Key

An Appreciative View of Psychology and Your Life
Problem focused coping is when you squarely face a problem and try to solve it. Emotion focused coping is when you try to manage your emotional reaction to the problem; perhaps by avoiding it, denying it, or rationalizing it. Approach coping is similar to problem focused coping in that it means actively engaging with the problem. Avoidance coping is when you avoid a problem or ignore it and is similar to some types of emotion focused coping.

Practice Test 1 Answers

1. a. No; this statement is correct.
   b. No; this statement is correct, humans have a number of biases that computers do not have.
   c. YES; this statement is incorrect, the complexity of the human brain allows us to plan complex and sophisticated learning goals, something a computer cannot do on its own.
   d. No; this statement is correct.

2. a. No; the development of the MRI scan is less important.
   b. THAT'S RIGHT; computers provide information about how the brain might work.
   c. No; in fact Skinner would never support cognitive psychology.
   d. No; the case of Genie is more important in linguistics.

3. a. No; concepts allow us to make generalizations.
   b. No; concepts allow us to relate experiences and objects.
   c. RIGHT; concepts do not make us feel tired after a workout.
   d. No; concepts allow us to remember associations.

4.   a.   No; the hindsight bias occurs independently of our use of concepts.

        b.   No; the critical learning period is not related to our use of concepts.

        c.   No; in fact, concepts make memory more efficient.

        d.   YES; generalizations are possible because of concepts.

5.   a.   No; a plan is needed.

        b.   RIGHT; this is a good strategy in establishing subgoals.

        c.   No; maybe, but this can limit our thinking.

        d.   No; subgoals must be ordered and logical, not random.

6.   a.   No; this describes heuristics.

        b.   No; the problem has already been identified; you don't need to identify again.

        c.   YES; this is the definition of algorithms.

        d.   No, asking questions is effective for framing problems.

7.   a.   No; inductive reasoning is reasoning from specific to general.

        b.   No; mindfulness is similar to critical thinking, which this person appears to lack.

        c.   YES; functional fixedness is failing to see other uses of an object.

        d.   No; hindsight bias is thinking that you knew it all along.

8.   a.   No; this is not an anagram.

        b.   CORRECT; the penny is being used in an unusual function.

        c.   No; heuristics are rules of thumb.

        d.   No, this involves a cognitive not a language challenge.

9.   a.   No; in this bias we seek out information that confirms our beliefs.

        b.   GOOD; analogies draw on inductive reasoning.

        c.   No; in this bias we show too much confidence in our decisions.

        d.   No; this is the tendency to hold on to a belief when there is contradictory evidence.

10.   a.   No; in this heuristic we use prototypes to make decisions.

        b.   No

        c.   No; inductive reasoning is going from specific to general.

        d.   YES; this is the definition of deductive reasoning.

11.   a.   No; this heuristic focuses on recalling the frequency of past occurrences.

        b.   No

        c.   No; this bias says that we use prototypes to make decisions.

        d.   YES; the hindsight bias says that people falsely report an event after it has occurred.

12.   a.   No; this heuristic focuses on recalling the frequency of past occurrences.

        b.   No

        c.   YES; this defines the representativeness heuristic.

        d.   No; this is a problem-solving strategy.

13.   a.   YES; the classical model is actually criticized because sometimes we include objects in concepts even if they don't share all the defining properties.
       b.   No; this model argues that we use the most typical case of the category in establishing the concept.
       c.   No
       d.   No; there is no such thing as a biased model of structure of concepts.

14.   a.   No; this takes place after we explain what the problem is.
       b.   No; this takes place after strategies have been tested.
       c.   YES; framing the problem is precisely considering different ways in which the problem may be explained and understood.
       d.   No; this is a type of problem-solving strategy.

15.   a.   No; in this strategy only the most common method is used.
       b.   YES; an algorithm guarantees a solution because it involves trying all possible strategies.
       c.   No; a mnemonic is a memory-enhancing device.
       d.   No; a mental set is an obstacle to problem solving.

16.   a.   No; this does facilitate problem solving.
       b.   No; being an expert does facilitate problem solving.
       c.   YES; a mental set is a fixation with solving problems in one particular way and ignoring other ways.
       d.   No; this is one of the most effective tools in problem solving.

17.   a.   No; this is a good critical-thinking question, asking about motivations.
       b.   No; this is also a good critical-thinking question, considering more than one perspective.
       c.   No; this is also a good critical-thinking question, asking for research evidence.
       d.   YES; this is not a good critical-thinking question, as it assumes that only one perspective must have the right answer.

18.   a.   No; Ashley is not seeking confirmation, she is just affirming that she knew all along.
       b.   No; in this instance, the availability of the information is not influencing Ashley's certainty.
       c.   No; in this instance, the representativeness heuristic is irrelevant.
       d.   YES; this is the bias we have to tend to think and claim that we knew things even when it was impossible to know them.

19. a. YES; the classical model assumes that all instances of a concept (all birds) share all the characteristics of birds.
    b. No; this model accounts for exceptions, such as penguins.
    c. No
    d. No; all these models are cognitive, but no specific one is referred to as the cognitive model of concept structure.

20. a. No; this office administrator is being mindless, since there are many other ways of communication (e.g., e-mail) that could be more effective.
    b. No; this person is being extremely mindless, since possibly not even simple decisions, such as waking time, are being made by the individual.
    c. No; this is also mindlessness, since the person drove in "automatic mode" and forgot a simple plan that was not part of the common trajectory home.
    d. YES; this involves mindfulness; using computers involves developing a number of skills, and the more familiar you are with the equipment and interface the easier it is to use; therefore, changing the type of computer used requires being open to new information, being mindful.

Practice Test 2 Answers

1. a. No; this includes multiple intelligences.
   b. No; this is a rather comprehensive definition.
   c. No; this includes several intelligences.
   d. YES; this is the least comprehensive definition of intelligence.

2. a. YES; reliability refers to the extent to which scores are consistent.
   b. No; standardization refers to developing uniform procedures for giving and scoring.
   c. No; norms are established standards of performance for a test.
   d. No; validity refers to the extent to which a test measures what it is supposed to measure.

3. a. YES; validity refers to the extent to which a test measures what it is supposed to measure.
   b. No; reliability refers to the extent to which scores are consistent.
   c. No; standardization refers to developing uniform procedures for giving and scoring.
   d. No; this is a reliability examining consistency in scores from two test versions.

4. a. No
   b. RIGHT
   c. No
   d. No

5.   a.   YES; MA/CA x 100; 8/10 x 100 = 80
     b.   No; MA/CA x 100
     c.   No; MA/CA x 100
     d.   No; MA/CA x 100

6.   a.   No
     b.   No; there are few scores at the extremes.
     c.   YES; a normal distribution is shaped like a bell with few scores on the ends.
     d.   No; that would not be a normal distribution.

7.   a.   No; this refers to solving problems in innovative ways.
     b.   YES; this refers to getting along in the world.
     c.   No; this is related to storing and retrieving information and to solving problems.
     d.   No; this is one of Gardner's types of intelligence.

8.   a.   No; intelligence tests are very well standardized.
     b.   YES; intelligence tests tend to favor certain backgrounds and classes.
     c.   No; intelligence tests have good reliability.
     d.   No; intelligence tests have good reliability or consistency.

9.   a.   No; there is a verbal component on the SOMPA.
     b.   YES
     c.   No; both tests can measure intelligence in children from different backgrounds.
     d.   No

10.   a.   YES; these types of items are the most widely criticized, because the "everyday life" is likely to be very different from children of different socioeconomic and ethnic backgrounds.
     b.   No; this is one of the ways in which culture-fair tests are developed.
     c.   No; this is one of the ways in which culture-fair tests are developed.
     d.   No; this is one of the ways in which culture-fair tests are developed.

11.   a.   No; this is consistent with the analytical intelligence.
     b.   No; this is consistent with the creative intelligence.
     c.   YES; this is not one of the types proposed by Sternberg; this type belongs in Gardner's categories.
     d.   No; this is consistent with the practical intelligence.

12.   a.   No; James's IQ is above average.
     b.   No; Barbara's IQ is average.
     c.   No; Andrew's IQ does not meet the cut-off of an IQ of 70 or below.
     d.   YES; Julia's case fits the definition of mental retardation.

13.   a.   YES; this is inconsistent with the findings about individuals with this condition; actually, adults with this disorder tend to become "invisible," which also possibly means that they become integrated into society; perhaps these people don't become doctors, but they may be able to hold jobs and have families.

        b.   No; cultural-familial retardation is usually detected in school.

        c.   No; tangible rewards do tend to be more effective with these children.

        d.   No; children with cultural-familial retardation are very sensitive to what others think about them and their expectations, so they could become upset if they feel that they are being treated differently.

14.   a.   No; this is not true about all gifted people; creativity seems to be different and separate from intelligence.

        b.   No; the gifted are not more likely to have mental problems than others.

        c.   YES; gifted people do tend to have positive social lives.

        d.   No; the gifted have a great ability to focus, even if they have many interests.

15.   a.   YES; while Csikszentmihalyi does recommend keeping a diary, he recommends that the person use it to find new patterns and interests, not as a tool to keep track of "to-do lists."

        b.   No; this would qualify as offering a surprise to someone else, and that is one of the recommendations.

        c.   No; this is one of the recommendations.

        d.   No; this is one of the recommendations.

16.   a.   No; this has been associated and has sparked significant controversy regarding the validity of intelligence tests.

        b.   YES; the workplace, which at least in our society involves adult labor, has not been studied in terms of its possible effect on intelligence assessments (at least no such studies are reported in this chapter).

        c.   No; this has been associated and has sparked significant controversy regarding the validity of intelligence tests.

        d.   No; this has been associated and has sparked significant controversy regarding the validity of intelligence tests.

Practice Test 3

1.   a.   No; in fact, this is a criticism of bilingual education.

        b.   CORRECT; also, they claim that bilingual education values others' culture.

        c.   No; the whole language approach is an approach to teaching children to read.

        d.   No; the whole language approach is an approach to teaching children to read.

2.   a.   No; this is a type of fixation that interrupts optimal problem solving.

        b.   No; heuristics are rules of thumb that do not guarantee solutions to problems.

        c.   No; semantics refers to the meaning of words and sentences.

        d.   YES; using finite sets of words and rules, we can create infinite sentences.

3. a. No; all words are made up of one or more morphemes.
    b. No; syntax refers to how words are combined to form phrases and sentences.
    c. No; semantics refers to the meaning of words and sentences.
    d. YES; a phoneme is a basic sound.

4. a. No; morphology refers to word formation.
    b. YES; semantics refers to the meaning of words and sentences.
    c. No; syntax refers to how words are combined to form phrases and sentences.
    d. No; using finite sets of words and rules, we can create infinite sentences.

5. a. YES; this is correct.
    b. No; actually this is the opposite of what Whorf argued..
    c. No; but this is what the research on Whorf's ideas has found.
    d. No; this sounds more like infinitive generativity.

6. a. No; this does not best describe the experts' consensus.
    b. No; this does not best describe the experts' consensus.
    c. YES; a combination of the two approaches is best.
    d. No; this does not best describe the experts' consensus.

7. a. No; it was Bandura who emphasized imitation.
    b. CORRECT; Skinner emphasized reinforcement in language acquisition, Chomsky emphasized pre-wired biological predispositions.
    c. No; close, but it is actually the other way.
    d. No; Chomsky focused on biological predispositions.

8. a. No; the opposite is true, since these findings have been considered consistent and supportive of Whorf's theory that language determines thinking.
    b. YES; this is correct; Sapir was a student of Whorf's.
    c. No; both concepts are virtually the same.
    d. No; the opposite is true.

9. a. No; Wernicke's area is associated with understanding language.
    b. No; the occipital lobe is associated with the processing of visual information (Chapter Three).
    c. No; the right hemisphere is too broad of an area, but in any case, language is associated with activity in the left hemisphere.
    d. YES; Broca's area is associated with the production of speech.

Chapter 10: Motivation and Emotion

Learning Goals
1. Describe evolutionary, drive reduction, and optimum arousal theories of motivation.
2. Explain the physiological basis of hunger and the nature of eating behavior.
3. Discuss the motivations for sexual behavior.
4. Characterize the positive psychology of motivation.
5. Summarize views of emotion.
6. Discuss the role of emotions in physical and psychological health and wellness.

After studying chapter 10, you will be able to:
- Describe what it means to be self-actualized, which is the highest need in Maslow's hierarchy;
- Understand how to avoid undermining intrinsic motivation;
- Describe how positive emotions can broaden perspective and build resources.

Chapter Outline
1. Theories of Motivation
- Motivation is _____

  _____

- The evolutionary approach emphasizes _____

  _____.

- Instinct is _____

  _____

- According to the evolutionary approach, the motivation for sex, aggression, and achievement is rooted in _____.
- A drive is _____
- A need is _____
  - An example of needs and drives working together is _____

    _____

- Drive reduction theory states _____

  _____

  - The goal of drive reduction is _____ which means

    _____.

- The Yerkes-Dodson law states _____

  _____

2. Hunger
- The basis for hunger is _____.
- Cholecystokinin (CCK) is a hormone that _____

  _____

- Glucose is important because _____

  _____

- Insulin is important because _____

  _____

- Leptin is a protein that _____
_____
  - Leptin may be able to help obese people lose weight.
- Activity in the _____ (part of the brain) contributes to hunger.
  - The lateral hypothalamus is involved in _____.
  - The ventromedial hypothalamus is involved in _____
  _____.

- Being obese or overweight puts an individual at risk for _____
_____.
- The _____ gene may contribute to obesity because it is related to the
production of _____.
- The tendency to be overweight can be inherited
- Weight set point is _____
_____
- Adipose cells are _____ and when they
are filled _____.
- Learned associations with time and place can affect eating behavior.
- Restrained eaters are _____
_____.
- Anorexia nervosa is _____
_____.
- Bulimia nervosa is _____
_____.

3. Sexuality
- Motivation for sexual behavior is centered in _____ (part of
the brain) and generated by _____.
- Orgasm is caused by _____ and the
relaxation experienced afterward is linked to _____.
- Estrogens _____.
- Androgens _____.
- For men, higher androgen levels are associated with _____
_____ but the relationship betweens hormones and sexual behavior
in women is _____.
- Human sexual response pattern:
  - _____
  _____
  - _____
  _____
  - _____
  _____
  - _____
  _____
- Sexual scripts are _____
_____.
- The sensory system of _____ predominates sexual activity.

- Cultural factors are also important in sexual motivation.
- _____ is a good predictor of delaying first sexual intercourse in adolescents.
- Sexual orientation refers to _____
  _____
- Studies show that children raised by gay men and women tend to be as well adjusted as children from heterosexual households.
- For gay men and women, having a positive gay identity, rejection of negative gay stereotypes, and gay activism correlate with _____.

4. Beyond Hunger and Sex: Approaches to Motivation in Everyday Life
- Maslow's hierarchy of needs states that _____
  _____.
  - See figure 10.7
  - Self actualization is _____
    _____
- Self determination theory asserts that there are 3 basic needs:
  - _____
  - _____
  - _____
- Intrinsic motivation is _____
  _____
- Extrinsic motivation is _____
  _____
- The problem with using reward as incentive is _____
  _____
  _____
- Self-regulation is _____
  _____

5. Emotion
- Emotion _____
  _____
- Anger and fear are associated with elevated _____
  activity.
- Happiness activates _____.
- _____ and _____
  _____ are two measures of arousal.
- Polygraphs err just under _____% of the time.
- James-Lange theory states that emotion results from _____
  _____.
  - For example, _____
    _____
    _____
- Cannon-Bard theory states that _____
  _____.
- The amygdala is activated when we experience _____ emotions.

- The _____ is likely activated when we experience positive emotions.
  - Neurotransmitters such as _____ and _____ might also be associated with positive emotions.
- The two-factor theory of emotion states that emotion is determined by _____ and _____.
  - When participants were injected with epinephrine to increase arousal, they _____ _____ _____

- In the primacy debate, Lazarus argued that _____ was a precondition for emotion because _____ _____.
- Zajonc argued that _____ _____ _____.

- According to the facial feedback hypothesis, _____ _____.
- The facial expressions of emotion _____ between cultures.
- Contrary to the stereotype, men and women _____ in the way they experience emotion.
- The circumplex model proposed by Plutchik says emotions have four dimensions:
  - _____
  - _____
  - _____
  - _____
- The two-dimensional approach classifies emotions by _____ _____.
- The broaden-and-build model of positive emotions proposed by _____ _____ states that _____ _____ _____.

- Catharsis is the _____.
  - The _____ perspective supports the use of catharsis.
  - Whereas the _____ perspective does not support the use of catharsis.
- Gratitude is a complex positive emotion associated with _____ _____.

6. Emotion and Health and Wellness

- Positive emotions have been linked to the release of _____
  _____ which antibody linked to _____
  _____.

  o Levels of this are also linked to using _____ as a coping
    strategy.

- Resilient individuals are _____
  _____.

  o Research on resiliency around September 11, 2001 found that

    _____
    _____
    _____
    _____.

Critical Controversy

- Extrinsic events, such as _____
  _____ can reduce enjoyment (intrinsic motivation) of tasks.

Intersection

- Delay of gratification is _____
  _____.

  o Delay of gratification is exhibited in studies by Walter Mischel where

    _____
    _____
    _____.

  o Hot thoughts are _____.
  o Cool thoughts are _____.

Clarifying Tricky Points

Unhappiness and overeating

It is commonly considered that when some people have just broken up with a boyfriend or
girlfriend or are just generally unhappy they overeat. This may be true for some people but it is
not one of the major factors in overeating. Individual differences in biological factors such as
genes, hypothalamus activity, the number of adipose cells and cultural factors such as learned
associations between eating and a certain time of day or a certain place are far more important
factors to consider in overeating behavior.

How to best reward good behavior

When someone you know does something good you might want to reward them somehow. But
what is the best way: a new iPod, a candy bar, or just a pat on the back? The answer is tricky
because if someone is doing something for intrinsically motivated reasons, then extrinsic rewards
like iPods or candy can actually undermine such motivation. Intrinsic motivation is generally
better than extrinsic motivation because it is associated with improved performance, persistence,
and creativity but the whole point of intrinsically motivated activities is that they are done simply
because you enjoy them, not because there is a prize to be won. So adding extrinsic rewards for

intrinsic behavior is not a good idea. However, not all activities can be intrinsically motivated. Some things just have to be done whether you want to or not, and for those activities extrinsic rewards can be just fine. See the Critical Controversy discussion in your text for more on this issue.

Emotion or physiological reaction: Which comes first?
You know you feel emotions all the time but you have probably not given much thought to how or why you feel emotions. The James-Lange theory says you feel emotion because of physiological changes in your body. Your hands get sweaty, so you feel nervous, which is not the same as you feel nervous, so your hands get sweaty. In the James-Lange model, the physiological change happens first; but the Cannon-Bard theory states that the experience of the emotion and the physiological change occur together and at the same time. Cannon-Bard essentially states that the body plays less of a role in the experience of emotions than the James-Lange model proposes. See figure 1.9 in your text for more on the differences between these two perspectives.

An Appreciative View of Psychology and Your Life
Barbara Fredrickson's broaden-and-build theory of positive emotions states that positive emotions can cause you to broaden your mind and see unusual possibilities that might not occur to you when you are in a bad mood. Additionally, positive emotions can lead to a building of resources, such as more friends, more physical activity, etc.
Describe a time when you were in a particularly good mood that might have caused you to broaden your mind or see things differently.

_____

_____

_____

_____

_____

Can you think of ways that this experience helped you build any resources such as those described above or in chapter 10?

_____

_____

_____

_____

_____

Practice Test 1
1.   "The question of why individuals behave, think, and feel the way they do" defines
   a.   motivation.
   b.   instinct.
   c.   emotion.
   d.   drive.

2.   Which aspect of motivation was supported by Darwin and Freud?
   a.   drives
   b.   instincts
   c.   needs
   d.   incentives

3.   A need is to a physiological state as a drive is to a(n)
   a.   innate state.
   b.   psychological state.
   c.   physical state.
   d.   biological state.

4.   Which of the following is an example of homeostasis?
   a.   An organism in pain cries out loudly.
   b.   A cold organism shivers to reduce heat loss.
   c.   A fearful organism huddles in the corner and cries.
   d.   Two friends who have been separated for months greet each other with hugs.

5.   Which of the following theories of motivation predicts that a person drinks water because she has an uncomfortable lack of fluids in her body?
   a.   optimum arousal theory
   b.   the cognitive approach
   c.   drive reduction theory
   d.   hierarchy of human needs

6.   The deprivation that energizes the drive to eliminate or reduce the deprivation is referred as a(n)
   a.   instinct.
   b.   drive.
   c.   homeostasis.
   d.   need.

7.   Which of the following biological factors is NOT associated with an increase in the hunger motivation?
   a.   insulin injections
   b.   the release of the hormone cholecystokinin (CCK)
   c.   low levels of glucose in the brain
   d.   low or no production of leptin

8.   All of the following are symptoms of bulimia nervosa, EXCEPT
   a.   extreme loss of weight.
   b.   a binge-and-purge eating pattern.
   c.   strong fear of becoming overweight.
   d.   depression.

9.   According to statistics, which of the following is at highest risk for anorexia nervosa?
   a.   21-year-old White college student who works 30 hours a week to pay for school
   b.   18-year-old African-American female whose parents are both teachers
   c.   16-year-old Hispanic female who works at a fast-food place after school
   d.   15-year-old White female whose parents are both lawyers

10.   According to drive reduction theory, we eat to reduce
   a.   food.
   b.   homeostasis.
   c.   instincts.
   d.   arousal.

11.   According to the Yerkes-Dodson theory, under which of the following conditions can we expect a novice dancer to perform best?
   a.   at home in front of the mirror
   b.   in front of/for the selection committee at a highly prestigious art school
   c.   at the dance studio where she works
   d.   in a new show in her community

12.   Which of the following biological factors does not contribute to overeating?
   a.   lower basal metabolism rate
   b.   heredity
   c.   damage to the ventromedial hypothalamus
   d.   having an average of 100 billion fat cells

Practice Test 2

1.   The highest and most elusive of needs, according to Maslow, is
   a.   self-esteem.
   b.   self-actualization.
   c.   love and belongingness.
   d.   safety.

2.   The desire to do a job well for its own sake is called
   a.   extrinsic motivation.
   b.   intrinsic motivation.
   c.   the Yerkes-Dodson law.
   d.   the Cannon-Bard theory.

3.   According to the James-Lange theory, an environmental stimulus
   a.   is perceived as emotional by the hypothalamus.
   b.   triggers emotional arousal, which is labeled by the brain.
   c.   is emotional because of cultural and social expectations.
   d.   causes arousal if it appears threatening.

4.   When first-graders work hard on a project in order to collect praise and gold stars from their teacher, what kind of motivation are they demonstrating?
a.   achievement motivation
b.   competence motivation
c.   extrinsic motivation
d.   intrinsic motivation

5.   Which of the following perspectives on motivation is the one that focuses on a person's ability to choose which behaviors they want to do?
a.   drive reduction theory
b.   evolutionary theory
c.   optimum arousal theory
d.   the cognitive approach

6.   Which of the following is NOT an example of an extrinsic motivator to do a house chore?
a.   the smile of a mother
b.   the desire to do it
c.   they keys to the parents' car
d.   the allowance

7.   Self-generated goals are important motivators. The following are examples of self-generated goals, EXCEPT
a.   restoring homeostasis.
b.   life tasks.
c.   personal projects.
d.   personal strivings.

8.   The second level of needs in Maslow's hierarchy involves concerns with
a.   love and belongingness.
b.   self-actualization.
c.   safety.
d.   esteem.

9.   A child who cleans up his room every day so he can receive his two-dollar allowance on Saturday is
a.   self-actualizing.
b.   extrinsically motivated.
c.   intrinsically motivated.
d.   high in the affiliation motivation.

10. Which of the following motivators in the workplace is more likely to result in productivity and high quality work?
    a. a high salary
    b. a good and understanding boss
    c. the challenge presented by the task
    d. a good work environment

11. In Maslow's hierarchy of needs, when are people concerned with having friends and stable family lives?
    a. after they satisfy their basic physiological needs
    b. before they become concerned with having a positive self-image
    c. after they have become self-actualized
    d. before they are concerned with their own safety

12. In Chapter 1 you learned about the main psychological perspectives. Which of the following perspectives would argue that we should study the fact that sometimes we do things and we don't really know why we do them?
    a. cognitive
    b. evolutionary
    c. sociocultural
    d. psychodynamic

Practice Test 3

1. Emotion is defined as
    a. a feeling that involves physiological arousal, conscious experience, and behavioral expression.
    b. a feeling that involves physiological arousal.
    c. physiological arousal.
    d. behavior that involves facial expressions.

2. According to the Yerkes-Dodson theory, your performance on an exam will be best if you are
    a. extremely aroused.
    b. minimally aroused.
    c. moderately aroused.
    d. extremely happy.

3. According to Schachter and Singer, the specific emotion we experience depends on the
    a. rate of firing of fibers leading from the hypothalamus to the neocortex.
    b. amount of serotonin released in the peripheral nervous system.
    c. specific pattern of heart rate, blood pressure, and skin resistance.
    d. environmental circumstances to which we attribute our arousal.

4.   The Cannon-Bard theory predicts that after witnessing a shocking event, a person will
      a.   first experience shock and then be motivated to turn away.
      b.   be motivated to turn away and then will experience shock.
      c.   experience cathartic shock as a release of anxiety.
      d.   experience physical and emotional reactions simultaneously.

5.   Researchers have found universality in each of the following, EXCEPT
      a.   facial expressions of happiness.
      b.   facial expressions of fear.
      c.   facial expressions of surprise.
      d.   facial expression of contentment.

6.   Plutchik suggests that our emotions can be classified according to four dimensions. Which of the following is not one of the four?
      a.   Emotions are primary or mixed.
      b.   Emotions are strong or weak.
      c.   Emotions are bright or dull.
      d.   Emotions are positive or negative.

7.   According to Plutchik, mixing primary emotions leads to
      a.   psychological difficulties.
      b.   polar opposites.
      c.   other emotions.
      d.   negative emotions.

8.   The following factors are associated with happiness, EXCEPT
      a.   being engaged by work and leisure.
      b.   extreme happiness increases the experience of happiness in the future.
      c.   having faith.
      d.   being extroverted.

9.   Which of the following theories of emotions is the one that argues that the way in which we explain our physiological arousal plays a central role in determining exactly which emotion we experience?
      a.   the two-factor theory
      b.   the James-Lange theory
      c.   the Cannon-Bard theory
      d.   the neural circuits explanation

10.   Which of the following facts explains why is it easier to acquire a fear than to get rid of the fear?
    a.   The amygdala participates in positive emotions.
    b.   There is a direct pathway involved in the communication of fear from the thalamus to the amygdala.
    c.   The amygdala sends more connections to the cerebral cortex than it gets back.
    d.   There is an indirect path involved in the communication of fear from the thalamus through the sensory cortex to the amygdala.

11.   Lazarus argues that cognition comes before emotion while Zajonc argues that emotion is followed by cognition. What is the variable that explains why they are both correct?
    a.   physiology
    b.   time
    c.   personality
    d.   culture

12.   Which of the following signs of emotional arousal is measured by a polygraph?
    a.   blood pressure
    b.   sweating
    c.   heart rate
    d.   body temperature

13.   Happiness is to the _____ hemisphere of the brain as disgust is to the _____ hemisphere of the brain.
    a.   left; occipital
    b.   right; left
    c.   left; right
    d.   temporal; parietal

14.   In some cultures, widows (who have just lost their husbands) express their sadness with very loud and uncontrollable crying, screaming, calling the name of the lost husband, and bouts of fainting. In other cultures, widows respond with a quiet sadness that is hardly interrupted by others. These differences are explained by the concept of
    a.   universal emotions.
    b.   display rules.
    c.   facial feedback hypothesis.
    d.   gender influences.

Answer Key

Practice Test 1 Answers

1.   a.   YES, this is the definition of motivation; it energizes, directs, and sustains behavior.
      b.   No; an instinct is an innate, biological pattern of behavior.
      c.   No; an emotion is a feeling that has physiological and behavioral components.
      d.   No; a drive is an aroused state that occurs because of a need.

2.   a.   No
      b.   RIGHT; Darwin and Freud believed that instincts motivate behavior.
      c.   No
      d.   No

3.   a.   No
      b.   YES; a drive involves a psychological state.
      c.   No
      d.   No

4.   a.   No; there is no indication that crying loudly leads to a return of a steady   state.
      b.   YES; homeostasis refers to the body's equilibrium or steady state.
      c.   No; there is no reference that this behavior returns the organism to equilibrium.
      d.   No; this does not involve a return to the body's equilibrium.

5.   a.   No; this question simply states that a person has a need and behaves to reduce the drive; it does not address the person's particular level of optimal hydration.
      b.   No; the motivation is physiological.
      c.   YES; the behavior is done to reduce the drive, thirst.
      d.   No; while physiological needs are at the base, the best answer in this question is item c.

6.   a.   No; an instinct is an unlearned pattern of behavior shared by a species.
      b.   No; a drive does not energize a drive.
      c.   No; homeostasis is restored when the need is eliminated.
      d.   YES; a need is a deprivation, a lack of something, that when provided will restore homeostasis.

7.   a.   No; this leads to hunger.
      b.   YES; CCK helps start digestion and travels to the brain through the bloodstream and signals you to stop eating; a contributor in this process is the neurotransmitter serotonin.
      c.   No; this increases hunger.
      d.   No; this increases hunger.

8. a. YES; people with bulimia nervosa tend to keep a normal weight range, whereas people with anorexia nervosa tend to weigh less than 85% of what is considered normal for their age and height.
    b. No; this is characteristic of bulimia nervosa.
    c. No; this is characteristic of bulimia nervosa as well as of anorexia nervosa.
    d. No; this is characteristic of bulimia nervosa as well as of anorexia nervosa.

9. a. No; this person does not have the highest risk.
    b. No; this person does not have the highest risk.
    c. No; this person does not have the highest risk.
    d. CORRECT; this person has the most risk factors (age, race, family background).

10. a. No; unless you are in a hotdog eating competition.
    b. YES; the goal of drive reduction is homeostasis, the body's tendency to maintain equilibrium.
    c. No; instincts are not reduced, they motivate behavior in a different way.
    d. No; arousal is a state of alertness and is unrelated to drive reduction.

11. a. No; this is likely to be a low arousal situation, and thus performance will not be peaked.
    b. No; this is likely to be a high arousal situation, and thus performance may be impaired.
    c. No; this, like item a, is likely to be a low arousal situation, and thus performance will not be peaked.
    d. YES; a new show for a novice dancer is likely to result in a moderate level of arousal, and thus result in the best performance, according to the Yerkes-Dodson theory.

12. a. No; this is associated with overeating and obesity.
    b. No; this is associated with overeating and obesity.
    c. YES; when this area has been destroyed in animal research, the animal eats profusely and quickly becomes obese.
    d. No; this is associated with overeating and obesity.

Practice Test 2 Answers

1. a. No; this is second from the top of the hierarchy.
    b. YES, this refers to developing one's full potential and sits on top of the hierarchy.
    c. No; this is third from the top of the hierarchy.
    d. No; this is fourth from the top of the hierarchy.

2. a. No; extrinsic motivation refers to an external reward for a job well done.
    b. YES, this illustrates intrinsic motivation since the desire is internal.
    c. No; this refers to the relationship between performance and arousal.
    d. No; this is an emotion theory.

3. a.   The Cannon-Bard theory of emotion includes the hypothalamus.
    b.   RIGHT; emotional arousal is interpreted or labeled by the brain to create emotion.
    c.   No; this theory doesn't directly include cultural and social expectations.
    d.   No; the brain first interprets arousal before anything is perceived as threatening.

4. a.   While children may want to accomplish something, this is not the best option.
    b.   No
    c.   YES; the children are receiving praise and gold stars, both of which are external.
    d.   No; the rewards are external.

5. a.   No; drive reduction is a biologically based theory.
    b.   No; evolutionary theory focuses on the role of instincts.
    c.   No; optimum arousal is a physiologically based theory.
    d.   YES; the cognitive approach focuses on how we think and consciously decide to engage in some behaviors and not in others.

6. a.   No; this is extrinsic, offered by the mother to the child.
    b.   YES; this is intrinsic, something that is internal.
    c.   No; this is a reward that is external.
    d.   No; this is a reward that is external.

7. a.   YES; restoring homeostasis is a biological process that is not self- generated.
    b.   No; life tasks are self-generated goals that involve problems the individual is currently working on.
    c.   No; personal projects are self-generated goals that range from trivial pursuits to life goals.
    d.   No; personal strivings are self-generated goals that represent what a person is typically trying to do, such as doing a good job, keeping the family together, making friends, etc.

8. a.   No; this is the third level.
    b.   No; this is the fifth and last level.
    c.   YES; concerns for safety follow the physiological needs.
    d.   No; this is the fourth level, right before self-actualization.

9. a.   No; self-actualization refers to fulfilling one's potential.
    b.   THIS IS CORRECT; extrinsic motivation involves external rewards for doing a task.
    c.   No; intrinsic motivation involves internal rewards for a task.
    d.   No; while this could be true, the question does not address the child's affiliation tendencies.

10.   a.   No; this is an extrinsic motivator that may actually diminish the achievement motivation.
       b.   No; this is an extrinsic motivator.
       c.   YES; this is an intrinsic motivator and thus it may be expected to have more positive outcomes than an extrinsic motivator.
       d.   No; this is an extrinsic motivator.

11.   a.   No; safety comes after the physiological need.
       b.   YES; according to Maslow, people go on to be concerned with esteem needs once the love and belongingness needs are satisfied.
       c.   No; self-actualization is the last level.
       d.   No; love and belongingness needs go after safety needs.

12.   a.   No; this perspective would focus on conscious motivations.
       b.   No; this perspective would focus on instincts as motivators; instincts are shared by all humans, and we engage in instinctual behavior because we are human.
       c.   No; this perspective focuses on broad social and cultural influences; we engage in those behaviors because of others.
       d.   YES; this perspective focuses on unconscious motivations.

Practice Test 3 Answers

1.   a.   RIGHT; these characteristics define emotion.
       b.   Emotion includes other components.
       c.   No; but you're partially correct.
       d.   No; there's more to emotion that this option.

2.   a.   Too much arousal will impair your performance.
       b.   No; too little arousal will impair your performance.
       c.   THAT'S RIGHT; moderate arousal tends to maximize performance.
       d.   No; the Yerkes-Dodson theory describes arousal and performance, not happiness.

3.   a.   No; this is not relevant in this theory.
       b.   No; Schachter and Singer do not consider serotonin.
       c.   No; the pattern of arousal is less important than the external cues for it.
       d.   THIS IS RIGHT; we look for reasons or external cues to explain our arousal.

4.   a.   No
       b.   No; this option sounds more like the James-Lange theory.
       c.   No
       d.   RIGHT; this theory says that physiological arousal and the emotion are experienced at the same time.

5.   a.   Happiness is expressed in a universal way.
       b.   Fear is expressed in a universal way.
       c.   Surprise is expressed in a universal way.
       d.   RIGHT; contentment is not expressed in a universal way.

6. a. Emotions can be primary or mixed.
    b. No; emotions can be strong or weak.
    c. RIGHT; Plutchik does not classify emotions in this way.
    d. No; emotions can be positive or negative.

7. a. No
    b. No; this is one of the four dimensions.
    c. CORRECT; mixing primary emotions leads to other emotions such disappointment.
    d. No; mixing primary emotions may lead to negative or positive emotions.

8. a. No; this has been associated with happiness.
    b. YES; actually, intense positive moments can diminish the sensation of future positive events.
    c. No; this has been associated with happiness.
    d. No; this has been associated with happiness.

9. a. YES; the two-factor theory says that emotions are determined by physiological arousal and cognitive labeling; cognitive labeling is a process of explaining the physiological arousal.
    b. No; this theory says that stimuli cause a physiological reaction, which in turn causes an emotion; however, it does not address the cognitive process.
    c. No; this theory says that the processing of the physiological reaction and the emotion occurs simultaneously.
    d. No; the neural circuits approach focuses on the role of certain parts of the brain, such as the amygdala, in receiving, processing, and sending out information about emotions.

10. a. No; this is a fact, but positive emotions do not contribute to fears.
    b. No; this is a fact, but it does not explain why it is easier to learn than to unlearn fears.
    c. YES; this is a fact, and it explains why once a fear is learned and "saved" in the amygdala, this information can more easily influence how we think (amygdala sending out messages to cortex); however, when we try to unlearn something we are engaging in activation on the cerebral cortex and sending the information back to the amygdala; there are fewer pathways back into the amygdala, thus less opportunity for connections to be established.
    d. No; this is a fact, but it does not explain why it is easier to learn than to unlearn fears.

11.   a.   No; physiology is a component of emotion.
        b.   YES; time is the key; Lazarus refers to a relationship between cognition and emotion across an extended period of time, such as thinking that your partner does not love you followed by feeling sad; however, Zajonc referred to more immediate situations, such as being scared by a scream; the emotion occurs immediately followed by an awareness and the thoughts of the situation.
        c.   No; personality does not play a role in this issue.
        d.   No; culture plays no role in this issue; this is more likely to be explained in terms of brain circuitry.

12.   a.   No; this is not measured by a polygraph.
        b.   No; don't confuse the polygraph with the galvanic skin response assessment, which measures the electrical conductivity of the skin when sweat glands increase activity.
        c.   YES; this is one of the measures taken by polygraphs, along with breathing and electrodermal response, an index detecting skin resistance to passage of a weak electrical current.
        d.   No; this changes with emotions but it is not measured by a polygraph.

13.   a.   No; while happiness is associated with the left hemisphere, occipital refers to a lobe, not a hemisphere.
        b.   No; the opposite is true.
        c.   YES; the left hemisphere of the brain is associated with approach-related emotions, such as happiness, while the right hemisphere is associated with withdrawal-related emotions, such as disgust.
        d.   No; these are lobes of the hemispheres, not hemispheres themselves.

14.   a.   No; while sadness is universal and crying is universally associated with sadness, the studies done by Ekman do not account for such dramatic differences in the expression of emotions.
        b.   YES; display rules are sociocultural standards that determine when, where, and how emotions should be expressed.
        c.   No; this hypothesis states that behavioral aspects of emotions can initiate the emotional experience.
        d.   No; the question is not about gender differences in the expression of sadness.

Chapter 11: Personality

Learning Goals
1. Define personality and summarize the psychodynamic perspectives.
2. Describe the humanistic perspectives.
3. Discuss the trait perspectives.
4. Discuss the personological and life story perspectives.
5. Explain the social cognitive perspectives.
6. Characterize the main methods of personality assessment.
7. Summarize how personality relates to health and wellness.

After studying chapter 11, you will be able to:
- Explain how humanistic perspectives stress the capacity for growth and the freedom to choose your own destiny;
- Understand the importance of self-efficacy and how you can increase it;
- Describe why optimism is important for health and well-being and how it can be learned.

Chapter Outline
1. Psychodynamic Perspectives
- Personality is _____
_____.
- Psychodynamic perspectives view personality as _____
_____.
  - o _____ (name) is most associated with psychodynamics.
- According to Freud, sex is _____.
- Hysteria refers to _____
_____.
  - o Overdetermined means _____
_____.
- Freud believed the unconscious was extensive. See figure 11.1 for an illustration of this point.
- Freud thought personality had three structures:
  - o _____
_____
    - ▪ Operates according to the _____principle.
  - o _____
_____
    - ▪ Operates according to the _____ principle.
  - o _____
_____
    - ▪ Also known as the _____.
- The purpose of defense mechanisms is to _____ and
_____.
  - o Repression _____
_____.

- o The two most important points about defense mechanisms is that they are
  _____ and, when used temporarily, are _____
  _____.
- Psychosexual development:
  - o Oral stage _____
    _____
  - o Anal stage _____
    _____
  - o _____
    _____
    - ▪ Oedipus complex _____
      _____
    - ▪ Castration anxiety _____
      _____
  - o Latency period _____
    _____
  - o Genital stage _____
    _____
- Fixation is a defense mechanism that _____
  _____.
- Critics of Freud note the following important points:
  - o _____
    _____
    _____
  - o _____
    _____
    _____
  - o _____
    _____
    _____
  - o _____
    _____
    _____
- Karen Horney insisted that _____
  _____ be considered in the study of personality.
  - o Research about women was limited because _____
    _____.
  - o From Horney's perspective, _____ not _____ is the
    primary motive.
- Carl Jung believed the roots of personality begin _____
  _____.
  - o Collective unconscious: _____
    _____.
  - o Archetypes: _____
    _____.

- ▪ _____ and _____ are the most common and mean _____
_____.

- In Alfred Adler's individual psychology, people are motivated by _____
_____.
  - ○ _____ factors are more important than _____
_____.
  - ○ Compensation: _____
_____.

2. Humanistic Perspectives

- The humanistic perspective emphasizes _____
_____.

- Abraham Maslow called the humanistic approach _____ because
_____.
  - ○ Self-actualization _____
_____.
  - ○ A person at the optimal level of existence would be _____
_____
_____

- Carl Rogers emphasized _____
_____
  - ○ Conditions of worth _____
_____.
  - ○ Self concept _____
_____
    - ▪ Real self is _____.
    - ▪ Ideal self is _____.
  - ○ Unconditional positive regard _____
_____.

3. Trait Perspectives

- A trait is _____
_____.

- Trait theories state that personality consists of _____
_____
_____.

- Gordon Allport stressed _____
_____
  - ○ Lexical approach: _____
_____.
  - ○ Factor analysis _____
_____.

- The big five factors of personality are: (Remember the acronym "O-C-E-A-N" can help you remember all five factors.)
  - ○ _____: _____
_____
_____

    o   _____ : _____
    _____
    _____

    o   _____ : _____
    _____
    _____

    o   _____ : _____
    _____
    _____

    o   _____ : _____
    _____
    _____

4. Personological and Life Story Perspectives

- Personological perspectives emphasize _____
_____ .

- Henry Murray thought that a person's _____
_____ was important to study.
  - o According to Murray, a person's motives are _____
  _____ .
  - o Thematic Apperception Test (TAT): _____
  _____
  _____

- Dan McAdams' life story approach emphasizes _____
_____ .

5. Social Cognitive Perspectives

- Social cognitive perspectives emphasize _____
_____ .

- Albert Bandura's social cognitive theory states that _____
_____ .
  - o Reciprocal determinism: _____
  _____

- Social cognitive theorists believe that we acquire behaviors, thoughts, and feelings through _____ .
- Self-efficacy is _____
_____ .
  - o It can be increased through the following strategies:
  - o   _____
  _____
  - o   _____
  _____
  - o   _____
  _____
  - o   _____
  _____
  - o   _____
  _____

- Walter Mischel emphasized the lack of _____ in personality research.
  - Situationism: _____
    _____

- Through the person-situation debate, researchers were able to show the following three important findings:
  - _____
    _____
    _____
    _____

  - _____
    _____
    _____
    _____

  - _____
    _____
    _____
    _____

- CAPS model stands for _____
  _____ and means _____
  _____.

6. Personality Assessment

- Self report tests are tests that _____
  _____
  - They are also called _____.
- The NEO-PI-R tests _____.
  - Face validity: _____
    _____

- The most widely used and researched self-report test is the _____.
- A projective test presents people with _____ and asks them to _____.
  - _____ and _____
    _____ are examples of projective tests.
- The TAT measures the following needs: _____
  _____.

- Behavioral assessment assesses personality by _____
  _____.

- Cognitive assessment is a strategy that might ask _____
  _____.

7. Personality and Health and Wellness

- _____ is the most important of the big five traits for health.
- Personal control is important for health because it _____
  _____.

- Type A behavior is characterized by _____
  _____.
  - Hostility is the component of Type A most associated with _____
    _____.

- Type B behavior is characterized by _____
  _____.

- Optimism is good for health as demonstrated by the following research findings:
  - ○ _____
    _____
  - ○ _____
    _____
  - ○ _____
    _____

- Hardiness is a trait characterized by _____
  _____.

Critical Controversy

- William James hypothesized that personality is basically set by age 30. Subsequent research by Paul Costa and Robert McCrae _____
  _____
  _____.

- Over time, however, some traits do change a little. As people get older, they also get
  _____.

Intersection

- Extraverts tend to be _____ compared to introverts.
- But, positive moods experienced by introverts may be more like _____
  _____, which is different than the positive mood experienced by extraverts.

Clarifying Tricky Points

Sex according to Freud

Most people who don't understand Freud well think all he talked about was sex. This is true to some extent but what Freud meant by sex is not necessarily what we call "sex" today. Freud defined sex as organ pleasure which includes things like smell, taste, bowel movements, etc. Basically, anything that uses any part of your body, not just your genitals, to bring you pleasure, is sex according to Freud's definition.

Factor Analysis

Factor analysis is a statistical procedure used to breakdown a large quantity of questions or words into fewer, more general, constructs. For example, outgoing, friendly, talkative, lively, entertaining, fun, loud, excited, and engaging are several words that all mean about the same thing: extraverted. If a person were administered a questionnaire with all those words, responses on these items would tend to "hang together," meaning a person would tend to respond to each item in a similar manner. Factor analysis uses statistics to identify those items that "hang together" and can therefore breakdown a 200 item personality questionnaire into just a few meaningful constructs such as the "big five" personality traits of neuroticism, extraversion, openness to experience, agreeableness, and conscientiousness.

Person Situation Debate

One of the most important points in the history of personality psychology was the person situation debate. Walter Mischel, who is now considered a personality psychologist, wrote in a book that research showed people do not behave similarly across different situations, which means personality traits (and personality more generally) doesn't really matter, only the situation matters. His argument was so compelling that personality psychology as a field was nearly destroyed. However, some thoughtful personality psychologists broke down Mischel's argument and found some areas where he got it wrong. For example, when people are in a casual situation, such as just lounging around the house, personality traits are good predictors of behavior. However, when people are in more compelling situations such as giving an important talk in front of a large group of people, personality is not a great predictor of behavior. After years of debate, the field has generally agreed now that behavior is best predicted by an interaction of personality and the situation, both parts being equally important.

An Appreciative View of Psychology and Your Life

Using the "big five" traits and the more specific traits that are related to health and wellness (optimism, hardiness, etc.), describe your personality.

_____
_____
_____
_____

Now, according to research discussed in your textbook, how does your personality affect your health? If the research indicates that your personality might not be good for your health, don't worry; instead describe actions you can take to reduce the negative impact of your personality on your health.

_____
_____
_____
_____
_____
_____

Practice Test 1

1. Which of the following concepts is not part of the definition of personality?
    a. thoughts
    b. emotions
    c. behaviors
    d. situations

2. According to psychodynamic theorists, personality is primarily
   a. unconscious.
   b. shaped by self-actualization.
   c. conscious.
   d. acquired through reinforcement and punishment.

3. According to Freud, which part of the personality is dominated by the pleasure principle?
   a. the id
   b. the conscience
   c. the ego
   d. the superego

4. According to Freud, the executive branch of the personality is called the
   a. ego.
   b. superego.
   c. id.
   d. conscience.

5. The moral branch of personality, according to the psychodynamic perspective, is
   a. ego.
   b. superego.
   c. id.
   d. regression.

6. _____ are the ego's protective methods for reducing anxiety by unconsciously distorting reality.
   a. Sublimations
   b. Archetypes
   c. Defense mechanisms
   d. Cardinal traits

7. During the Oedipus complex,
   a. the child enters the anal stage.
   b. the child develops an intense desire to replace the parent of the same sex.
   c. the child represses all interest in sexuality.
   d. the genital stage begins.

8. During what Freudian stage of development does the child focus on social and intellectual skills?
   a. the oral stage
   b. the anal stage
   c. the latency stage
   d. the genital stage

9. Which of the following is not a criticism of Freud's ideas about personality?
    a. Sexuality is not the pervasive underlying force Freud believed it to be.
    b. Experiences after 5 years of age are powerful in shaping adult personality.
    c. Conscious thoughts play little role in our personality.
    d. Sociocultural factors are much more important than Freud argued.

10. If a person tries to conceal her weaknesses in an exaggerated way, she might be showing _____, according to Adler.
    a. overcompensation
    b. compensation
    c. fixation
    d. situationism

11. According to Jung, archetypes
    a. are conscious events.
    b. are responsible for hallucinations and delusions.
    c. are derived from the collective unconscious.
    d. cause inferiority and superiority complexes.

12. Which of the following is NOT one of the archetypes proposed by Carl Jung?
    a. anima (female)
    b. mandala (self)
    c. wheel (technology)
    d. animus (male)

13. The following are criticisms of the psychodynamic perspective, EXCEPT
    a. the perspective is too positive and optimistic.
    b. early life experiences are the most important in determining personality.
    c. the perspective has a largely male, Western bias.
    d. the main concepts of this theory are difficult to test.

Practice Test 2

1. Which of the following accurately list the big five factors of personality?
    a. neuroticism, optimism, conscientiousness, extraversion, agreeableness
    b. hostility, pessimism, neuroticism, self-conscious, conscientiousness
    c. neuroticism, extraversion, openness to experience, agreeableness, conscientiousness
    d. extraversion, conscientiousness, extraversion, archetype, optimism

2. If you are interested in creating a new questionnaire and you begin with a dictionary to see how many words are used to describe what you are interested in, what approach are you taking?
    a. lexical
    b. archetype
    c. psychodynamic
    d. cognitive

3.   The study of the whole person, as outlined by Henry Murray, is
        a.   personality psychology.
        b.   personology.
        c.   psychodynamics.
        d.   behavioral-cognitive approach.

4.   Psychologists who rely on narrative accounts of life experiences are taking what
        approach to studying personality?
        a.   life story approach
        b.   psychodynamic approach
        c.   lexical approach
        d.   humanistic approach

5.   According to Walter Mischel, a key to understanding personality is the concept of
        a.   delay of gratification.
        b.   repression.
        c.   unconditional positive regard.
        d.   central traits.

6.   According to Rogers, acceptance of another person regardless of the person's
        behavior is called
        a.   self-esteem.
        b.   unconditional positive regard.
        c.   self-actualization.
        d.   hierarchy of motives.

7.   Rogers would describe a person who is open to experience, not very defensive, and
        sensitive to others as being
        a.   fixed in the anal stage.
        b.   receiving conditional positive regard.
        c.   a fully functioning person.
        d.   striving for superiority.

8.   Unconditional positive regard and conditions of worth are important
        concepts in
        a.   the behavioral perspective.
        b.   the social cognitive perspective.
        c.   the humanistic perspective.
        d.   trait theory.

9.   Each of the following is considered one of the five main factors in personality except
  a.   extraversion.
  b.   emotional stability.
  c.   agreeableness.
  d.   intellect.

10.   According to the humanistic perspective, which of the following is not consistent with the fully functioning person?
  a.   being very defensive
  b.   being aware of and sensitive to the self
  c.   being sensitive to the external world
  d.   being open to experience

11.   Which of the following perspectives is the most optimistic regarding our ability to control our lives and basically choose our personalities?
  a.   psychodynamic
  b.   behavioral
  c.   humanistic
  d.   social cognitive

12.   According to Rogers, human relations must be based on all the following, EXCEPT
  a.   being a sensitive listener and understanding another's true feelings.
  b.   being open with our feelings and dropping pretenses and facades.
  c.   accepting others as long as they do the things that are considered right in our society.
  d.   unconditional positive regard.

Practice Test 3
1.   What specific component of Type A personality is associated with heart problems?
  a.   competitiveness
  b.   neuroticism
  c.   pessimism
  d.   hostility

2.   The trait of hardiness is:
  a.   really just extraversion.
  b.   characterized by commitment, control, and perceiving problems as challenges.
  c.   characterized by being pretty happy most of the time no matter what happens.
  d.   highly correlated with mental health problems.

3. Which personality theorists would place the most emphasis on cognitive factors
    mediating the environment's effects on the personality?
    a. psychoanalysts
    b. behaviorists
    c. social cognitive theorists
    d. humanists

4. Which of the following stresses the interaction between behavior, environment, and
    person/cognitive variables?
    a. humanistic
    b. psychodynamic
    c. behavioral
    d. social cognitive

5. According to Bandura, the belief that a person has mastery over a situation and the ability
    to produce positive outcomes is called
    a. self-efficacy.
    b. self-esteem.
    c. self-concept.
    d. self-actualization.

6. Which of the following concepts is relevant to the social cognitive perspective of
    personality?
    a. fixation
    b. unconditional positive regard
    c. reciprocal determinism
    d. projective tests

7. Self-efficacy can be increased by
    a. ignoring old successes and focusing on the future.
    b. doing difficult tasks before easier tasks.
    c. doing something that you can expect to be able to do.
    d. choosing new and challenging projects.

8. An individual's belief about whether the outcomes of his actions depend on what he
    does or on events outside of his personal control is referred to as
    a. self-esteem.
    b. self-concept.
    c. delayed gratification.
    d. locus of control.

9. Optimism is associated with all the following, EXCEPT
    a. good physical health.
    b. coming up with stable explanations for bad events.
    c. coming up with external explanations for bad events.
    d. avoidance of depression.

10.   "This is a test of your imagination. I am going to show you some pictures, and I want you to tell me an interesting story about each one. What is happening, how did it develop, and how will it end?" These instructions are part of the preparation for the
a.   Thematic Apperception Test.
b.   Rorschach Inkblot test.
c.   MMPI.
d.   self-report test.

11.   A basic assumption of behavioral assessment is that
a.   the unconscious always influences behavior.
b.   personality cannot be evaluated apart from the environment.
c.   traits are consistent even in varying situations.
d.   personality is inherited.

12.   Which type of personality test is designed to elicit the individual's unconscious feeling?
a.   self-report tests
b.   the MMPI
c.   NEO-PI-R
d.   projective tests

13.   Serena scored very high in optimism on the optimism scale developed by Martin Seligman. She just received a letter from her top-choice university saying that she was not admitted into the freshman class. Serena is likely to come up with the   following explanation for the rejection letter:
a.   I'm not smart enough for that university.
b.   I'll never get into a good school.
c.   This must have been a tough year to get into that university.
d.   I knew I needed better SATs.

14.   One of the main differences between the behavioral and the social cognitive perspectives is that
a.   social cognitive theorists emphasize the extent to which we can control our environments.
b.   behaviorists emphasize reciprocal determinism.
c.   social cognitive theorists focus on unconscious influences on personality.
d.   behaviorists define personality based on how people act, think, and feel.

Answer Key
An Appreciative View of Psychology and Your Life

- Conscientiousness, optimism, personal control, and hardiness (among others) are all traits that have a positive impact on health. Hostility, excessive competitiveness, and pessimism (among others) are all traits that have a negative impact on health.
- Optimism can be learned. When you think pessimistic thoughts, reframe as more optimistic. Increase your sense of personal control, or self-efficacy, by selecting projects that are feasible. Don't ignore your failures, but don't ignore your successes either. Write down when you succeed at something and what you did to succeed, etc.

Practice Test 1 Answers

1.   a.   No; cognition is part of the definition of personality.
     b.   No; these mental processes are also part of the definition of personality.
     c.   No; actions are part of the definition of personality.
     d.   YES; situations is not a concept addressed in the definition of personality.

2.   a.   YES; personality is shaped by unconscious processes.
     b.   No; this sounds too much like the humanistic perspective.
     c.   No; remember that personality is mostly out of awareness.
     d.   No; this option describes the behavioral viewpoint.

3.   a.   YES; the id is dominated by the pleasure principle.
     b.   No; the ego operates according to the reality principle.
     c.   No; the ego operates according to the reality principle.
     d.   No; the superego is often described as being our conscience.

4.   a.   YES; the ego deals with the demands of reality.
     b.   No; the superego is the moral branch of the personality.
     c.   No; the id always seeks pleasure and avoids pain.
     d.   No; this is not one of the three components of personality according to Freud.

5.   a.   No; the ego deals with the demands of reality.
     b.   YES; the superego is the moral branch of the personality.
     c.   No; the id always seeks pleasure and avoids pain.
     d.   No; this is not one of the three components of personality according to Freud.

6.   a.   No; sublimation is an example of a defense mechanism.
     b.   No; archetypes are emotion-laden ideas and images in the collective unconscious.
     c.   YES; this is the definition of defense mechanism.
     d.   No; cardinal traits are a type of trait proposed by Allport.

7.   a.   No; the anal stage occurs earlier.

      b.   YES; the child also has the desire to enjoy the affections of the opposite-sex parent.

      c.   No; this describes the latency stage, which appears following the Oedipus complex.

      d.   No; the genital stage is the fifth Freudian stage, appearing after the Oedipus complex.

8.   a.   No; the mouth is center of pleasure in this stage.

      b.   No; this is associated with pleasure regarding the eliminative function.

      c.   YES; this is related to going to school.

      d.   No; this coincides with puberty, where there is a sexual reawakening.

9.   a.   No; this is a criticism.

      b.   No; this is a criticism.

      c.   YES; in fact, conscious thoughts play a large role in our personality.

      d.   No; this is a criticism.

10.   a.   YES; this is the definition of overcompensation.

      b.   No; the key is that she is trying to conceal her weakness, not trying to overcome.

      c.   No; fixation refers to receiving too much or too little stimulation.

      d.   No; situationism is the notion that personality changes according to the situation.

11.   a.   No; the opposite is true.

      b.   No; they are unrelated to such experiences.

      c.   YES; archetypes are emotion-laden ideas and images from collective unconscious; examples are the anima and the animus.

      d.   No; they are not related to those aspects of personality.

12.   a.   No; this represents our feminine side.

      b.   No; this is a figure within a circle and it has shown up in art through the ages.

      c.   YES; the wheel is a specific technology and this is inconsistent with the concept of collective unconscious.

      d.   No; this represents our masculine side.

13.   a.   YES; this is not a criticism.

      b.   No; this is the position of this theory, for which is has been criticized.

      c.   No; this is one of the criticisms of this perspective.

      d.   No; this is a serious problem with this perspective; if it can't be tested, it can't be supported.

Practice Test 2 Answers

1.   a.   No.

      b.   No.

      c.   Yes, this is the correct listing of the big five traits.

      d.   No.

2.　a.　Yes, if you begin with a dictionary, you are probably taking the lexical approach.
　　b.　No.
　　c.　No.
　　d.　No.

3.　a.　No.
　　b.　Yes, Henry Murray coined the term "personology" to describe the study of the whole person.
　　c.　No.
　　d.　No.

4.　a.　Yes, this is correct.
　　b.　No.
　　c.　No.
　　d.　No.

5.　a.　YES; this refers to the ability to defer immediate gratification for something better in the future.
　　b.　No; repression is an example of a defense mechanism from the psychodynamic view.
　　c.　No; unconditional positive regard is a concept from the humanistic perspective.
　　d.　No; these are traits that are adequate enough to describe someone's personality.

6.　a.　No; self-esteem is the person's overall evaluation of his or her self-worth or self-image.
　　b.　CORRECT
　　c.　No; this term refers to the motivation to develop one's full potential.
　　d.　No; this is a way to order an individual's needs from physiological needs to self-actualization.

7.　a.　No; this pertains to the psychodynamic perspective.
　　b.　No; while Rogers addressed this issue, the question refers to another aspect of his theories.
　　c.　CORRECT; these characterize the fully functioning person.
　　d.　No; this is a concept associated with the work of Adler.

8.　a.　No; the behavioral perspective emphasizes reinforcement.
　　b.　No; this perspective underscores learning and cognitive processes.
　　c.　YES; these are important concepts in the humanistic perspective.
　　d.　No; traits stress broad dispositions that lead to characteristic responses.

9.　a.　No; this is one of the "big five."
　　b.　No; this is one of the "big five."
　　c.　No; this is one of the "big five."
　　d.　YES; this is not among the "big five."

10. a.   YES; this is inconsistent, as the fully functioning person is not very defensive.
     b.   No; this is characteristic of the fully functioning person.
     c.   No; this is characteristic of the fully functioning person.
     d.   No; this is characteristic of the fully functioning person.

11. a.   No; this perspective, it could be argued, is very pessimistic in this respect.
     b.   No; this perspective argues that personality is shaped by the environment, not the individual.
     c.   YES; this perspective views people as being innately good and able to self-actualize.
     d.   No; the reciprocal determinism view characteristic of the social cognitive perspective strikes a compromise between person/cognitive, environmental, and behavioral influences.

12. a.   No; this is the definition of empathy and Rogers considered this very important in human relations.
     b.   No; this is the definition of genuine and Rogers considered this very important in human relations.
     c.   YES; Rogers believed that people should be accepted and valued, even if they did things we didn't like.
     d.   No; this is very important in human relations, according to Rogers.

Practice Test 3 Answers

1.   a.   No, while competitiveness is associated with Type A, it is not the aspect most associated with heart problems.
     b.   No.
     c.   No.
     d.   Yes, hostility is associated with developing heart problems.

2.   a.   No.
     b.   Yes.
     c.   No.
     d.   No.

3.   a.   No; unconscious processes play the primary role in personality for psychoanalysts.
     b.   No; the behaviorists would say that cognitive factors play no role in personality.
     c.   YES; these theorists would say that behavior, environment, and cognitive factors interact with one another.
     d.   No; the humanists stress self-actualization, positive regard, and self-concept.

4.   a.   No; the humanistic perspective stresses personal growth and freedom to choose.
     b.   No; unconscious processes play the primary role in personality for psychoanalysts.
     c.   No; this perspective focuses on the role of the environment in personality.
     d.   CORRECT

5.   a.   CORRECT; this defines self-efficacy, and it is one of the cognitive/person factors.
     b.   No; self-esteem is how we evaluate and feel about our self-concept.
     c.   No; this is an individual's overall perception of ability, behavior, and personality.
     d.   No; this term refers to the motivation to develop one's full potential.

6.   a.   No; this concept is associated with the psychodynamic perspective and the psychosexual stages of development.
     b.   No; this concept is associated with Rogers' humanistic perspective.
     c.   YES; this is a concept proposed by Bandura to describe the way behavior, environment, and cognitive factors interact to create personality.
     d.   No; projective tests measure unconscious influences, and these are not of interest to social cognitive psychologists.

7.   a.   No; to increase self-efficacy, it is recommended that the person consider old successes
     b.   No; to increase self-efficacy, the opposite is recommended.
     c.   YES; to increase self-efficacy, it is recommended that we engage in something at which we know we are likely to succeed.
     d.   No; before doing this, we are advised to do something we know we are able to do.

8.   a.   No; self-esteem is the sense of self-worth that a person has.
     b.   No; self-concept involves the beliefs that a person has about his or her own abilities.
     c.   No; delayed gratification refers to the ability people have to choose how and when their behaviors will be reinforced.
     d.   YES; this concept and the scale to measure it were developed by Julian Rotter.

9.   a.   No; this is associated with optimism; people who had been classified as optimistic at age 25 were healthier at ages 45 to 60 than those classified as pessimistic.
     b.   YES; this is actually consistent with pessimism.
     c.   No; this is consistent with the optimistic explanatory style.
     d.   No; this is one of the positive mental health factors associated with optimism.

10. a. CORRECT; the TAT is made up of pictures that elicit information about personality.
    b. No; this test involves asking individuals what they see in inkblots.
    c. No; the MMPI is a self-report test.
    d. No; these tests directly ask people whether items describe their personality or not.

11. a. No; in fact, this is not assumed in behavioral assessment, but is in psychodynamic.
    b. YES; this is an important assumption of behavioral assessment.
    c. No
    d. No

12. a. No; these tests directly ask people whether items describe their personality or not.
    b. No; the MMPI is an example of self-report test.
    c. No; this is an example of self-report test that assesses the five main factors.
    d. YES; these tests are designed to elicit unconscious feelings.

13. a. No; this is an internal explanation for a bad event, an explanation more characteristic of pessimism.
    b. No; this is a stable explanation ("never") for a bad event.
    c. YES; this is a temporary/unstable explanation for a bad event, likely to be thought of by an optimistic person.
    d. No; this is also an internal explanation for the bad event.

14. a. YES; behaviorists focus only on the effects of the environment, but social cognitive theorists add the aspect of personal control to understanding personality.
    b. No; social cognitive theorists are the ones who emphasize reciprocal determinism.
    c. No; the psychodynamic perspective is the one that focuses on the unconscious.
    d. No; behaviorists focus only on actions.

Chapter 12: Social Psychology

Learning Goals
1. Describe how people think about the social world.
2. Identify how people are influenced in social settings.
3. Discuss intergroup relations.
4. Explain the nature of close relationships.
5. Describe social processes affecting health and wellness.

After studying chapter 12, you will be able to:
- Explain the importance of self-esteem and positive illusions;
- Understand the relationship between empathy and altruism;
- Articulate the role social support plays in physical and mental health.

Chapter Outline
1. Social Cognition
- Social judgments are affected by _____ _____.
- Stereotype: _____ _____
- The power of first impressions is likely due to _____ _____.
- Attribution is _____ _____.
- Attribution theory views people as motivated to _____ _____.
    - o Attributions vary along three dimensions:
        - ▪ _____ _____
        - ▪ _____ _____
        - ▪ _____ _____
- When people commit the fundamental attribution error, they _____ _____ _____.
- The availability heuristic leads to mistakes because _____ _____.
- False consensus effect: _____ _____
- Positive illusions are _____ _____ and are generally possessed by _____.
- Self-serving bias: _____ _____

- Self-objectification refers to the tendency to _____ _____.

- Stereotype threat: _____ _____

  - o   Example: _____ _____ _____

- Social comparison is the process by which _____ _____.

  - o   Downward social comparison is _____ _____.

- Attitudes are _____ _____.

  - o   Attitudes can predict behavior when:

    - ▪ _____ _____

    - ▪ _____ _____

    - ▪ _____ _____

    - ▪ _____ _____

- Cognitive dissonance was developed by _____ (name) and is _____ _____.

  - o   Cognitive dissonance can be reduced by _____ _____ or _____ _____.

- Effort justification: _____ _____

- Self- perception theory reflects ideas about _____ _____ _____.

- The following are factors in persuasion and attitude change:
  - o   _____

    - ▪ Example: _____ _____ _____

  - o   _____

    - ▪ Example: _____ _____ _____

  - o   _____ _____

- Example: _____

  _____

  _____

  o _____

  _____

  - Example: _____

    _____

    _____

  o The elaboration likelihood model explains _____

    _____.

    - Central route: _____

      _____

    - Peripheral route: _____

      _____

2. Social Behavior

- Altruism: _____

  _____

- Egoism: _____

  _____

- Empathy happens when _____

  _____ and can produce _____

  _____.

- Bystander effect: _____

  _____

  o Example: _____

    _____

    _____

- The following are examples of different factors in aggression:
  o Biological influences:
    - Evolution: _____

      _____

    - Genes: _____

      _____

    - Neurobiological: _____

      _____

      _____

      _____

      _____

  o Psychological factors:
    - Frustration: _____

      _____

    - Cognitive: _____

      _____

    - Observational: _____

      _____

  o Sociocultural:

- Cultural variations: _____
    _____
    _____
    _____

- Media: _____
    _____
    _____
    _____

  o Gender: _____
    _____

3. Social Influence
- Conformity: _____
    _____

    o Example: _____
    _____
    _____

- Asch's conformity experiment found that _____
    _____
    _____
    _____.

- A confederate is _____
    _____.

- Informational social influence refers to _____
    _____.

- Normative social influence refers to _____
    _____.

- Obedience: _____
    _____

    o Milgram's study found that _____
    _____
    _____
    _____

- Deindividuation occurs when _____
    _____.

- Social contagion is _____
    _____.

- Social facilitation occurs when _____
    _____.

- Social loafing refers to _____
    _____.

- Group decision making involves the following aspects:
    o Risky shift: _____
    _____

    o Group polarization effect: _____
    _____

- o Groupthink: _____
  _____

  - ▪ Example: _____
    _____
    _____

  - ▪ Symptoms of groupthink include _____
    _____
    _____.

  - ▪ Groupthink can be prevented by _____
    _____
    _____.

4. Intergroup Relations

- Social identity refers to _____
  _____.

  - o It differs from personal identity because _____
    _____.

- Social identity theory states that _____
  _____.

  - o In-group: _____
  - o Out-group: _____
- Ethnocentrism: _____
  _____.

- Prejudice: _____
  _____.

- Explicit racism: _____
  _____

- Implicit racism: _____
  _____

  - o It is measured by _____
    _____.

  - o Breaking down racism into explicit/implicit is necessary because _____
    _____
    _____.

- Prejudice can develop for the following reasons:
  - o _____
    - ▪ Example: _____
      _____
  - o _____
    - ▪ Example: _____
      _____
  - o _____
    - ▪ Example: _____
      _____
  - o _____
    - ▪ Example: _____
      _____

- Discrimination is _____
  _____.

- Interethnic relations can be improved by:
  - _____
  - _____

5. Close Relationships

- Mere exposure effect means that _____
  _____.

- Consensual validation explains why _____
  _____.
  - We generally prefer to be around other people who _____
    _____.

- The evolutionary perspective shows that in mating men focus on _____
  _____ whereas women focus on _____
  _____.

- The difference between romantic love and affectionate love is _____
  _____
  _____
  _____
  _____.

- Social exchange theory states that _____
  _____.

- Adult attachment styles:
  - _____
    _____
    _____
    _____
  - _____
    _____
    _____
    _____
  - _____
    _____
    _____
    _____

- Investment model: _____

6. Social Psychology and Health and Wellness

- Social isolation and mortality are related in that _____
  _____
  _____.

- Social support is important and comes in the following forms:
  - _____
    _____
    _____
  - _____
    _____
    _____

   o _____

      _____

      _____

      _____

- The following are some ways to counteract loneliness and become better connected with other people:

   o _____

      _____

   o _____

      _____

   o _____

      _____

   o _____

      _____

Critical Controversy

- Craig Anderson's research found that, in the laboratory, playing violent video games is associated with _____.

Intersection

- _____ (type of self-esteem) is most related to aggression.

Clarifying Tricky Points

Definitions

You probably noticed while reading chapter 12 that there are a lot of keywords. Social psychology is a big area and there is a lot to learn about it. Each keyword represents a key theory or phenomenon, so it is important to learn them all. Take some time while studying and write a list of all the keywords (many are already included in the chapter outline). Next challenge yourself to write a definition for each keyword. Use this study guide to then focus on the definitions you couldn't come up with or got mixed up.

Attitudes and behavior

In the last chapter on personality, you learned how traits and situations can predict behavior. Social psychology, however, is more interested in whether or not attitudes predict behavior. Your parents may have told you "Do as I say, not as I do," which implies people's attitudes don't always predict their behaviors. But, generally speaking, attitudes are a pretty good predictor of behavior, particularly when a person's attitudes are strong and relevant to the behavior, and when the issue is important to the person. Sometimes, however, attitudes and behaviors don't match up, in which case the person is likely to experience cognitive dissonance, and either the attitude or behavior must change in order to relieve the dissonance.

Different types of racism

It's not a very controversial statement to say racism exists in America. But if a scientist is interested in researching racism and asks people on a questionnaire "Are you racist?" nearly everybody would say "No," because it is no longer socially acceptable to be racist. Yet people are treated unfairly due to the color of their skin, so some people out there must be racist. This observation led social psychologists to distinguish between explicit racism and implicit racism.

Explicit racism is how racist you say you are, and is a good predictor of what you say to people in minority groups. Implicit racism is more subtle and more difficult to measure because it's not how racist you say you are, rather it is measured by a sophisticated technique that surreptitiously measures the extent to which you feel positively or negatively towards people of a different race. Implicit racism is a good predictor of how closely you will sit next to someone of a different race and your facial expressions towards the person.

An Appreciative View of Psychology and Your Life

Having friends is important for your health and well-being. Friends provide us with social support, which is basically feedback from others, assuring you that you are loved and valued as a person. It's just as important to give social support as it is to receive social support. Think back to a time when a friend of yours was struggling and you offered some social support. As you learned in chapter 12, social support has three different types of benefits. What type of social support did you offer and how?

_____

_____

Now describe, based on the research outlined in your textbook, how the social support you provided helped your friend physically and psychologically.

_____

_____

_____

_____

Practice Test 1

1.   What are the three dimensions that are used in the attributions people make?
       a.   internal or external, stable or unstable, and controllable or uncontrollable
       b.   internal or external, primary or secondary, and chronic or acute
       c.   stable or unstable, controllable or uncontrollable, and primary or secondary
       d.   stable or unstable, primary or secondary, and interpersonal or intrapersonal

2.   Which of the following most clearly illustrates an internal attribution?
       a.   John believes his sister plays the piano to make a good impression on others.
       b.   Larry believes that his father is hostile because of the difficulties at work.
       c.   Maria believes Rob gossips about others because of a mean and spiteful streak.
       d.   Diane believes her son lies to her to avoid possible punishment.

3.   Which of the following is not a component of social perception?
       a.   developing impressions of others
       b.   gaining self-knowledge from our perceptions of others
       c.   presenting ourselves to others to influence them
       d.   trying to persuade someone to change their attitudes

4. Which of the following is true of individuals experiencing cognitive dissonance?
   a. They show an inability to make up their mind.
   b. They have lost their sense of self and the ability to make decisions.
   c. They are preoccupied with how they are perceived by others.
   d. They are experiencing a conflict between their attitudes and behavior.

5. People are interested in discovering the causes of behavior, according to
   a. cognitive dissonance.
   b. self-perception theory.
   c. attribution theory.
   d. catharsis.

6. "Whenever I do well on an exam, it is because I studied hard. Whenever I do poorly on an exam, it is because the test was unfair." This demonstrates
   a. the fundamental attribution error.
   b. implicit personality.
   c. prototypes.
   d. the self-serving bias.

7. "First impressions are lasting impressions" according to
   a. the primacy effect.
   b. the latency effect.
   c. attribution theory.
   d. the social comparison theory.

8. _____ are beliefs or opinions about people, objects, and ideas.
   a. Attributions
   b. Altruisms
   c. Stereotypes
   d. Attitudes

9. Our own attitudes and behavior are supported when another's attitudes and behavior are similar to ours, according to
   a. the matching hypothesis.
   b. consensual validation.
   c. altruism.
   d. cognitive dissonance.

10. It's the first day of classes and your professor just fell flat on her back as she was walking into the classroom. Considering the fundamental attribution error, which of the following attributions is most likely to be shared by the students in the class?
    a. "The floor must have been slippery."
    b. "It's the first day of classes, these things happen."
    c. "The professor is clumsy."
    d. "Someone must have startled her."

11.   If we asked each member of a married couple what percentage of housework each does, and one says 75% and the other says 60%, we are seeing evidence of
    a.   prejudice.
    b.   the self-serving bias.
    c.   stereotyping.
    d.   romantic love.

12.   Raoul is a young African-American college student. According to Leon Festinger's theory of social comparison, when Raoul evaluates himself, he is more likely to compare himself to
    a.   a young causasian college student.
    b.   an older African-American female.
    c.   another African-American male.
    d.   an adult college student.

Practice Test 2
1.   Conformity is lowest
    a.   when group opinion is unanimous.
    b.   among individuals with low self-esteem.
    c.   if group members are experts.
    d.   when there are dissenters in the group.

2.   The type of social influence that involves seeking approval or avoiding disapproval is called
    a.   obedience.
    b.   social facilitation.
    c.   informational social influence.
    d.   normative social influence.

3.   In Milgram's research, it was discovered that obedience decreased
    a.   as people were paid more to participate.
    b.   when the authority figure was perceived to be legitimate.
    c.   when the authority figure was close by.
    d.   when the victim was made to seem more human.

4.   Omar is frustrated because there are people in his committee who are just not pulling their weight and doing their assigned tasks. This lack of effort is called
    a.   social loafing.
    b.   social facilitation.
    c.   deindividuation.
    d.   groupthink.

5. Tajfel's social identity theory provides an explanation for
    a. prejudice.
    b. the risky shift.
    c. group leadership.
    d. social loafing.

6. If Simone changes her behavior to better fit with a group standard, then _____ is said to have occurred.
    a. obedience
    b. conformity
    c. groupthink
    d. ethnocentrism

7. When individuals make decisions on their own, their decisions tend to be more conservative than the decision they will agree to in a group. The tendency for a group's decision to be more daring is called
    a. deindividuation.
    b. emergent boldness.
    c. disinhibition.
    d. the risky shift.

8. Don was in need of help on a very busy highway. No one stopped to help. No one accepted responsibility, since everyone assumed that someone else would stop. This is best explained by
    a. the bystander effect.
    b. risky shift.
    c. groupthink.
    d. the matching hypothesis.

9. Which of the following situations is more likely to lead to conformity?
    a. a group that has dissenters
    b. a group in which some members established a commitment to their attitudes before joining the group
    c. if there is a lot of diversity in the group
    d. if the group members are from a collectivistic culture

10. When the man is expected to open the door for a woman, this is referred to as
    a. the norms of the group.
    b. the roles in the group.
    c. consummate love.
    d. affectionate love.

11. According to social facilitation theory, when we are good at something, our performance is _____ in the presence of others. Also, when we are not so good at something, our performance is _____ in the presence of others.
    a. impaired; impaired
    b. enhanced; enhanced
    c. enhanced; impaired
    d. impaired; enhanced

12. Which of the following individuals is least likely to engage in social loafing when assigned to a group project in a class?
    a. a Chinese female
    b. an American female
    c. a French male
    d. a Japanese male

13. Terrorist organizations are likely to attract individuals who share a common bias, such as dislike of government. Once these individuals join a group, their ideas become more extreme. Which of the following social factors better explains this tendency?
    a. impression management
    b. group polarization
    c. minority influence
    d. leadership

Practice Test 3
1. Research on improved interethnic relations in shared facilities disregards placing importance on
    a. task-oriented cooperation.
    b. the jigsaw classroom.
    c. intimate contact.
    d. competition.

2. Which of the following statements about research on gender differences in aggression is incorrect?
    a. Males are more aggressive than females in all cultures.
    b. More aggression by males than females is found in animals as well as humans.
    c. Males are found to be more aggressive than females as early as two years of age.
    d. In verbal aggression, no differences are found between adult males and females.

3. The matching hypothesis of attraction states that
    a. individuals prefer a person more attractive than themselves.
    b. individuals are uncomfortable around attractive people.
    c. individuals choose someone close to their level of attractiveness.
    d. in enduring relationships, physical attractiveness becomes more important.

4. Why does intimate contact tend to facilitate interethnic relations?
    a. It allows people to discover their similarities.
    b. It allows people to confirm their stereotypes.
    c. It encourages people to re-categorize others.
    d. It reinforces ethnic and cultural differences.

5. What do behavioral and social cognitive theorists argue about the cause of aggression?
    a. Aggression is biologically based.
    b. Aggression is the result of unconscious needs that go unmet.
    c. Aggression is learned through observational learning and reinforcement.
    d. Aggression is the result of frustration.

6. What is the unselfish interest in helping someone else called?
    a. agonist
    b. egoism
    c. altruism
    d. catharsis

7. Ken and Barbie have a love relationship characterized by passion, intimacy, and commitment. According to Sternberg, this is called
    a. a temporary situation.
    b. romantic love.
    c. consummate love.
    d. affectionate love.

8. According to social identity theory, prejudice occurs because
    a. people identify the other group as evil.
    b. people have a hard time connecting to their groups.
    c. people want to achieve self-esteem through their group identity.
    d. people do not trust the members of their own group, therefore they trust those in another group even less.

9. Prejudice
    a. is less likely in a person with an authoritarian personality.
    b. can be caused by competition between groups.
    c. is limited by our social cognitive processes.
    d. is innate.

10. Stereotype is to _____ as discrimination is to _____.
    a. attitude; cognition
    b. cognition; attitude
    c. behavior; cognition
    d. cognition; behavior

11.   A good strategy to promote collaboration is
        a.   assigning different tasks to each group member that he or she must share with the group.
        b.   bringing people of different backgrounds to work together in a project.
        c.   creating a social-oriented situation, in which the group members first have to get along before they can proceed with the task.
        d.   discouraging intimate contact between the group members.

12.   Aggression is less likely if
        a.   an undesirable stimulus is unexpected.
        b.   an undesirable stimulus was intentionally delivered.
        c.   receiving an undesirable stimulus is perceived as unfair.
        d.   an undesirable stimulus was caused by a source that was not completely in control.

13.   Which of the following clichés has been supported by the research in interpersonal attraction?
        a.   opposites attract
        b.   birds of a feather flock together
        c.   killing two birds with one stone
        d.   time flies

Answer Key
An Appreciative View of Psychology and Your Life
- Social support can provide tangible assistance, information, and/or emotional support.
- Social support helps people cope with stress and can buffer against depression, anxiety, and loss of self-esteem. Social support can also provide information about how to better manage your time or how to study harder for the next exam, etc. Perhaps, most importantly, having supportive friends around is associated with greater longevity.

Practice Test 1 Answers
1.   a.   YES; these are the dimensions of attributions.
        b.   No; these concepts do not correspond to the dimensions of attributions.
        c.   No; these concepts do not correspond to the dimensions of attributions.
        d.   No; these concepts do not correspond to the dimensions of attributions.

2.   a.   No; John is attributing his sister's playing to some external factor.
        b.   No; Larry is attributing his father's hostility to some external factor.
        c.   YES; Maria is attributing Rob's behavior to a personality or disposition.
        d.   No; Diane is attributing her son's lying to an external factor.

3.   a.   No; this is part of social perception.
        b.   No; this is part of social perception.
        c.   No; this is part of social perception.
        d.   YES; this is another aspect of our social behaviors but does not fall under social perception.

4. a. No; cognitive dissonance contributes to their making up their mind.
    b. No; cognitive dissonance is a normal phenomenon not associated with losing a sense of self.
    c. No; this sounds like a very high level of self-monitoring.
    d. YES; we are motivated to reduce the dissonance caused by inconsistency.

5. a. No; this is the motivation to reduce the discomfort caused by inconsistent thoughts.
    b. No; this theory says that we make inferences about our own attitudes by perceiving our behavior.
    c. YES; attributions are explanations for behavior.
    d. No; this is the release of anger by directly engaging in anger or aggression.

6. a. No; this is the tendency to overestimate the importance of traits and underestimate the importance of the situations when explaining someone's behavior.
    b. No; implicit personality refers to how a layperson understands how traits go together.
    c. No; these are abstract categorizations of traits that describe a particular personality type.
    d. YES; we attribute successes to internal factors and failures to external factors.

7. a. YES; the primacy effect refers to the tendency to remember initial information.
    b. No; the latency effect refers to the tendency to remember information that is presented later.
    c. No; attribution theory describes how we explain behavior.
    d. No; this theory describes how we compare our thoughts and behaviors to other people.

8. a. No; attributions are the suspected underlying causes of behavior.
    b. No; altruism is an unselfish interest in helping someone else.
    c. No; stereotypes are generalizations about a group's characteristics that ignore individual variation.
    d. YES; this is the definition of attitudes.

9. a. No; this refers to the tendency to select others who have similar level of attractiveness as we do.
    b. YES; others' attitudes and behaviors validate our attitudes and behaviors.
    c. No; altruism is unselfish interest in helping others.
    d. No; cognitive dissonance refers to differences in attitudes within the person, not between people.

10.   a.   No; this is an external attribution.
       b.   No; this is also an external attribution.
       c.   YES; this is an internal attribution for the professor's behavior.
       d.   No; this is an external attribution.

11.   a.   No; the opinions of married couples about house chores do not involve prejudice.
       b.   YES; clearly both partners believe that they are doing more than what they are in fact doing, since 75% and 60% add up to a lot more than 100% of the housework; they are exaggerating their positive beliefs about themselves.
       c.   No; this scenario does not involve stereotyping.
       d.   No; this question is not addressing the level of love that this married couple is experiencing.

12.   a.   No; the ethnic difference would probably make this comparison not very informative for Raoul.
       b.   No; as in item a, there are many differences between Raoul and this person, therefore the comparison would not be as informative.
       c.   YES; while age or education have not been specified, this is the one option that presents most similarity with Raoul and thus he is more likely to obtain an accurate appraisal from that comparison.
       d.   No; this person may not share much in common with Raoul.

Practice Test 2 Answers

1.   a.   No; this contributes to conformity.
       b.   No; this contributes to conformity.
       c.   No; this contributes to conformity.
       d.   YES; when the opinions are not unanimous, conformity decreases.

2.   a.   No; obedience is behavior that complies with an authority figure's explicit orders.
       b.   No; this describes an individual's performance that improves in the presence of others.
       c.   No; this is social influence that involves the desire to be right.
       d.   YES; we conform in order to be liked and accepted by others.

3.   a.   No; this was not an issue in the experimental procedure.
       b.   No; this tends to increase obedience.
       c.   No; this tends to increase obedience.
       d.   YES; this encouraged disobedience.

4. a. YES; social loafing occurs when individuals do not expend much effort when in a group because of reduced monitoring.
    b. No; this describes how an individual's performance improves in the presence of others.
    c. No; deindividuation refers to a lost of identity when in the presence of a group.
    d. No; this describes how groups make poor decisions.

5. a. YES; we tend to think of our group as an in-group and other groups as out-groups.
    b. No; social identity theory does not address this social phenomenon.
    c. No; social identity theory does not address this social phenomenon.
    d. No; social identity theory does not address this social phenomenon.

6. a. No; obedience is behavior that complies with explicit demands of an authority.
    b. YES; this is the definition of conformity, and it can take many different forms.
    c. No; groupthink is the tendency of groups to make impaired decisions.
    d. No; this refers to the tendency to favor one's own group over other groups.

7. a. No; deindividuation refers to a lost of identity when in the presence of a group.
    b. Incorrect
    c. Incorrect
    d. YES; this is the definition of the risky shift.

8. a. YES; the presence of others reduces the chance that any one person will help.
    b. No; groups tend to make more risky choices.
    c. No; groupthink refers to impaired decision making in a group.
    d. No; this refers to the tendency we have to choose someone who is close to our own level of attractiveness.

9. a. No; this means that there is not unanimity and this reduces conformity.
    b. No; being committed to an attitude makes it harder for people to conform to a different attitude in the group.
    c. No; the more similar the group members, the higher the conformity.
    d. YES; collectivistic cultures encourage conformity.

10. a. No; norms are the rules that apply to all group members.
    b. YES; this question presents roles for the man and the woman that are different within the group/couple.
    c. No; the question does not address love.
    d. No; the question does not address love.

11. a. Incorrect
     b. Incorrect
     c. YES; when we are good and skilled at something, doing it in the presence of others actually facilitates and enhances our performance; however, if we are new at what we are doing, having to do it in front of others actually impairs our performance.
     d. Incorrect; the opposite is true.

12. a. YES; this person has two characteristics that make her less likely to engage in social loafing: she is a female and she is from a collectivistic culture.
     b. No; while this person is a female, she is also from an individualistic culture.
     c. No; this is the most likely to engage in social loafing, a male from an individualistic culture.
     d. No; while this person is from a collectivistic culture, he is also a male.

13. a. No; impression management is not a group dynamic.
     b. YES; group polarization is the tendency for an original bias to become strengthened and in some cases more extreme.
     c. No; in groups where people share a bias, it is not likely for there to be a minority influence; basically, there is no minority in such groups.
     d. No; while leadership can play a role in the development of terrorist organizations, this question does not address that factor.

Practice Test 3 Answers

1. a. No; this contributes to interethnic relations.
    b. No; the jigsaw classroom requires that all individuals make contributions, which aids interethnic relations.
    c. No; intimate contact allows others to see people as individuals and contributes to interethnic relations.
    d. YES; competition does not contribute to interethnic relations.

2. a. No; this is a correct statement.
    b. No; this is a correct statement.
    c. No; this is a correct statement.
    d. YES; the type of aggression is important to consider when examining gender differences in aggression (females tend to display more verbal aggression).

3. a. No; this may be true in the abstract, but it is not the matching hypothesis.
    b. No; this may be true, but it does not summarize the matching hypothesis.
    c. YES; we choose others who are close to our own level of attractiveness.
    d. No; in fact, attractiveness becomes less important.

4. a. YES; we discover that there is more similarity with the out-group than difference.
    b. No; this would tend to deteriorate interethnic relations.
    c. No; this would reinforce our perceptions of an in-group and out-group.
    d. No; this could reinforce stereotypes and encourage prejudice.

5. a. No; this sounds like the view that ethologists take.
    b. No; a psychoanalyst would adopt this argument.
    c. YES; social learning focuses on the role of observational learning and reinforcement.
    d. No; this is most consistent with the frustration-aggression hypothesis.

6. a. No; this is a type of drug (from Chapter 3).
    b. No; this is selfish.
    c. YES; altruism is unselfish, no gains are expected.
    d. No; this is a way of releasing aggression.

7. a. No; this is not a type of love.
    b. No; Ken and Barbie seem to share more than romantic love.
    c. YES; consummate love includes passion, intimacy, and commitment.
    d. No; affectionate love includes intimacy and commitment.

8. a. No; social identity theory did not address such attributions.
    b. No; actually identifying with a group seems to be very easy.
    c. YES; this is the main postulate of this theory.
    d. No; actually, people favor the people in their group, even when the reasons they are together in a group are meaningless.

9. a. No; the opposite is true.
    b. YES; competition over valued resources tends to breed prejudice.
    c. No; actually, some of our social cognitive processes tend to contribute to prejudice, such as our tendency to categorize people into groups to facilitate our management of social information.
    d. No; prejudice is an attitude and attitudes are learned; however, the roots of prejudice may have some innate/evolutionary basis.

10. a. No; prejudice is an attitude, and stereotypes are cognitions.
    b. No; while stereotypes are cognitions, discrimination is not an attitude.
    c. No; the opposite is true.
    d. YES; stereotypes are thoughts and discrimination is an action.

11. a. YES; this is the basic idea in the jigsaw approach to cooperation and integration in classrooms.
    b. No; diversity will not, by itself, lead to collaboration.
    c. No; creating a task-oriented situation may be better to foster collaboration.
    d. No; on the contrary, intimate contact should be encouraged.

12.   a.   No; when we don't expect an aversive action, we tend to react more aggressively.

          b.   No; if we perceive that the person intended to harm us, we do tend to respond more aggressively.

          c.   No; if receiving an aversive action is perceived as not fair or justified, that increases aggression.

          d.   YES; if the source is not perceived as completely responsible or not in control of the undesirable stimulus, our aggression is lowered.

13.   a.   No; the opposite is true.

          b.   YES; similarity says that we tend to associate with people who are similar to us.

          c.   Incorrect

          d.   Incorrect

Chapter 13: Industrial and Organization Psychology

Learning Goals
1. Discuss the roots and evolution of industrial and organizational psychology.
2. Describe the perspective and emphases of industrial psychology.
3. Identify the main focus of organizational psychology and describe some important business factors that organizational researchers have studied.
4. Define organizational culture and describe factors relating to positive and negative workplace environments.
5. Name some common sources of job-related stress and cite strategies for coping with stress in the workplace.

After studying chapter 13, use the space below to list the top 3 most interesting things you learned that help you appreciate I/O psychology more.

- _____
- _____
- _____

Chapter Outline
1. Origins of Industrial and Organizational Psychology
- Scientific management: _____
  _____
  _____

  - Taylor's guidelines:
    - _____
      _____
    - _____
      _____
    - _____
      _____
    - _____
      _____

- Ergonomics: _____
  _____

- The Hawthorne studies found:
  - _____
  - _____
  - _____
- Hawthorne effect: _____
  _____

- Major implication of the Hawthorne studies was _____
  _____

- Human relations approach: _____
  _____

2. Industrial Psychology

- Industrial psychology: _____
  _____

- Job analysis: _____
  _____

  - ○ Three critical elements:
    - ▪ _____
    - ▪ _____
    - ▪ _____
  - ○ Two types: _____
    _____
    - ▪ KSA: _____
      _____

- ADA: _____
  _____

- Job evaluation: _____
  _____

- Testing: (Use space below to outline the importance and methods of testing.)
  - ○ _____
  - ○ _____
  - ○ _____
  - ○ _____
  - ○ _____
  - ○ _____

- Orientation: _____
  _____

- Training: _____
  _____
  - ○ _____
    _____

- Mentoring: _____
  _____

- Performance appraisal: (Use space below to outline methods and biases in appraisal.)
  - ○ _____
  - ○ _____
  - ○ _____

○ _____

_____

○ _____

_____

- Organizational citizenship behavior: _____

_____

   ○ Example: _____

_____

3. Organizational Psychology

- Organizational psychology: _____

_____

   ○ Different from industrial psychology because _____

_____

_____.

- Management: (Use the space below to outline all approaches to management. Be sure to include W. E. Deming, Theories X and Y, waigawa, D. Clifton, and strengths-based management.)

   ○ _____

_____

     ■ _____

_____

   ○ _____

_____

     ■ _____

_____

   ○ _____

_____

     ■ _____

_____

   ○ _____

_____

     ■ _____

_____

- Job satisfaction: _____

_____

   ○ Measurement: _____

_____

   ○ Factors related to job satisfaction:

     ■ _____

     ■ _____

     ■ _____

   ○ Cultural differences: _____

_____

_____

- Employee commitment: (Use the space below to define each type of commitment and provide examples.)
  - _____
    _____
    - _____
      _____
  - _____
    _____
    - _____
      _____
  - _____
    _____
    - _____
      _____

- Three different ways to think about an occupation:
  - _____
    _____
  - _____
    _____
  - _____
  - "Calling" is unique because _____
    _____
    _____.

- Job crafting: _____
  _____

- Leadership (Describe transactional and the four elements of transformational.)
  - _____
    _____
    - _____
      _____
  - _____
    _____
    - _____
    - _____
    - _____
    - _____

- Organizational identity: _____
  _____.

4. Organizational Culture

- _____
  _____

- Four types:
  - _____
    _____

- o _____
  _____
- o _____
  _____
- o _____
  _____

- Factors contributing to a positive culture:
  - o _____
  - o _____
  - o _____
- Factors contributing to a negative culture:
  - o _____
  - o Sexual harassment: _____
    - Related to:
      - _____
      - _____
      - _____
      - _____
    - Two types:
      - _____
        _____
      - Example: _____
        _____
      - _____
        _____
      - Example: _____
        _____
  - o Workplace violence: _____
    _____
    - _____
      _____
      _____

5. I/O Psychology and Health and Wellness
- Role conflict: _____
  _____
- Things associated with job stress:
  - o _____
  - o _____
  - o _____
  - o _____
  - o _____
  - o _____
- Ways to manage stress:
  - o _____
  - o _____

○ _____

○ _____

- Flow: _____

  _____

Critical Controversy

- On one hand, _____

  _____.

- But on the other hand, _____

  _____.

- I think _____

  _____.

Intersection

- Personality psychology has identified the following important things related to I/O psychology:

    ○ _____

    ○ _____

    ○ _____

    ○ _____

Clarifying Tricky Points

The difference between the I and the O of I/O psychology

Industrial and organization (I/O) psychology are almost always talked about together but they are actually two distinct areas of psychology, each with a different focus. Basically, industrial psychology focuses on the company whereas organizational focuses on the person. Industrial psychology spends time evaluating how the company can perform more efficiently, create more precise job descriptions, testing and interview procedures that are most likely to find the best candidate, and how to train and evaluate employees. Organizational psychology, conversely, spends more time trying to find the best way for managers to interact with their workers to enhance job satisfaction and commitment to the organization. Leadership and citizenship are also important areas of organizational psychology.

Conclusions of the Hawthorne studies

The Hawthorne studies are considered landmark studies in the field of I/O psychology. When they were first conducted, the researchers concluded that employees will perform better if management pays attention to them and makes them feel important. Things like ideal lighting and comfortable chairs aren't as important as just being made to feel special. But these studies were conducted in the late 1920s, and since then several researchers have gone back to the data and drawn some different conclusions. Most notably, during the time of the Hawthorne studies the Great Depression occurred. During the Great Depression jobs were scarce and money scarcer so all people worked harder, regardless of the delicate experimental manipulations employed by the researchers of the Hawthorne studies. Would the same effects originally described in the Hawthorne studies be found if the study were conducted during the 1990s (a relatively stable and positive economic period)? It's hard to know, but one conclusion of the Hawthorne studies that is still with us today is that, as companies spend more time on micro-level aspects of a job, such as nit-picking over efficiency, the more workers feel alienated from the job they are doing, the people they work with, and the company they work for.

The relationship between job satisfaction and pay

Most college students look forward to the fact that their degree will help them make more money. Money is obviously important and today's modern life is expensive. But does more money mean more satisfaction? When it comes to your job, the answer is no. Research has found that people can make minimum wage and be satisfied with their job or they can make $500,000 and be dissatisfied with their job. More important than amount of pay is the perception that your pay is fair. It is also important for job satisfaction that you feel a sense of social support and have opportunities for advancement. Your general emotional disposition is also important.

An Appreciative View of Psychology and Your Life

In this chapter you learned that there are different ways to view your occupation. You can view it as a job, career, or calling. Viewing your occupation as a calling has many benefits but can everybody hear a "calling"? Maybe, maybe not, but it is important to realize that a "calling" doesn't need to be something as extreme as hearing a supreme being "call" you into a ministry or something deep inside your soul that compels you to join the Peace Corps and save Africa. You can transform almost any job into a calling by making relatively small changes in perception and the way you do your job.

Describe the benefits to viewing an occupation as a calling?

_____
_____
_____
_____
_____

Describe how you can transform your job, or a job you have previously held or will hold in the future, into a calling and reap the benefits you described above.

_____
_____
_____
_____
_____

Practice Test 1

1.   The managerial philosophy that focuses on efficiency and the worker as a "well-oiled machine" is
      a.   industrial psychology.
      b.   scientific management.
      c.   Theory Y.
      d.   Hawthorne approach.

2. Ergonomics are
    a. human factors studied by combining engineering and psychology.
    b. the scientific approach to the work place.
    c. only important in manufacturing jobs.
    d. an advanced interview technique.

3. In the Hawthorn studies on room lighting,
    a. only the group with the most light showed increased performance.
    b. the group with the least light showed increased performance.
    c. no group showed good performance.
    d. both groups showed increased performance.

4. The tendency to perform better just because you are made to feel important is called the
    a. Hawthorne effect.
    b. KSA.
    c. integrity.
    d. halo effect.

5. To endorse a human relations approach is to
    a. stress the importance of efficiency.
    b. stress factors such as morale and values.
    c. endorse the idea of scientific management.
    d. be a Theory X manager.

6. _____ psychology focuses on the company and the efficient use of resources.
    a. Organizational
    b. I/O
    c. Industrial
    d. Social

7. Job analysis is essentially
    a. a job description.
    b. a performance review.
    c. an interview.
    d. related to waigawa.

8. KSAOs or KSAs are associated with
    a. a job oriented description.
    b. waigawa.
    c. a person-oriented job analysis.
    d. ergonomics.

9.   Aspects of a job that are desirable but not necessary are
        a.   nonessential functions.
        b.   essential functions.
        c.   human factors.
        d.   KSAs.

10.   The Americans with Disabilities Act (ADA) mandates that people cannot be denied a job
        due to their inability to complete
        a.   essential functions.
        b.   KSAs.
        c.   an interview.
        d.   nonessential functions.

11.   The act of scientifically evaluating the monetary value of a job is _____ and relies
        on _____.
        a.   a job analysis; compensable factors
        b.   a job evaluation; compensable factors
        c.   a job analysis; non-compensable factors
        d.   a job evaluation; non-compensable factors

12.   If an interviewer asks "Do you think white lies are okay?" they might be conducting a(n)
        a.   360-degree interview.
        b.   biographical inventory.
        c.   integrity test.
        d.   Hawthorne test.

13.   If a colleague says to you "Oh, I always know if an applicant is telling the truth just by
        feeling them out," they are likely exhibiting the
        a.   interviewer illusion.
        b.   halo effect.
        c.   Hawthorne effect.
        d.   strengths-based approach.

14.   The process of asking specific questions that methodically seek useful information is
        a.   biographical inventory.
        b.   integrity test.
        c.   overlearning.
        d.   a structured interview.

15.   Training that tries to make a skill automatic is
        a.   overlearning.
        b.   ergonomics.
        c.   Theory Y.
        d.   operant conditioning.

Practice Test 2

1. If Carolina is nice and gets along well with her coworkers, and on a performance evaluation her supervisor Karem gives her high marks on everything, Karem has just exhibited
    a. the Hawthorne effect.
    b. the halo effect.
    c. the overlearning effect.
    d. classical conditioning.

2. When a performance review seeks information from supervisors, coworkers, and clients, it is an example of
    a. biographical inventory.
    b. structured interview.
    c. 360 degree feedback.
    d. scientific management

3. Organizational citizenship refers to
    a. an employee's actions that promote the company but aren't required.
    b. voting.
    c. being nice to co-workers.
    d. tedious jobs people don't want to do, but must.

4. _____ psychology emphasizes the psychological factors of the worker.
    a. Industrial
    b. I/O
    c. Personality
    d. Organizational

5. The Japanese management style is best characterized by a focus on
    a. efficiency.
    b. well-being.
    c. quality.
    d. thinking outside the box.

6. Theory X managers assume
    a. that work is enjoyable.
    b. that work is innately unpleasant.
    c. that a job is a calling.
    d. that waigawa is necessary.

7. Theory Y managers assume
    a. that working hard is natural to humans.
    b. that work is innately unpleasant.
    c. that "callings" aren't real.
    d. human relations waste company time.

8.   When any employee, from the assembly line all the way to the executive board room, can approach the CEO with new ideas, this is an example of what type of system?
    a.   Theory X.
    b.   Theory Y.
    c.   Japanese.
    d.   waigawa.

9.   If a manager seeks to find unique talents in each employee and puts them to good use, the manager is probably employing the _____ approach.
    a.   strengths based
    b.   Theory X
    c.   Theory Y
    d.   Japanese

10.   The following are all positively related to job satisfaction
    a.   well-being, pay
    b.   emotional disposition, ergonomics
    c.   emotional disposition, social support,
    d.   social support, pay

11.   A person with a high _____ identifies closely with the goals of his or her company.
    a.   continuance commitment
    b.   normative commitment
    c.   social commitment
    d.   affective commitment

12.   The sense of obligation an employee feels towards his or her company is called
    a.   normative commitment.
    b.   continuance commitment.
    c.   social commitment.
    d.   affective commitment.

13.   People who see their occupation simply as a job
    a.   focus primarily on the material benefits of work (money).
    b.   focus on opportunities for advancement.
    c.   experience a great deal of fulfillment.
    d.   are most likely to engage in citizenship behaviors.

14.   Individuals who feel their job is a calling tend to
    a.   view their position as a stepping stone for advancement.
    b.   experience work as meaningful and fulfilling.
    c.   focus on the material benefits of work (money).
    d.   focus on waigawa.

15.   A transformational leader focuses on
      a.   enforcing the rules.
      b.   "keeping the ship steady."
      c.   changing the rules.
      d.   working within the goals of the existing organizational system.

Practice Test 3

1.   An organization's shared values, beliefs, and norms is
      a.   organizational culture.
      b.   organizational identity.
      c.   normative commitment.
      d.   affective commitment.

2.   In a power culture
      a.   teams are used to solve problems.
      b.   authority is delegated.
      c.   power is centralized to only a few people.
      d.   open communication is encouraged.

3.   Compassion and virtuousness
      a.   contribute to positive organizational culture.
      b.   take away from efficiency.
      c.   tend to cause companies to downsize.
      d.   only exist in an organization with a person culture.

4.   Sexual harassment that includes sexual favors as a condition of employment is an
    example of
      a.   workplace incivility harassment.
      b.   hostile work environment sexual harassment.
      c.   ipso facto sexual harassment.
      d.   quid pro quo sexual harassment.

5.   A father who is stressed out because of his responsibilities at work and his desire to spend
    more time with his kids is likely experiencing
      a.   job stress.
      b.   role conflict.
      c.   burnout.
      d.   continuance commitment.

6.   Symptoms such as emotional exhaustion and low motivation for work indicate
      a.   role conflict.
      b.   normative commitment.
      c.   burnout.
      d.   waigawa.

7. An unwillingness to take vacations is associated with
   a. career advancement.
   b. heart disease.
   c. role conflict.
   d. flow.

8. When we meet a challenge that is optimally matched with our skills, we are likely to experience a state of
   a. flow.
   b. overlearning.
   c. affective commitment.
   d. halo.

Answer Key
An Appreciative View of Psychology and Your Life
- Viewing an occupation as a calling is associated with experiencing work as more meaningful and fulfilling, being more satisfied with life and work, engaging in more citizenship behaviors, and missing work less.
- Any job can be transformed into a calling by engaging in job crafting or finding a way to place a personal stamp on your workplace.

Practice Test 1 Answers
1. a. No
   b. Correct
   c. No
   d. No

2. a. Correct
   b. No
   c. No
   d. No

3. a. No
   b. No
   c. No
   d. Correct

4. a. Correct
   b. No
   c. No
   d. No

5. a. No
   b. Correct
   c. No
   d. No

6.   a.   No
     b.   No
     c.   Correct
     d.   No

7.   a.   Correct
     b.   No
     c.   No
     d.   No

8.   a.   No
     b.   No
     c.   Correct
     d.   No

9.   a.   Correct
     b.   No
     c.   No
     d.   No

10.   a.   No
     b.   No
     c.   No
     d.   Correct

11.   a.   No
     b.   Correct
     c.   No
     d.   No

12.   a.   No
     b.   No
     c.   Correct
     d.   No

13.   a.   Correct
     b.   No
     c.   No
     d.   No

14.   a.   No
     b.   No
     c.   No
     d.   Correct

15. a. Correct
    b. No
    c. No
    d. No

Practice Test 2 Answers
1. a. No
   b. Correct
   c. No
   d. No

2. a. No
   b. No
   c. Correct
   d. No

3. a. Correct
   b. No
   c. No
   d. No

4. a. No
   b. No
   c. No
   d. Correct

5. a. No
   b. No
   c. Correct
   d. No

6. a. No
   b. Correct
   c. No
   d. No

7. a. Correct
   b. No
   c. No
   d. No

8. a. No
   b. No
   c. No
   d. Correct

9. a. Correct
    b. No
    c. No
    d. No

10. a. No
    b. No
    c. Correct
    d. No

11. a. No
    b. No
    c. No
    d. Correct

12. a. Correct
    b. No
    c. No
    d. No

13. a. Correct
    b. No
    c. No
    d. No

14. a. No
    b. Correct
    c. No
    d. No

15. a. No
    b. No
    c. Correct
    d. No

Practice Test 3 Answers

1. a. Correct
    b. No
    c. No
    d. No

2. a. No
    b. No
    c. Correct
    d. No

3. a. Correct
    b. No
    c. No
    d. No

4. a. No
    b. No
    c. No
    d. Correct

5. a. No
    b. Correct
    c. No
    d. No

6. a. No
    b. No
    c. Correct
    d. No

7. a. No
    b. Correct
    c. No
    d. No

8. a. Correct
    b. No
    c. No
    d. No

Chapter 14: Psychological Disorders

Learning Goals
1. Discuss the characteristics, explanations, and classifications of abnormal behavior.
2. Distinguish among the various anxiety disorders.
3. Compare the mood disorders and specify risk factors for depression and suicide.
4. Describe the dissociative disorders.
5. Characterize schizophrenia.
6. Identify the behavior patterns typical of personality disorders.
7. Explain how psychological disorders affect health and describe how individuals with disorders can improve their quality of life.

After studying chapter 14, use the space below to list the top 3 most interesting things you learned that help you appreciate the study of psychological disorders more.

- _____
- _____
- _____

Chapter Outline
1. Defining and Explaining Abnormal Behavior
- Abnormal behavior: _____
  _____
  - ○ _____
  - ○ _____
  - ○ _____
- Biological approach
  - ○ _____
  - ○ _____
  - ○ _____
  - ○ _____
- Psychological approach
  - ○ _____
  - ○ _____
  - ○ _____
  - ○ _____

- Sociocultural approach (Describe factors involved, and define internalizing and externalizing disorders.)
    - ○ _____
      _____
    - ○ _____
      _____
    - ○ _____
      _____
    - ○ _____
      _____

- Interactionist approach:
    - ○ _____
      _____
    - ○ _____
      _____

- Benefits of classification
    - ○ _____
      _____
    - ○ _____
      _____
    - ○ _____
      _____

- DSM-IV: _____
  _____
    - ○ _____
    - ○ _____
    - ○ _____
    - ○ _____
    - ○ _____

- DSM-IV criticism:
    - ○ _____
      _____
    - ○ _____
      _____
    - ○ _____
      _____

2. Anxiety Disorders

- _____
  _____

- Generalized anxiety disorder: _____
  _____
    - ○ Symptoms:
        - _____
        - _____
        - _____

- o Etiology:
    - • _____
    - • _____
    - • _____
- • Panic disorder: _____

    _____
    - o Symptoms:
        - • _____
        - • _____
        - • _____
    - o Etiology:
        - • _____
        - • _____
        - • _____
    - o Agoraphobia: _____

    _____

- • Phobic disorders: _____

    _____
    - o Symptoms:
        - • _____
        - • _____
        - • _____
    - o Etiology:
        - • _____
        - • _____
        - • _____
    - o Social phobia: _____
- • Obsessive-compulsive disorder: _____

    _____
    - o Symptoms:
        - • _____
        - • _____
        - • _____
    - o Etiology:
        - • _____
        - • _____
        - • _____
- • Post-traumatic stress disorder: _____

    _____

  o Symptoms:

    • _____

    • _____

    • _____

  o Etiology:

    • _____

    • _____

    • _____

3. Mood Disorders

 • Depressive disorders: _____

    _____

  o Major depressive disorder: _____

    _____

    ▪ Symptoms:

      • _____

      • _____

      • _____

      • _____

  o Dysthymic disorder: _____

    ▪ Symptoms:

      • _____

      • _____

      • _____

      • _____

 • Bipolar disorder: _____

    _____

  o Symptoms:

    ▪ _____

    ▪ _____

    ▪ _____

 • Etiology of mood disorders

  o _____

    ▪ _____

    ▪ _____

    ▪ _____

    ▪ _____

    ▪ _____

  o _____

    ▪ _____

    ▪ _____

    ▪ _____

    ▪ _____

    ▪ _____

  o _____

- ▪ _____
- ▪ _____
- ▪ _____

- Suicide: _____

  _____

  - ○ _____
    - ▪ _____
    - ▪ _____

  - ○ _____
    - ▪ _____
    - ▪ _____

  - ○ _____
    - ▪ _____
    - ▪ _____

4. Dissociative Disorders

- ● _____

  _____

- Dissociative amnesia: _____

  _____

- Dissociative fugue: _____

  _____

- Dissociative identity disorder: _____

  _____

  - ○ _____
  - ○ _____
  - ○ _____

5. Schizophrenia

- ● _____

  _____

  - ○ Positive symptoms: _____

    _____

    - ● _____
    - ● _____
    - ● _____
    - ● _____
    - ● _____

  - ○ Negative symptoms: _____

    _____

    - ● _____
    - ● _____
    - ● _____

  - ○ Cognitive symptoms: _____

    _____

- • _____
- • _____
- • _____

- • Disorganized schizophrenia: _____
  _____

- • Catatonic schizophrenia: _____

- • Paranoid schizophrenia: _____

- • Undifferentiated schizophrenia: _____

- • Etiology of schizophrenia
  - ○ _____
    - • _____
    - • _____
  - ○ _____
    - • _____
    - • _____
  - ○ _____
    - • _____
    - • _____

6. Personality Disorders

- • _____
  _____

- • Odd/eccentric cluster
  - ○ _____
    _____
  - ○ _____
    _____
  - ○ _____
    _____

- • Dramatic/emotionally problematic cluster
  - ○ _____
    _____
  - ○ _____
    _____
  - ○ _____
    _____
  - ○ _____
    _____

- • Chronic-fearfulness/avoidant cluster
  - ○ _____
    _____
  - ○ _____
    _____

      ○ _____

         _____

      ○ _____

         _____

7. Psychological Disorders and Health and Wellness

- _____

    _____

- _____

    _____

- _____

    _____

Critical Controversy

- Dimensional approach: _____

    _____

      ○ Example: _____

         _____

         _____

Intersection

- Developmental psychopathology: _____

    _____

    _____

Clarifying Tricky Points

Anxiety and "impairment to function in the world"

Most people feel anxious sometimes. Some of us more than others, but everybody can relate to that tight feeling in your chest and the sensation of your heart beating at what seems to be a million times a minute. If everybody experiences anxiety, how then do you distinguish between a normal level of anxiety and an abnormal level that warrants a diagnosis of generalized anxiety disorder or panic disorder? A key feature of diagnosable anxiety disorders is impairment in the person's ability to function in the world. For example, if you feel anxious before given an important interview, that is, of course, normal. However, if you feel so anxious that when you park your car outside the office of where you are interviewing, you can't get out of the car, then the problem is more serious. By not being able to complete the interview, the anxiety has impaired your ability to function in the world.

The ups and downs of bipolar disorder

Phrases like bipolar disorder or manic-depressive are sometimes thrown about casually when people feel uneven or down one moment and up the next. An important feature of bipolar disorder, however, is the length and space between depressed and manic episodes. Every one feels down sometimes and up at other times. Once in a while these ups and downs are significant, but it doesn't necessarily indicate bipolar disorder. According to the DSM-IV, manic episodes (the "up" period when a person feels euphoric) must last at least 1 week but on average they last around 3 months.

Dissociative identity disorder (aka: multiple personality disorder)
Dissociative identity disorder (DID; formerly known as multiple personality disorder) is excellent fodder for movies or TV dramas, but it is actually quite rare. It is difficult to know exactly how rare because it is often misdiagnosed as schizophrenia but until the 1980s, only 300 cases total had been reported. Most people that have been diagnosed with DID have been the victims of sexual abuse, but even among those who have been sexually abused, development of DID is exceedingly rare.

An Appreciative View of Psychology and Your Life
As you learned in this chapter, many people are able to lead successful and fulfilling lives with or without a psychological disorder. Just as we hear about people beating cancer or living with HIV, people overcome or learn to live with psychological disorders such as depression, anxiety, and even schizophrenia. One aspect of psychological disorders that is hard to overcome actually has nothing to do with the person diagnosed with the disorder: people with psychological disorders are often stigmatized and treated differently because of negative stereotypes that have no basis in reality.

How does the experience of stigma affect an individual with a psychological disorder?

_____

_____

_____

_____

_____

The next time you meet or hear about a person being diagnosed with a psychological disorder, how can you help alleviate the experience of stigma?

_____

_____

_____

_____

_____

Practice Test 1
1. Which of the following is not an important factor in psychological disorders?
    a. biological factors
    b. psychological factors
    c. sociocultural factors
    d. technological factors

2. Abnormal behavior is
    a. always bizarre.
    b. very different from normal behavior.
    c. treatable.
    d. easy to distinguish from normal behavior.

3.   Barbara's psychological disorder is keeping her from going to work. The fact that this disorder is interfering with her ability to function effectively means that her behaviors are
   a.   deviant.
   b.   maladaptive.
   c.   personally distressing.
   d.   atypical.

4.   Each of the following is an axis on the DSM multiaxial system, EXCEPT
   a.   personality disorders.
   b.   psychological stressors in the individual's recent past.
   c.   the individual's highest level of functioning in the past year.
   d.   potential treatments for the individual.

5.   Which of the following is a criticism of the DSM-IV?
   a.   Five axes are not sufficient for the classification of all mental disorders.
   b.   The classification is not comprehensive enough.
   c.   The classification is not current enough.
   d.   Labels can become self-fulfilling prophecies.

6.   Mr. Dodge engages in very rigid and structured behavior. He is preoccupied with cleanliness. He washes his hands more than twenty times per day and brings two changes of underwear to work with him. He would probably be diagnosed as suffering from a(n)
   a.   conversion disorder.
   b.   schizophrenia.
   c.   generalized anxiety disorder.
   d.   obsessive-compulsive disorder.

7.   The fear cluster centered on public places and an inability to escape or find help should one become incapacitated is called
   a.   agoraphobia.
   b.   social phobia.
   c.   compulsion.
   d.   generalized anxiety disorder.

8.   The fear-of-fear hypothesis refers to
   a.   agoraphobias being a fear of public places.
   b.   fear of death.
   c.   agoraphobias being a fear of having a panic attack in a public place.
   d.   fear of pain.

9. An example of the personal distress criterion of abnormal behavior is
   a. Chad's inability to stop exercising even when he knows that there are other things he should be doing
   b. Chad's schedule of exercising three hours a day, seven days a week
   c. Chad's embarrassment and concern that people might find out that he always has to do his workout in the same order and if he can't he has to start all over again
   d. Chad's insistence on wearing the exact same workout clothes everyday

10. A person who behaves very differently from what the social norms indicate can be argued to fulfill the _____ criterion of abnormal behavior.
    a. personal distress
    b. deviance
    c. maladaptiveness
    d. dysfunction

11. Among the psychological factors of psychological disorders, the humanistic perspective argues that
    a. disorders are a result of unconscious conflict.
    b. disorders are caused by a person's inability to fill one's potential.
    c. disorders are caused by environmental factors such as rewards and punishments.
    d. disorders are caused by having a high self-concept.

12. Women are to _____ disorders as men are to _____ disorders.
    a. externalized; internalized
    b. unconscious; conscious
    c. internalized; externalized
    d. conscious; unconscious

13. The following are issues addressed in the axes of the DSM-IV, EXCEPT
    a. general medical condition.
    b. psychosocial issues.
    c. environmental problems.
    d. labeling problems.

14. _____ involves an intense fear of being humiliated or embarrassed in social situations.
    a. A social phobia
    b. Generalized anxiety disorder
    c. Schizophrenia
    d. Obsessive-compulsive disorder

15. The following are symptoms of post-traumatic stress disorder (PTSD), EXCEPT
    a. flashback memories.
    b. impulsive behaviors, such as aggressiveness.
    c. difficulties in concentration.
    d. a fear of a specific object or situation.

16. When a mental health professional is using the DSM-IV to diagnose a disorder, he will ask a number of questions to the individual and/or family members to see where the individual stands in each of the five axes. Which of the following questions is unlikely to be asked by a mental health professional in the process of determining a diagnosis with the DSM-IV?
    a. Has the individual been previously diagnosed with a psychological disorder or mental retardation?
    b. What type of therapy would the individual prefer?
    c. How well is the individual functioning in comparison to previous levels of functioning?
    d. Does the individual have diabetes?

17. Labels can become self-fulfilling prophecies because
    a. labels encourage people to develop mental competence.
    b. labels are used only for the most severe psychological disorders.
    c. labels legitimize the belief that there is something wrong and permanent about having a psychological disorder.
    d. labels of psychological disorders are rarely associated with other personality characteristics.

18. The causes of psychological disorders include the following, EXCEPT
    a. specific genes.
    b. insanity.
    c. a person's community.
    d. how a person thinks about the disorder.

Practice Test 2

1. A disorder characterized by unexpected travel away from home and a new identity is called
    a. dissociative identity disorder.
    b. dissociative amnesia.
    c. dissociative fugue.
    d. panic disorder.

2. Which of the following has not been associated with dissociative identity disorder?
    a. sexual abuse
    b. brain trauma
    c. rejecting mothers
    d. alcoholic fathers

3.   Which of the following is NOT a type of mood disorder?
        a.   bipolar disorder
        b.   major depressive disorder
        c.   dysthymic disorder
        d.   obsessive-compulsive disorder

4.   Which of the following refers to a biological cause of mood disorders?
        a.   heredity
        b.   learned helplessness
        c.   personality factors
        d.   childhood experiences

5.   According to Aaron Beck, a depressed person is more likely than a non-depressed person to engage in
        a.   productive thinking.
        b.   creative thinking.
        c.   catastrophic thinking.
        d.   reactive thinking.

6.   The "hidden observer" concept has been used to explain _____ disorders.
        a.   somatoform
        b.   anxiety
        c.   dissociative
        d.   personality

7.   Which of the following statements is NOT true about the mania aspect of bipolar disorder?
        a.   Fewer than 10% of bipolar individuals tend to experience manic-type episodes and not depression.
        b.   A manic episode involves feelings of euphoria.
        c.   During a manic episode, the person often experiences fatigue.
        d.   Mania is associated with impulsiveness.

8.   Which of the following psychological disorders has an etiology of sexual and physical abuse during early childhood?
        a.   phobic disorder
        b.   histrionic personality disorder
        c.   paranoid schizophrenia
        d.   dissociative identity disorder

9.   Which of the following is not true about dissociative identity disorder?
        a.   It is rare.
        b.   It runs in families.
        c.   Some psychologists believe that in the past it has been misdiagnosed as schizophrenia.
        d.   Most of the people diagnosed with the disorder are adult males.

10.   A person experiencing major depressive disorder is unlikely to
     a.   be impulsive.
     b.   lose weight.
     c.   have a hard time concentrating.
     d.   have problems sleeping.

11.   Which of the following disorders has been associated with a decrease in metabolic activity in the cerebral cortex?
     a.   catatonic schizophrenia
     b.   panic disorder
     c.   major depressive disorder
     d.   narcissistic personality disorder

Practice Test 3

1.   Martha has been sitting in a hunched-over position on her hospital bed for several hours. When you speak to her, her position remains unchanged, and she doesn't answer. When you lift her arm, she remains sitting motionless, with her arm in a raised position. Martha is most likely suffering from which type of schizophrenia?
     a.   paranoid
     b.   catatonic
     c.   disorganized
     d.   undifferentiated

2.   Which of the following is not a symptom of a schizophrenic disorder?
     a.   hallucinations
     b.   delusions
     c.   bizarre motor behavior
     d.   manipulation of people

3.   _____ disorders are chronic, maladaptive cognitive-behavioral patterns that are thoroughly integrated into an individual's personality.
     a.   Anxiety
     b.   Personality
     c.   Schizophrenic
     d.   Dissociative

4.   Which theory argues that a biogenetic disposition and stress cause schizophrenia?
     a.   diathesis-stress view
     b.   disorganized-stress theory
     c.   dopamine hypothesis
     d.   psychoanalytic theory

5.   An individual who engages in stealing and vandalism, who cannot uphold financial obligations, and who shows no remorse after harming someone may be considered to have a(n)
    a.   panic disorder.
    b.   bipolar disorder.
    c.   anxiety disorder.
    d.   antisocial personality disorder.

6.   Which of the following characterizes antisocial personality disorder?
    a.   It usually begins in middle adulthood.
    b.   It affects males and females equally.
    c.   Most adolescents grow out of the disorder.
    d.   Those with the disorder show no remorse when harming someone.

7.   Andrea has an excessive need to be the center of attention. At work, she is highly competitive and gets very angry if anyone criticizes her. She constantly manipulates others, especially younger coworkers. With which personality disorder are these behaviors associated?
    a.   paranoid
    b.   borderline
    c.   schizoid
    d.   narcissistic

8.   What is the main difference between schizophrenia and dissociative personality disorder?
    a.   The schizophrenic has one personality that has disintegrated.
    b.   The schizophrenic has one integrated personality.
    c.   The schizophrenic never has more than one alternate personality.
    d.   The schizophrenic always has more than two alternate personalities.

9.   Esther has been diagnosed with schizophrenia. One of her cognitions involves the belief that when the light switches in her home are turned on, her neighbor to the north is able to hear what she is thinking. Esther's type of schizophrenia is
    a.   disorganized.
    b.   catatonic.
    c.   paranoid.
    d.   undifferentiated.

10.   Habeeba has a very hard time connecting with other people. She is shy and has never shown much interest in intimate friendships or romantic relationships; actually, most co-workers think of her as a cold person. Habeeba could possibly be diagnosed as experiencing
    a.   schizoid personality disorder.
    b.   depression.
    c.   schizotypal personality disorder.
    d.   antisocial personality disorder.

11. A father who is always late to his kids' little league games, often forgets when their school tuition is due, is not flexible with the children, and tends to look for excuses to avoid spending time with his wife and the kids may be diagnosed with _____ personality disorder.
   a. antisocial
   b. dependent
   c. schizotypal
   d. passive-aggressive

Answer Key
An Appreciative View of Psychology and Your Life

- Feelings of stigma are a major source of stress. The experience of stigma related stress takes away time and energy that could be devoted to overcoming or learning to cope with a psychological disorder. Stigma can also lead health workers and everyday people to avoid helping those with psychological disorders overcome non-psychological health related problems such as obesity, smoking, drinking, and just overall fitness.

- The next time you hear about a person being diagnosed with a psychological disorder, don't let that diagnosis come to define that person. Treat him or her just like you always did or just like anybody else. Just as when a friend is diagnosed with the flu or an ACL injury doesn't change the way you feel about the person, neither should the diagnosis of a psychological disorder.

Practice Test 1 Answers

1. a. No; biological factors are important in psychological disorders.
   b. No; psychological factors also contribute to psychological disorders.
   c. No; sociocultural factors also contribute to psychological disorders.
   d. YES; technological factors are not a category of variables considered in the study of psychological disorders.

2. a. No; this is a myth, because people diagnosed with a disorder often cannot be distinguished from other people.
   b. No; many times the problems is a poor fit between the behavior and the situation; however, the behaviors may be similar.
   c. YES; most people diagnosed with psychological disorders can be successfully treated.
   d. No

3. a. No; the question does not address the deviance criteria of abnormal behavior; her behaviors are not described as atypical or uncommon.
   b. YES; Barbara used to be able to work and now she can't; therefore, the behaviors are maladaptive.
   c. No; the question does not address Barbara's level of distress.
   d. No; this is similar to item a, in the sense that deviant and atypical are equivalent concepts.

4. a. No; personality disorders are placed on Axis II.
    b. No; psychological stressors are indicated on Axis IV.
    c. No; information on functioning is placed on Axis V.
    d. YES; treatment options are not among the axes in the DSM.

5. a. No; the more accurate the classifications, the better the diagnosis will be.
    b. No; great effort has been put into making the classifications comprehensive.
    c. No; the classifications have been revised in a timely manner.
    c. YES; this is a criticism since the DSM does have a strong medical focus and looks more at pathology and problems than at other aspects of psychology.

6. a. No; there are no physical symptoms.
    b. No; Mr. Dodge is not experiencing hallucinations or other important symptoms of schizophrenia.
    c. No; his concern is focused on cleanliness.
    d. YES; obsessive-compulsive disorder includes the types of thoughts and rituals that Mr. Dodge is experiencing.

7. a. YES; this is the definition of agoraphobia, often associated with panic disorder.
    b. No; social phobias are intense fears of being embarrassed in social situations.
    c. No; this is a phobia, not a pattern of behaviors.
    d. No; the phobia is specific, not a generalized anxiety.

8. a. No; the fear-of-fear hypothesis challenges this popular conceptualization of agoraphobia.
    b. No; this is the definition for thanatophobia.
    c. YES; this hypothesis proposes that agoraphobia is the fear of being afraid and experiencing a panic attack in a public situation.
    d. No; this is the definition of algophobia.

9. a. No; this is an example of maladaptiveness.
    b. No; this is an example of deviant behavior.
    c. YES; he is aware that his behaviors are different, and this causes him stress.
    d. No; this is an example of deviant behavior.

10. a. No; this question does not address the person's level of distress caused by the behavior.
    b. YES; deviant behavior is behavior that is different according to social standards such as norms.
    c. No; the question does not address the functionality of the behavior.
    d. No; the behavior is not described as dysfunctional or maladaptive.

11.   a.   No; this is the view of the psychodynamic perspective.
       b.   YES
       c.   No; this is consistent with the behavioral perspective.
       d.   No; humanists would argue that disorders may be caused by having a low self-concept.

12.   a.   No; the opposite is true; see item c.
       b.   No; no evidence is presented in this chapter that suggests that there are gender differences on the issue of conscious versus unconscious influences.
       c.   YES; women are more likely to suffer from anxiety disorders and depression, which have symptoms that are turned inward, whereas men are more likely to have externalized disorders that involve aggression and substance abuse.
       d.   No

13.   a.   No; this information is collected in Axis III.
       b.   No; this information is collected in Axis IV.
       c.   No; this information is also part of Axis IV.
       d.   YES; although being labeled with a diagnosis can have lasting effects, it is unlikely that those issues will be addressed in the process of determining the diagnosis.

14.   a.   YES; these individuals are often afraid of saying the wrong thing and may avoid public situations.
       b.   No; in this question, the fear is focused.
       c.   No; in a social phobia, the person is not experiencing hallucinations or delusions.
       d.   No; while this is also an anxiety disorder, obsessive-compulsive disorder involves other fears and concerns.

15.   a.   No; this is one of the main symptoms of PTSD.
       b.   No; this is also a symptom of PTSD.
       c.   No; this is also a symptom of PTSD.
       d.   YES; this is not a symptom of PTSD, it is a symptom of a phobic disorder, another type of anxiety disorder.

16.   a.   No; this is an important question in reference to both Axes I and II.
       b.   YES; this is not a typical question in the process of diagnosis, since the mental health professional has not even classified the disorder yet.
       c.   No; this is an important question in reference to Axis V.
       d.   No; this is also an important question in reference to Axis III; a person with diabetes may be taking medication that could interact with possible treatment for a psychological disorder.

17. a.   No; on the contrary, because of their negative connotations, labels motivate people to get rid of the bad aspects of the mental disorder but don't necessarily encourage the person to work with the disorder and develop mental competence even if the challenges of the disorder continue.

    b.   No; this is incorrect, labels have been developed even for mild problems, such as caffeine-use disorder, making the effect of labels even more pervasive.

    c.   YES; once people are labeled with a disorder they are more likely to give into the belief that a psychological disorder is a terrible thing that will not go away, and they may buy into the social stigma attached to psychological diagnosis.

    d.   No; being labeled as having a psychological disorder is usually associated with being incompetent, dangerous, and socially unacceptable.

18. a.   No; there are specific genes that have been associated with specific disorders, such as the genetic markers for schizophrenia on chromosomes 10, 13, and 22.

    b.   YES; insanity is a legal concept and not a cause of psychological disorder.

    c.   No; a person's community can be a sociocultural contributor to psychological disorders.

    d.   No; cognition is an important aspect of psychological disorders; how a person thinks about the disorder may contribute to the disorder.

Practice Test 2 Answers

1. a.   No; this is the current name for what used to be called multiple personality disorder.

    b.   No; dissociative amnesia is not associated with travel and change of identity.

    c.   YES; these are the characteristics of dissociative fugue.

    d.   No; these are not the symptoms or characteristics of panic disorder.

2. a.   No; this has been associated with dissociative identity disorder, since sexual abuse occurred in 56% of reported cases.

    b.   YES; brain trauma has not been associated with this disorder; it seems to have strong psychological contributors.

    c.   No; this is one of the patterns observed in individuals with dissociative identity disorder.

    d.   No; this is also one of the patterns observed in individuals with dissociative identity disorder.

3.   a.   No; bipolar disorder is a mood disorder.
     b.   No; major depressive disorder is a mood disorder.
     c.   No; dysthymic disorder is a mood disorder and is more chronic.
     d.   YES; obsessive-compulsive disorder is an anxiety disorder and it is also a name used to refer to a particular pattern of personality disorder.

4.   a.   CORRECT; heredity refers to genetics and is a biological cause of mood disorders.
     b.   No; learned helpless is a psychosocial explanation.
     c.   No; personality factors do not refer to biological causes.
     d.   No; childhood experiences are not related to biological causes.

5.   a.   No; Beck does not make reference to productive thinking.
     b.   No; Beck does not make reference to creative thinking.
     c.   YES; Beck focuses on how negative thoughts shape person's experience.
     d.   No; Beck does not make reference to reactive thinking.

6.   a.   No; somatoform disorders involve the manifestation of a psychological problem in physical symptoms.
     b.   No; the cognitive component of anxiety disorders involves apprehensive expectations and thoughts.
     c.   YES; the hidden observer is a concept Hilgard used to explain hypnosis; it involves a person's ability to have a divided state of consciousness; it has been argued that people with dissociative disorders can effectively integrate the different dimensions of consciousness.
     d.   No; personality disorders don't involve the issue of the hidden observer.

7.   a.   No; this is correct, most cases of bipolar disorder involve the movement from one extreme to the other.
     b.   No; this is correct and the main symptom of mania.
     c.   YES; this is incorrect, because fatigue is a symptom of depression; during manic episodes, a person feels full of energy.
     d.   No; this is correct and is one of the main reasons why people experiencing manic episodes can get in serious trouble as their behavior becomes more risky and impulsive.

8.   a.   No; phobic disorders involve extreme fears of specific objects or situations, and etiology studies reveal that most phobias can be associated with a traumatic experience but not of sexual or physical abuse.
     b.   No; this personality disorder involves an excessive desire of attention, and it is more common in women than in men.
     c.   No; the etiology of schizophrenic disorders indicates that they have a very strong genetic component.
     d.   YES; the etiology of the disorder that used to be called multiple personality indicates that this disorder is characterized by an inordinately high rate of sexual or physical abuse during early childhood.

9.   a.   No; this is true about this disorder.
       b.   No; this is true about this disorder.
       c.   No; this is true about this disorder.
       d.   YES; most people diagnosed with this disorder are adult females.

10.   a.   YES; this is a characteristic of people experiencing mania.
       b.   No; this could happen, or gaining weight.
       c.   No; this is one of the characteristic problems in thinking.
       d.   No; this is one of the main symptoms of the disorder, possibly due to the lesser amount of slow-wave sleep and the faster arrival at REM that depressive individuals experience.

11.   a.   Incorrect
       b.   Incorrect
       c.   YES; the metabolic activity in the cerebral cortex decreases during depression and, for bipolar individuals, increases during mania.
       d.   No

Practice Test 3 Answers

1.   a.   No; there is no indication of delusions.
       b.   YES; Martha shows bizarre motor behavior.
       c.   No; these symptoms do not fit a diagnosis of disorganized schizophrenia.
       d.   No; these symptoms do fit a particular type of schizophrenia.

2.   a.   No; this is a symptom of a schizophrenic disorder.
       b.   No; this is a symptom of a schizophrenic disorder.
       c.   No; this is a symptom of a schizophrenic disorder.
       d.   YES; this implies that the person is in control to manipulate others, and that does not apply to schizophrenic disorders.

3.   a.   No; these involve motor tension, hyperactivity, and apprehensive expectations.
       b.   YES; this is the definition of personality disorders.
       c.   No; these disorders involve disturbances in thought, emotion, and motor behavior.
       d.   No; dissociative disorders involve changes in memory and identity.

4.   a.   YES; the diathesis refers to the disposition.
       b.   No
       c.   No; but dopamine is a neurotransmitter that may play a role in schizophrenia.
       d.   No

5. a. No; this is an anxiety disorder.
    b. No; this disorder involves extreme moods such as mania and depression.
    c. Incorrect
    d. YES; these characterize antisocial personality disorder.

6. a. No; typically the disorder starts in adolescence.
    b. No; this disorder affects more males than females.
    c. No; in fact, people do not "grow out" of personality disorders.
    d. YES; people with this disorder show no remorse.

7. a. No; this disorder involves mistrust and suspiciousness.
    b. No; it refers to emotional instability and impulsiveness.
    c. No; schizoid personality disorder involves problems with social relationships.
    d. YES; Andrea shows an exaggerated sense of self-importance.

8. a. YES; schizophrenia is not "split personality."
    b. No; in schizophrenia, the personality has disintegrated.
    c. No; this is not an accurate description of schizophrenia.
    d. No; this is not an accurate description of schizophrenia.

9. a. No; Esther is not described as being withdrawn.
    b. No; Esther is not described as engaging in bizarre motor behavior.
    c. YES; Esther has an elaborate delusion of persecution.
    d. No; only one symptom was presented in the question, and it can be associated with the paranoid schizophrenia pattern.

10. a. YES; the schizoid disorder is characterized by all the tendencies of Habeeba, plus a difficulty expressing anger.
    b. No; the question does not address the emotional state of Habeeba.
    c. No; the schizotypal person tends to be hostile and overtly aggressive.
    d. No; antisocial individuals are guiltless, law-breaking, exploitive, irresponsible, self-indulgent, and intrusive.

11. a. No; this man is not directly taking advantage of his family members or others.
    b. No; there is no evidence in this scenario that this person lacks self-confidence and needs others to make decisions for him.
    c. No; this man is not directly being hostile or aggressive.
    d. YES; this man is sabotaging the success of this family by doing things that make them less effective.

Chapter 15: Therapies

Learning Goals
1. Describe the biological therapies.
2. Define psychotherapy and characterize four types of psychotherapy.
3. Explain the sociocultural approaches and issues in treatment.
4. Evaluate the effectiveness of psychotherapy.
5. Discuss therapy's larger implications for health and wellness, and characterize the client's role in therapeutic success.

After studying chapter 15, use the space below to list the top 3 most interesting things you learned that help you appreciate therapies more.

- _____
- _____
- _____

Chapter Outline
1. Biological Therapies

- _____
  _____

- Drug therapy
  - ○ _____
    - Example: _____
  - ○ _____
    - Types:
      - _____
      - _____
      - _____
      - _____
  - ○ _____
    - _____
    - Tardive dyskinesia: _____
      _____
    - _____

- Electroconvulsive therapy: _____
  _____
  - ○ _____
  - ○ _____
  - ○ _____
  - ○ _____

- Psychosurgery: _____
  _____
  - ○ _____
  - ○ _____

2. Psychotherapy

- Insight therapy: _____
  _____

  o Psychodynamic therapy: _____
    _____

    ▪ Psychoanalysis: _____
      _____

      - _____
        _____
        _____

      - _____
        _____
        _____

      - _____
        _____
        _____

      - _____
        _____
        _____

      - _____
        _____
        _____

      - _____
        _____

    ▪ _____

    ▪ _____
      _____
      _____

  o Humanistic therapy: _____
    _____

    ▪ Client-centered therapy: _____
      _____

      - _____
        _____

      - _____
        _____

      - _____
        _____

      - _____
        _____
        _____

- _____
  _____
  _____

  - _____
    _____
    _____

- Gestalt therapy: _____
  _____

  - _____
    _____
    _____

  - _____
    _____
    _____

  - _____
    _____
    _____

- Behavior therapy: _____
  _____

  o Classical conditioning: _____
    _____

    - _____
      _____

      - _____
        _____
        _____

      - _____
        _____
        _____

    - _____
      _____

      - _____
        _____
        _____

      - _____
        _____
        _____

  o Operant conditioning: _____
    _____

    - _____
      _____

    - _____
      _____

- Cognitive therapy: _____
  _____

o Rational-emotive: _____

_____

    ■ _____

_____

o _____

_____

    ■ _____

    ■ _____

_____

o Cognitive-behavior therapy: _____

_____

    ■ _____

    ■ _____

    ■ _____

_____

o Uses of cognitive therapy:

    ■ _____

    ■ _____

    ■ _____

    ■ _____

    ■ _____

3. Sociocultural Approaches and Issues in Treatment

• _____

_____

• Group therapy: _____

_____

  o _____

_____

    ■ _____

    ■ _____

    ■ _____

    ■ _____

    ■ _____

    ■ _____

• _____

_____

  o _____

  o _____

  o _____

  o _____

• Couples therapy: _____

_____

- Self help support groups: _____

    _____

    o _____

    _____

    o _____

    _____

    o _____

    _____

    o _____

    _____

- Community mental health: _____

    _____

    o _____

    _____

    o _____

    _____

    o _____

    _____

    o _____

    _____

- Culture, ethnicity, gender: _____

    o _____

    _____

    o _____

    _____

    o _____

    _____

    o _____

    _____

4. The Effectiveness of Psychotherapy

- _____

    _____

- _____

    _____

- _____

    _____

- Common elements of successful therapy:

    o _____

    o _____

    o _____

    o

    o Therapeutic alliance: _____

    _____

- Integrative therapy: _____

    _____

      ○ _____

- Guidelines for seeking professional help:
  - ○ _____
  - ○ _____
  - ○ _____

5. Therapies and Health and Wellness

- _____

- _____

- _____

- _____

- _____

- _____

- _____

Critical Controversy

- Problems associated with children and antidepressants:
  - ○ _____
  - ○ _____
  - ○ _____
  - ○ _____
  - ○ _____

Intersection

- Cognitive therapy can change the brain in the following ways:
  - ○ _____
  - ○ _____
  - ○ _____
  - ○ _____

Clarifying Tricky Points

Effectiveness of therapy

Psychotherapy is not perfect and does not work miracles. But, as figure 15.11 in your textbook shows, it does help and is certainly better than doing nothing. Generally speaking, however, studies have shown that no one type of therapy is better than another. What is important is that a person seeking therapy finds a type of therapy and a therapist with which they are comfortable. How long will it take to feel better is another issue when considering the effectiveness of therapy. With a physical problem, such as the common cold, we are accustomed to going to the doctor, getting some pills and usually feeling better within a week or so. However, psychological disorders are far more complex and therefore require more time, usually about 6 months before most people show substantial improvement (see figure 15.12 in your textbook).

Where does group therapy fit?

Chapter 15 began by discussing drug therapies, the insight therapies of psychoanalysis and client-centered therapy, and cognitive and behavioral therapies. But what type of therapy is group therapy? The answer, for many types of group therapy at least, is all of the above. Group therapy takes the best aspects of psychodynamics, humanistic approaches, cognitive, and behavioral therapy. Also, many people in group therapy are simultaneously seeing a psychiatrist that may be administering drug therapy. Indeed, many individual therapists do not fit neatly into the categories outlined in your textbook. Most therapists are trained in multiple forms of therapy and, while certainly demonstrating a proclivity towards one form or another, they often take the best aspects from multiple forms of therapy.

An Appreciative View of Psychology and Your Life

Therapy is not always directed by a highly trained and very expensive professional. It is estimated that more than 1 million people belong to at least one type of self-help support group. Self-help support groups are often led by someone with experience in the particular issue and that has been trained informally by a professional. Universities often have several support groups that students can use when they encounter a problem that they just can't handle alone.

Take some time to look up some support groups that are available on your campus or in your community. You never know when you or somebody you care about will need extra support so it is important to be aware of what resources are available. List a few in the space below.

_____

_____

_____

_____

Practice Test 1

1.   Neuroleptics are widely used to reduce symptoms of
   a.   depression.
   b.   schizophrenia.
   c.   bipolar disorder.
   d.   multiple personality.

2.   Electroconvulsive therapy (ECT) is
        a.   the most effective treatment for major depressive disorder.
        b.   comparable in effectiveness to cognitive therapy and drug therapy.
        c.   more effective than cognitive therapy, but not as effective as drug therapy.
        d.   less effective than both cognitive therapy and drug therapy.

3.   Electroconvulsive therapy is used in treating severe
        a.   schizophrenic disorder.
        b.   bipolar disorder.
        c.   multiple personality.
        d.   depression.

4.   The following are anti-anxiety drugs, EXCEPT
        a.   Xanax.
        b.   Valium.
        c.   Prozac.
        d.   Buspirone.

5.   The use of benzodiazepines has been associated with
        a.   alertness.
        b.   birth defects.
        c.   agitation.
        d.   lack of addiction.

6.   MAO (monoamine oxidase) inhibitors are used to treat
        a.   schizophrenia.
        b.   anxiety disorders.
        c.   mood disorders.
        d.   personality disorders.

7.   Neuroleptics, the most widely used class of antipsychotic drugs; relieve the
        symptoms of schizophrenia because
        a.   they inhibit MAO.
        b.   they block the dopamine system's action in the brain.
        c.   they increase the level of norepinephrine and serotonin.
        d.   they bind to the receptor sites of neurotransmitters that become overactive during
                anxiety.

8.   It may be argued that one of reasons people with schizophrenia stop drug
        treatment is because
        a.   the symptoms usually don't reappear or become milder.
        b.   these drugs keep them in the hospital longer than they want to be there.
        c.   of their concern with developing tardive dyskinesia.
        d.   they need the excess dopamine in the brain to feel good.

9. When psychosurgery is used today, it usually involves the lesioning of
    a. the area connecting the frontal lobe and the thalamus.
    b. a part of the limbic system.
    c. the prefrontal lobe.
    d. the frontal lobe of the cerebral cortex.

Practice Test 2
1. The process used by mental health professionals to help individuals recognize, define, and overcome their psychological and interpersonal difficulties is called
    a. biological therapy.
    b. drug therapy.
    c. electroconvulsive therapy.
    d. psychotherapy.

2. The psychoanalytic term to explain a client who suddenly begins missing appointments and becomes hostile in therapy sessions is
    a. resistance.
    b. transference.
    c. free association.
    d. catharsis.

3. The release of emotional tension associated with reliving an emotionally charge experience is called
    a. catharsis.
    b. resistance.
    c. free association.
    d. unconditional positive regard.

4. Which of the following is not a focus of humanistic therapy?
    a. conscious thoughts
    b. past experiences
    c. personal growth
    d. self-fulfillment

5. According to Carl Rogers, client-centered therapy requires all of the following except which one?
    a. unconditional positive regard
    b. genuineness
    c. interpretation
    d. active listening

6. Gestalt therapy is similar to psychoanalytic therapy in that they both
    a. assume that problems stem from past unresolved conflicts.
    b. assume that the client can find solutions in the right atmosphere.
    c. expect resistance and transference to occur.
    d. deny the importance of dreams in understanding a person.

7.   The term insight therapy applies to both psychodynamic therapy and
     a.   behavior therapy.
     b.   humanistic therapy.
     c.   biomedical therapy.
     d.   aversive conditioning.

8.   Vigorously challenging and questioning clients about critical issues and forcing them to face their problems are techniques used in
     a.   psychodynamic therapy.
     b.   humanistic therapy.
     c.   Gestalt therapy.
     d.   client-centered therapy.

9.   Your roommate Rachel has terrifying memories of having been bitten by a pit bull when she was a child. To this day, she gets extremely nervous if a dog is anywhere near her. In order to help Rachel overcome this fear of dogs, you have brought home a puppy and intend to use systematic desensitization. Which of the following best describes your procedure?
     a.   bringing the puppy closer and closer to Rachel after she has been given time to completely relax
     b.   keeping the puppy in a separate room where Rachel does not have to interact with it
     c.   forcing Rachel to hold the dog because fear of a puppy is ridiculous
     d.   letting young children handle the dog in front of Rachel

10. The principles of operant and classical conditioning are extensively used by practitioners of
     a.   psychoanalysis.
     b.   Gestalt therapy.
     c.   group therapy.
     d.   behavior therapy.

11. A technique of behavior therapy that pairs an undesirable behavior with an unpleasant stimulus is
     a.   token economy.
     b.   systematic desensitization.
     c.   aversive conditioning.
     d.   rational-emotion therapy.

12. Cognitive therapists are likely to be concerned with
     a.   an individual's thoughts.
     b.   unconditional positive regard.
     c.   the manifest content of dreams.
     d.   unconscious motives.

13. Which approach is most likely to be concerned with irrational and self-defeating beliefs?
    a. Beck's cognitive therapy
    b. Ellis' rational-emotional behavior therapy
    c. systematic desensitization
    d. operant therapy

14. The following are characteristics of Beck's cognitive therapy, EXCEPT
    a. this therapy tends to be confrontational.
    b. this therapy aims at getting individuals to reflect on their personal issues.
    c. this therapy encourages people to explore inaccuracies in their beliefs.
    d. this therapy involves an open dialogue between the therapist and the individual.

15. Development of social skills is most immediately facilitated in which type of therapy approach?
    a. behavior therapy
    b. individual
    c. group
    d. client-centered

16. Which of the following is not a technique used in psychoanalysis?
    a. dream analysis
    b. systematic desensitization
    c. free-association
    d. catharsis

17. If a patient started treating the psychotherapist in the same way he treats his mother, a psychoanalyst would argue that the person is engaging in
    a. catharsis.
    b. resistance.
    c. transference.
    d. free-association.

18. Heinz Kohut is a contemporary psychoanalyst. Which of the following issues is not emphasized in Kohut's therapeutic approach?
    a. having the person seek out appropriate relationships with others
    b. early relationships with attachment figures
    c. analysis of dreams by the psychotherapist
    d. having people develop a realistic understanding of relationships

19. Client-centered therapy is an approach consistent with the _____ theory of personality.
    a. psychodynamic
    b. humanistic
    c. behavioral
    d. social cognitive

20.   When a behavioral therapist is trying to help a person associate smoking with a bad thing, such as getting nauseous, the technique being used is
    a.   systematic desensitization.
    b.   token economy.
    c.   aversive conditioning.
    d.   operant conditioning.

21.   The cognitive-behavior technique(s) that teach individuals how to modify their own behaviors are called
    a.   psychoanalysis.
    b.   rational-emotive behavior therapy.
    c.   self-instructional methods.
    d.   client-centered therapy.

22.   Cognitive therapists test the misinterpretations of people experiencing panic disorder by
    a.   trying to change the behaviors associated with the panic disorder.
    b.   asking the person to free-associate to explore the possible reasons for the panic disorder.
    c.   inducing an actual panic attack.
    d.   telling the patient to relax and get over it.

Practice Test 3
1.   What is the main advantage of an integrative approach to psychotherapy?
    a.   It is usually more cost effective.
    b.   It is usually less time consuming.
    c.   It requires less formal training on part of the psychotherapist.
    d.   It utilizes the strengths of a variety of approaches to meet the specific needs of the client.

2.   Based on the most current research, is psychotherapy effective?
    a.   yes, overall
    b.   no, not very effective
    c.   only for those with schizophrenia
    d.   only for those with phobias

3.   There is _____ between number of therapy sessions and improvement in the psychological disorder.
    a.   a negative correlation
    b.   a positive correlation
    c.   no correlation
    d.   no relationship

4.   If you were to consider seeking professional psychological help, you would do all of the following except which one?
        a.   research the services offered by potential therapists
        b.   identify the professional credentials of potential therapists
        c.   pick a therapist from the Yellow Pages and make an appointment
        d.   set specific therapy goals and frequently assess whether these goals are being met

5.   A criticism of the managed health care system for providing psychotherapy is the
        a.   emphasis on long-term psychotherapy.
        b.   emphasis on short-term psychotherapy.
        c.   development of explicit and measurable treatment plans.
        d.   lack of certified practitioners.

6.   A _____ is a therapist who because of graduate training is able to prescribe medication for psychological disorders.
        a.   psychiatrist
        b.   clinical psychologist
        c.   social worker
        d.   counselor

7.   Which of the following is the type of prevention that involves efforts made to reduce the number of new cases of psychological disorders?
        a.   primary
        b.   secondary
        c.   tertiary
        d.   psychological

8.   Sociocultural approaches to therapy understand that the person
        a.   benefits most from individual therapy.
        b.   is part of a social system of relationships.
        c.   is less likely to improve a psychological problem if he or she must share it with other people.
        d.   should not be concerned with the credentials of the therapist.

9.   One of the reasons group therapy is effective is because it helps people realize that they are not alone in their problem. This is a feature of group therapy referred to as
        a.   altruism.
        b.   information.
        c.   corrective recapitulation.
        d.   universalism.

10.   The credibility of peers in the psychological problem contributes to the effectiveness of
        a.   family therapy.
        b.   cognitive therapy.
        c.   self-help support groups.
        d.   rational-emotive behavioral therapy.

11. Which of the following practices is not associated with the community mental health approach?
    a. training teachers and ministers on psychological issues
    b. preventing psychological disorders
    c. the use of mental health institutions as the primary source of psychological treatment
    d. deinstitutionalization

12. Which of the following is not one of the common elements in effective psychotherapies?
    a. establishing a plan of expectations with the client
    b. encouraging the client to take control of the therapeutic process
    c. arousing of emotions that motivate the client
    d. actively changing bad behaviors into more adaptive behaviors

Answer Key
Practice Test 1 Answers
1. a. No; neuroleptics are antipsychotic drugs and depression is a mood disorder.
   b. YES; neuroleptics are antipsychotic drugs.
   c. No; neuroleptics are antipsychotic drugs and bipolar disorder is a mood disorder.
   d. No; neuroleptics are antipsychotic drugs and this disorder is a dissociative disorder.

2. a. No; this is not a conclusion of the study presented in the textbook.
   b. YES; it is comparable to cognitive therapy and drug therapy in effectiveness.
   c. No; this ECT is not more effective than cognitive therapy or less effective as drugs.
   d. No; this is not a conclusion of the study presented in the textbook.

3. a. No; antipsychotic drugs are used to treat schizophrenic disorders.
   b. No; lithium is generally used to treat bipolar disorder.
   c. No; ECT is not used to treat multiple personality.
   d. YES; it is used to treat depression.

4. a. No; Xanax is a benzodiazepine used to treat anxiety disorders.
   b. No; Xanax is a benzodiazepine used to treat anxiety disorders.
   c. YES; Prozac is a selective serotonin reuptake inhibitor used to treat mood disorders.
   d. No; buspirone is a nonbenzodiazepine used to treat generalized anxiety disorder.

5. a. No; these drugs have the side effect of drowsiness.
    b. YES; these drugs have been linked to abnormalities in babies born to mothers who were taking these medications during pregnancy.
    c. No; these drugs have the side effect of fatigue.
    d. No; these drugs can be addictive.

6. a. No; antipsychotics are used to treat schizophrenia.
    b. No; MAO is associated with mood regulation.
    c. YES; Nardil is an example of an MAO inhibitor; these drugs are used less that tricyclics because they are more toxic and have dangerous side effects.
    d. No; personality disorders are not usually treated with drug therapy.

7. a. No; MAO inhibitors are used to regulate mood.
    b. YES; schizophrenia is characterized by an excess of dopamine.
    c. No; this is what tricyclics, the antidepressants, do.
    d. No; this is what benzodiazepines do in the process of relieving anxiety disorders.

8. a. No; this is incorrect, the symptoms return when the drugs are not used.
    b. No; the use of drug therapy actually reduces the hospital stay time.
    c. YES; tardive dyskinesia is a very disruptive side effect of neuroleptic drugs.
    d. No; the excess dopamine is what causes the undesirable symptoms.

9. a. No; this is what used to be referred to as prefrontal lobotomy.
    b. YES; small and precise lesions are made in the amygdala or another part of the limbic system.
    c. No; these were extreme measures that are not currently performed.
    d. No; this is the area in charge of higher processing and it is not lesioned or removed in psychosurgery to treat psychological disorders.

Practice Test 2 Answers

1. a. No; biological therapies are designed to change symptoms directly by altering how the body works.
    b. No; this is a type of biological therapy.
    c. No; this is a type of biological therapy.
    d. YES; psychotherapy is often used in conjunction with biological therapy.

2. a. YES; resistance refers to unconscious defense strategies.
    b. No; this is the person's relating to the analyst in a way that resembles another relationship.
    c. No; in free association the person says aloud whatever comes to mind.
    d. No; this is the release of emotional tension when having an emotional experience.

3.   a.   YES; this is the release of emotional tension when having an emotional experience.

     b.   No; resistance refers to unconscious defense strategies.

     c.   No; in free association the person says aloud whatever comes to mind.

     d.   No; this is acceptance of another person without any strings attached.

4.   a.   No; conscious thought is a focus of humanistic therapy.

     b.   YES; humanists tend to focus on the here and now.

     c.   No; humanistic therapy emphasizes personal growth.

     d.   No; self-fulfillment is a focus of humanistic therapy.

5.   a.   No; this is required in client-centered therapy.

     b.   No; this is required in client-centered therapy.

     c.   YES; this is not required in client-centered therapy since it is nondirective.

     d.   No; this is required in client-centered therapy.

6.   a.   YES; this is an assumption of both Gestalt therapy and psychoanalytic therapy.

     b.   No; the client cannot finds solutions without the assistance of a therapist.

     c.   No; Gestalt therapy makes no requirement on resistance and transference.

     d.   No; psychoanalytic therapy makes use of dream analysis in understanding a person.

7.   a.   No; behavior therapy does not use insight.

     b.   YES; both therapies assume the client needs to gain insight and awareness.

     c.   No; insight is not required for the biomedical therapies.

     d.   No; in this therapy a behavior is paired with some unpleasant stimulus.

8.   a.   No; this is not a technique in psychoanalysis.

     b.   No; the humanistic therapies would not be so active in confronting individuals.

     c.   YES; the therapist often confronts individuals.

     d.   No; client-centered therapy would not be so confrontational.

9.   a.   YES; the person is gradually exposed to the feared object while remaining relaxed.

     b.   No; this is not systematic desensitization.

     c.   No; this is not systematic desensitization.

     d.   No; this is not systematic desensitization.

10.   a.   No; psychoanalysis stresses the importance of the unconscious mind.

     b.   No; this therapy includes challenging and confronting the client.

     c.   No; these principles are not extensively used in group therapy.

     d.   YES; behavior therapy is based on the idea that maladaptive behaviors are learned.

11. a. No; in this technique, behavior is reinforced with tokens that can be later redeemed.
     b. No; the technique uses relaxation and anxiety-producing situations.
     c. YES; this is the definition of aversive conditioning.
     d. No; this focuses on irrational and self-defeating beliefs as causes of problems.

12. a. YES; cognitive therapists focus on irrational beliefs and faulty thinking.
     b. No; this is a concept from client-centered therapy.
     c. No; the manifest content of dreams would be determined in psychoanalysis.
     d. No; psychoanalytic therapy would emphasize unconscious motives.

13. a. No; even though Beck does focus on cognitions and the therapy is less directive.
     b. YES; Ellis believed that our self-statements are often irrational and self-defeating.
     c. No; the technique uses relaxation and anxiety-producing situations.
     d. No; operant therapy primarily focuses on the use of reinforcement.

14. a. YES; this is a characteristic of the rational-emotive behavioral therapy of Ellis. While there are a number of similarities between the approaches of Ellis and Beck, Beck's cognitive therapy is not as confrontational.
     b. No; this is one of the characteristics of Beck's cognitive therapy.
     c. No; this is one of the characteristics of Beck's cognitive therapy.
     d. No; this is one of the characteristics of Beck's cognitive therapy.

15. a. No; behavior therapy uses principles of learning to address maladaptive behaviors.
     b. No
     c. YES; the development of social skills is facilitated in group therapy.
     d. No; this therapy creates an atmosphere in which the person can gain insight.

16. a. No; dream analysis is the technique of interpreting dreams to figure out their unconscious content.
     b. YES; this is a behavioral therapy approach.
     c. No; this is the technique of asking the person to share freely whatever comes to mind.
     d. No; this is the technique of liberating pent-up emotions and issues.

17. a.   No; catharsis is another psychoanalytic issue.
    b.   No; resistance is when the person starts interrupting the therapeutic process.
    c.   YES; the person has transferred his issues with his mother to the therapist.
    d.   No; free-association is asking the person to share whatever comes to mind.

18. a.   No; this is one of the issues Kohut emphasizes in his therapy.
    b.   No; this is also one of the issues that Kohut emphasizes in his therapy.
    c.   YES; Kohut focuses more on being empathic and understanding and encouraging people to strengthen their sense of self; this would be inconsistent with a therapist figuring out the meaning of dreams.
    d.   No; this is also one of the issues that Kohut emphasizes in his therapy.

19. a.   No; the psychodynamic approach, at least in the original version, tended to be more "therapist-centered," because the therapist was the one making all the interpretations.
    b.   YES; this type of therapy was developed by Carl Rogers.
    c.   No; behavioral therapy assumes that the therapist is more knowledgeable than the person about how to solve the problems.
    d.   No; this therapy came out of the humanistic approach.

20. a.   No; systematic desensitization is used with phobic disorders.
    b.   No; the person is not being offered a token as a reward.
    c.   YES; classical conditioning is being used to have the person stop doing the undesirable behavior.
    d.   No; actually, aversive conditioning is a type of classical conditioning.

21. a.   No; this is the therapy that focuses on unconscious influences and early life experiences.
    b.   No; this is a cognitive therapy, but it focuses on facing irrational beliefs.
    c.   YES; these methods are used to teach the client to manage his or her own way of thinking.
    d.   No; this is the term used by Rogers to refer to his humanistic approach to therapy.

22. a.   No; this would be more consistent with behavioral therapy.
    b.   No; this would be more consistent with psychoanalysis.
    c.   YES; by inducing the panic attack the therapist can help the person realize that his or her thoughts are irrational.
    d.   No; this is a simplistic statement unlikely to be used by a psychologist, not even a rational-emotive behavioral therapist.

Practice Test 3 Answers

1. a. No; while this could be an advantage, it is not the main one.
    b. No; this is not an advantage.
    c. No; in fact, the psychotherapist must be competent in several diverse therapies.
    d. YES; this is the main advantage of integrative psychotherapy.

2. a. YES; different therapies are more effective for specific types of problems.
    b. No; this is not correct.
    c. No; there are psychotherapies that are effective for certain types of disorders.
    d. No; other disorders can be effectively treated using psychotherapy.

3. a. No; a negative correlation would indicate that the more therapy sessions, the less the improvement in the disorder.
    b. YES; in a study by Anderson and Lambert (2001) it was found that the more therapy sessions the person attended, the higher the rate of improvement, as rated by the individuals undergoing therapy.
    c. No; there is a correlation.
    d. No; there is a relationship, and it is a positive correlation.

4. a. No; this would be sensible advice.
    b. No; this is an appropriate thing to do.
    c. YES; this is not a very good way to pick a psychologist.
    d. No; seeking professional psychological help would involve setting specific goals.

5. a. No; managed care has attempted to eliminate long-term psychotherapy.
    b. YES; this is a criticism of managed care.
    c. No; this is not a criticism.
    d. No; however, managed care has been criticized for increasingly using mental health professionals with less experience and constraining the services offered by psychiatrists and clinical psychologists.

6. a. YES; a psychiatrist is a medical doctor who specializes in psychological disorders.
    b. No; clinical psychologists do not engage in graduate medical training.
    c. No; social workers may work as mental health providers but do not have medical training.
    d. No; counselors have at least a master's degree in psychology but do not have medical training.

7. a. YES; this is the definition of primary prevention.
    b. No; secondary prevention involves the screening for early detection of problems and early intervention.
    c. No; tertiary prevention involves efforts to reduce the psychological disorders.
    d. No; this is too broad a concept.

8. a. No; actually, the sociocultural approach argues that the person will benefit from exploring the problem in a social context.
    b. YES; these approaches consider exploring the problems with the people who are involved.
    c. No; on the contrary, sociocultural approaches are based on the assumption that being in a social setting encourages effective therapy.
    d. No; even in collective therapies, the credentials of the therapist are important.

9. a. No; this refers to the sympathy and support that groups provide.
    b. No; this refers to receiving information about the disorder from a therapist as well as from others with the disorder.
    c. No; this refers to viewing the group as a family.
    d. YES; this helps people deal with some of the fears associated with having the disorder.

10. a. No; in family therapy it is not common for all family members to be peers in the psychological problem; in other words, they don't go to family therapy because they all have depression.
    b. No; this is an individual therapy, thus the role of peers is irrelevant.
    c. YES; another person who has the same problem has credibility when he or she shares experiences.
    d. No; this is an individual therapy.

11. a. No; this is one of the practices that started with this movement.
    b. No; prevention is considered a priority in the community mental health approach.
    c. YES; the community mental health approach emphasized that psychological problems can be targeted at many other levels in the community.
    d. No; this is the transfer of mental health care from institutions such as mental hospitals to community-based facilities.

12. a. No; this is one of the common elements of effective psychotherapies.
    b. No; this is one of the common elements of effective psychotherapies.
    c. No; this is one of the common elements of effective psychotherapies.
    d. YES; this is the approach in behavioral therapies, but not all effective approaches focus on changing behaviors.

Chapter 16: Health Psychology

Learning Goals
1. Describe the scope of health psychology and behavioral medicine.
2. Describe the various theoretical models of change.
3. Discuss psychological and social tools that promote effective life change.
4. Describe strategies for cultivating good habits in five important realms of life.
5. Explain why positive psychology is the essence of psychology and how psychology applies to your physical health and well-being.

After studying chapter 16, use the space below to list the top 3 most interesting things you learned that make you appreciate the role of health psychology in your life more.

- _____
- _____
- _____

Chapter Outline
1. What You Already Know About Health Psychology

- _____
  _____
- _____
  _____
  _____
- _____
  _____
- _____
  _____

2. Making Positive Life Changes

- _____
  _____

- Theory of reasoned action: _____
  _____
  - Example: _____
    _____

- Stages of change model: _____
  _____
  - _____
    _____
    - Example: _____
      _____
  - _____
    _____
    - Example: _____
      _____
  - _____
    _____

- Example: _____
_____

  o _____
_____

    - Example: _____
_____

  o _____
_____

    - Example: _____
_____

  o Relapse: _____
_____

    - _____
_____

3. Tools for Effective Life Change

(For each heading, write down how each construct relates to health and list two important sub-points from your textbook.)

- Self-efficacy: _____
_____

  o _____
_____

  o _____
_____

- Motivation: _____
_____

  o _____
_____

  o _____
_____

- Religious faith: _____
_____

  o _____
_____

  o _____
_____

4. Cultivating Good Habits

- _____
_____

- General adaptation syndrome: _____
_____

  o _____
_____

  o _____
_____

  o _____
_____

- Psychoneuroimmunology: _____
  _____
  - ○ _____
    _____
  - ○ _____
    _____
  - ○ _____
    _____
  - ○ _____
    _____
  - ○ _____
    _____

- Stress, disease, and cancer
  - ○ _____
    _____
  - ○ _____
    _____
  - ○ _____
    _____
  - ○ _____
    _____

- Stress management programs
  - ○ _____
    _____
  - ○ _____
    _____
  - ○ _____
    _____

- Physical activity and health
  - ○ _____
    _____
  - ○ _____
    _____
  - ○ _____
    _____
  - ○ _____
    _____
  - ○ _____
    _____
  - ○ _____
    _____

- Diet and health
  - ○ _____
    _____
  - ○ _____
    _____

- o _____
- o _____
- o _____
- o _____

- **Quitting smoking**
  - o _____
  - o _____
  - o _____
  - o _____
  - o _____
  - o _____

- **Safe sex: unwanted pregnancy**
  - o _____
  - o _____
  - o _____
  - o _____
  - o _____
  - o _____

- **Safe sex: sexually transmitted infections**
  - o _____
  - o _____
  - o _____
  - o _____
  - o _____

○ _____
_____

5. Integrating Psychology and Health and Wellness

- _____
_____
_____

- _____
_____

Critical Controversy

- Cardiorespiratory fitness (CRF): _____
_____

    ○ _____
_____

    ○ _____
_____

Intersection

- Motivation and bad behaviors

    ○ _____
_____

    ○ _____
_____

    ○ _____
_____

Clarifying Tricky Points

Relapse is a part of change

Change is a slow process that often means taking several steps forward while taking a few steps backwards. Relapse is an expected occurrence according to the stages of change model and does not mean that change cannot occur. If you are trying to adhere to a diet and eat a piece of cake with butter cream frosting at a wedding, it does not mean you cannot change or that you should give up your goal. Rather, those who are successful at dieting are those who do not get too down on themselves when they relapse. Change occurs by taking more steps forward than backward, not necessarily by taking only steps forward.

Stress and health

Stress is bad for you. Most likely you have heard this before and know that when you are stressed out, your immune system suffers (which is why everybody on a college campus always seems to catch a cold during exam week!). But the relationship between stress and health is more complicated than just how stress affects your body. Stress also affects you psychologically and often leads to decreased ability to self-regulate and maintain healthy behaviors. For example, people who are chronically stressed are more likely to smoke, drink, eat poorly, and avoid exercising; all of which are factors that only compound on the weakness the stressed out body is already experiencing due to lowered immune functioning.

An Appreciative View of Psychology and Your Life
Throughout your textbook, the author has emphasized taking an "appreciative view" of psychology by pointing out how psychological research actually matters for everyday people going through everyday life. Take a moment to flip to the table of contents for your textbook and list some ways in which you have learned how to integrate psychology into your life. Maybe you have a better idea of how to take care of your brain and keep you memory sharp. Or maybe you have a better understanding of how to set and achieve goals. Each chapter has something in it that can be applied to your life. List a few that you think are the most important for your life.

_____
_____
_____
_____
_____
_____
_____

Practice Test 1
1. A model that is used in the field of health psychology emphasizes a combination of influences on health. This model is called the _____ model.
    a. psychodynamic
    b. general adaptation syndrome
    c. hardiness
    d. biopsychosocial

2. During the alarm stage of the general adaptation syndrome, the body_____ to deal with the stressor.
    a. shuts down temporarily
    b. releases hormones.
    c. increases immune system activity.
    d. activates the central nervous system.

3. Individuals who have high self-efficacy are least likely to do which of the following?
    a. persist in the face of obstacles
    b. expend effort in coping with stress
    c. experience less stress in challenging situations
    d. perceive that they have no control over the situation

4. Behavioral medicine is an interdisciplinary field that
    a. focuses on operant conditioning.
    b. promotes health and reduces illness.
    c. focuses on classical conditioning.
    d. uses psychotherapy to treat physical problems.

5.   Which of the following is NOT a health behavior?
   a.   safe sex
   b.   dieting
   c.   going to school
   d.   exercise

6.   _____ contends that effective change requires specific intentions and a positive attitude towards the new behavior.
   a.   The theory of reasoned action
   b.   The stages of change model
   c.   Generalized adaptation syndrome
   d.   The positive behavior change model

7.   The precontemplation stage
   a.   occurs when you are not thinking about changing.
   b.   happens just before relapse.
   c.   occurs when you acknowledge the problem.
   d.   occurs after successful change.

8.   Relapse is a challenge during the _____ stage.
   a.   contemplation
   b.   action
   c.   preparation
   d.   maintenance

9.   When you are no longer consciously engaged in maintaining a relatively new healthy lifestyle, you are experiencing
   a.   relapse
   b.   transcendence
   c.   contemplation
   d.   determination

10.   The belief that you can master a situation and produce positive outcomes is called
   a.   extrinsic motivation
   b.   implementation
   c.   self-efficacy
   d.   intrinsic motivation

Practice Test 2

1.   Selye's three-stage pattern of reaction to stress is known as the
   a.   cognitive appraisal scale.
   b.   social readjustment scale.
   c.   personality adjustment system.
   d.   general adaptation syndrome.

2. According to Selye, the immune system effectively fights off infection in the _____ stage of the general adaptation syndrome.
   a. alarm
   b. resistance
   c. exhaustion
   d. None of the answers are correct.

3. If you were a psychoneuroimmunologist, you would be most likely to read which fictitious journal?
   a. Journal of Humanistic Psychology
   b. Journal of Motor Skills
   c. Journal of Dream Analysis
   d. Journal of the Behavior and Health

4. Having implementation intentions for dealing with challenges is associated with
   a. successfully changing.
   b. relapse.
   c. extrinsic motivation.
   d. failure to change.

5. Stress is formally defined as
   a. inconveniences associated with work.
   b. anything that negatively affects your body and mind.
   c. response to stressors that tax coping abilities.
   d. anything you personally find upsetting.

6. People who experience work related stress for one month are
   a. about 5 times more likely to catch a cold than those without stress.
   b. no more or less likely than anybody else to get sick.
   c. will develop cardiovascular disease.
   d. are at risk for HIV infection.

7. Hostility and cardiovascular disease are _____ correlated.
   a. not
   b. positively
   c. negatively
   d. inversely

8. A program that teaches how to appraise stressful events and develop coping skills is called a _____.
   a. generalized adaptation program
   b. health behavior inducement
   c. contemplative program
   d. stress management program

9.   Weight loss in overweight individuals is associated with all of the following except
        a.   lower probability of cardiovascular disease
        b.   improved cognitive functioning
        c.   increased self-esteem
        d.   increased lung capacity

10.   A good nutritional plan includes the consideration of
        a.   fats and carbs.
        b.   calories only.
        c.   calories, fat, carbs, proteins, vitamins, and water.
        d.   calories, water, and protein.

Practice Test 3

1.   Most experts recommend that adults engage in _____ minutes or more of moderate-intensity physical activity on most days of the week.
        a.   5
        b.   15
        c.   30
        d.   60

2.   Exercise reduces risk of heart attack
        a.   only if you don't smoke.
        b.   only if you also eat right.
        c.   despite weight, blood pressure, and smoking.
        d.   only if you engage in it at least 4 times a week.

3.   The best predictor of getting a sexually transmitted disease is
        a.   being homosexual.
        b.   having sex with multiple partners.
        c.   living in a large urban city.
        d.   being between the ages of 16 and 22.

4.   Successful dieters
        a.   keep at their diet plan despite relapses.
        b.   completely change their plan after relapse.
        c.   tend to skip breakfast and snacks.
        d.   count calories only.

5.   Overall, smoking in the US is
        a.   declining among teenagers.
        b.   declining.
        c.   increasing among teenagers but decreasing among adults.
        d.   increasing.

6.   To engage in aversive conditioning to quit smoking, a person might
       a.   try a nicotine patch.
       b.   take a pill designed to help people quit.
       c.   think about the feeling of smoking an entire pack of cigarettes in one sitting.
       d.   upon craving a cigarette, imagine inhaling a cigarette but not actually doing so.

7.   Condoms are
       a.   90-99% effective at preventing unwanted pregnancy.
       b.   60-79% effective at preventing unwanted pregnancy.
       c.   about 50% effective at preventing unwanted pregnancy.
       d.   not effective at preventing unwanted pregnancy.

8.   In which of the following ways can HIV be transmitted?
       a.   kissing
       b.   vaginal intercourse
       c.   sharing silverware
       d.   All of the answers are correct.

9.   Proper condom use can reduce the occurrence of or transmission of
       a.   HIV.
       b.   pregnancy.
       c.   HIV and syphilis.
       c.   pregnancy, HIV, syphilis, gonorrhea, and Chlamydia.

10.   Sexually transmitted infections can affect
       a.   cancer risk.
       b.   future fertility.
       c.   life expectancy.
       d.   All of the answers are correct

Answer Key
Practice Test 1 Answers
1   a.   No
       b.   No
       c.   No
       d.   Correct

2.   a.   No
       b.   Correct
       c.   No
       d.   No

3. a. No
    b. No
    c. No
    d. Correct

4. a. No
    b. Correct
    c. No
    d. No

5. a. No
    b. No
    c. Correct
    d. No

6. a. Correct
    b. No
    c. No
    d. No

7. a. Correct
    b. No
    c. No
    d. No

8. a. No
    b. No
    c. No
    d. Correct

9. a. No
    b. Correct
    c. No
    d. No

10. a. No
    b. No
    c. Correct
    d. No

Practice Test 2 Answers

1   a. No
    b. No
    c. No
    d. Correct

2. a. No
    b. Correct
    c. No
    d. No

3. a. No
    b. No
    c. No
    d. Correct

4. a. Correct
    b. No
    c. No
    d. No

5. a. No
    b. No
    c. Correct
    d. No

6. a. Correct
    b. No
    c. No
    d. No

7. a. No
    b. Correct
    c. No
    d. No

8. a. No
    b. No
    c. No
    d. Correct

9. a. No
    b. No
    c. No
    d. Correct

10. a. No
    b. No
    c. Correct
    d. No

Practice Test 3 Answers

1.   a.   No
     b.   No
     c.   Correct
     d.   No

2.   a.   No
     b.   No
     c.   Correct
     d.   No

3.   a.   No
     b.   Correct
     c.   No
     d.   No

4.   a.   Correct
     b.   No
     c.   No
     d.   No

5.   a.   No
     b.   Correct
     c.   No
     d.   No

6.   a.   No
     b.   No
     c.   Correct
     d.   No

7.   a.   Correct
     b.   No
     c.   No
     d.   No

8.   a.   No
     b.   Correct
     c.   No
     d.   No

9.   a.   No
     b.   No
     c.   No
     d.   Correct

10.   a.   No
        b.   No
        c.   No
        d.   Correct